# ADVANCING TRINITARIAN THEOLOGY

# Proceedings of the
# Los Angeles Theology Conference

This is the second volume in a series published by Zondervan Academic. It is the proceedings of the Los Angeles Theology Conference held under the auspices of the School of Theology in Fuller Theological Seminary, with the support of Biola University, in January 2014. The conference is an attempt to do several things. First, it provides a regional forum in which scholars, students, and clergy can come together to discuss and reflect on central doctrinal claims of the Christian faith. It is also an ecumenical endeavor. Bringing together theologians from a number of different schools and confessions, the LATC seeks to foster serious engagement with Scripture and tradition in a spirit of collegial dialogue (and disagreement), looking to retrieve the best of the Christian past in order to forge theology for the future. Finally, each volume in the series focuses on a central topic in dogmatic theology. It is hoped that this endeavor will continue to fructify contemporary systematic theology and foster a greater understanding of the historic Christian faith among the members of its different communions.

Oliver D. Crisp and Fred Sanders, Editors

# ADVANCING TRINITARIAN THEOLOGY

## EXPLORATIONS IN CONSTRUCTIVE DOGMATICS

---CONTRIBUTORS---

Lewis Ayres • Stephen R. Holmes • Karen Kilby
Thomas H. McCall • Fred Sanders

ZONDERVAN

*Advancing Trinitarian Theology*
Copyright © 2014 by Oliver D. Crisp and Fred Sanders

This title is also available as a Zondervan ebook. Visit www.zondervan.com/ebooks.

Requests for information should be addressed to:

Zondervan, 3900 *Sparks Dr. SE, Grand Rapids, Michigan 49546*

Library of Congress Cataloging-in-Publication Data

Los Angeles Theology Conference (2014)
    Advancing Trinitarian theology : explorations in constructive dogmatics / Oliver D. Crisp and Fred Sanders, editors.
        pages cm
    Proceedings of the Los Angeles Theology Conference.
    Includes index.
    ISBN 978-0-310-51709-2 (softcover)
    1. Trinity—History of doctrines—21st century—Congresses. I. Crisp, Oliver, editor. II. Title.
    BT111.3.L68 2014
    231ʺ.044—dc23                                                        2014012259

*Cover design: Michelle Lenger*
*Cover photography or illustration: Bridgeman Art Library*
*Interior design: Matthew Van Zomeren*

*Printed in the United States of America*

14 15 16 17 18 19 20 /DCI/ 22 21 20 19 18 17 16 15 14 13 12 11 10 9 8 7 6 5 4 3 2 1

To Claire and Susan
Because you're worth it

# CONTENTS

# ACKNOWLEDGMENTS

THE EDITORS WOULD LIKE TO THANK Dr. Howard Loewen, the Dean of the School of Theology at Fuller Theological Seminary, and the staff and faculty of the school for their assistance with and support for the Second Los Angeles Theology Conference (LATC) in January of 2014, out of which these published proceedings grew. Daniel Salyers worked untiringly on the practical end of things as the administrative assistant to the conference at Fuller, as did Victoria Smith and Christian Drez, who made it run as smoothly as it did. We are grateful to them. Thanks too to Biola University for its ongoing support of LATC. Once again, we are particularly grateful to our editor and colleague, Katya Covrett, for her organization and "encouragement" of the editors in their work. Thanks too to the Zondervan Team—Jesse Hillman, Kari Moore, Josh Kessler, Ron Huizinga, and Verlyn Verbrugge—who have distinguished themselves in the production of this volume. Stan Gundry, editor-in-chief of Zondervan Academic, has been an indefatigable supporter of this endeavor from its inception, for which we are very thankful.

The support of our families has been a real boon in the development of LATC and this volume. We want to thank them for their patience, care, and lovingkindness. This second volume in the series is dedicated to our respective spouses, with great affection.

# LIST OF CONTRIBUTORS

Lewis Ayres—is professor of Catholic and Historical Theology at Durham University in the UK. He studied at the University of St. Andrews, where he obtained his MTheol degree, and the University of Oxford, where he earned his DPhil.

Stephen R. Holmes—is Senior Lecturer in St. Mary's College, University of St. Andrews, UK. He is an ordained Baptist minister and holds a BA degree from the University of Cambridge, an MTh from Spurgeon's College, London, and a PhD from King's College, London.

Karen Kilby—is the Bede Professor of Catholic Theology at Durham University, UK, having recently moved from the University of Nottingham. She gained her BA and PhD at Yale University and also earned postgraduate degrees in Mathematics and in Theology at the University of Cambridge.

Thomas H. McCall—is Associate Professor of Biblical and Systematic Theology at Trinity Evangelical Divinity School in Illinois, where he is also the Director of the Carl F. H. Henry Center for Theological Understanding. He holds a BA from Hobe Sound Bible College, the MA from Wesley Biblical Seminary, and the PhD from Calvin Theological Seminary.

Fred Sanders—is Associate Professor in the Torrey Honors Institute, Biola University, and the cofounder of the LA Theology Conference with Oliver Crisp. He earned degrees from Murray State University (BA), Asbury Theological Seminary (MDiv), and the Graduate Theological Union (PhD).

Jason S. Sexton—is Research Associate at the Center for Religion and Civic Culture, University of Southern California. He holds a BA in Theology from The Master's College, an MDiv and ThM in Systematic Theology from The Master's Seminary, and a PhD from The University of St. Andrews, UK; he has done postdoctoral work at Oak Hill Theological College, London, and has taught theology at Ridley

Hall, University of Cambridge, and Golden Gate Baptist Seminary in California.

R. Kendall Soulen—is Professor of Systematic Theology at Wesley Theological Seminary. He was educated at Yale University (BA), Emory University (MDiv), and Yale University (PhD).

Kyle C. Strobel—is Assistant Professor of Spiritual Theology at Talbot School of Theology, Biola Univerisity, and Research Associate at the University of the Free State, Bloemfontein, South Africa. He holds a BA from Judson University, two MA degrees in New Testament and Philosophy of Religion and Ethics from Talbot School of Theology, Biola University, and a PhD from the University of Aberdeen.

Darren O. Sumner—is an adjunct professor at Fuller Theological Seminary, Northwest. He earned his BA from Seattle Pacific University, an MA from Wheaton College Graduate School, an MDiv from Princeton Theological Seminary, and a PhD from the University of Aberdeen.

# ABBREVIATIONS

AB    Anchor Bible
*AJT*    *American Journal of Theology*
*CD*    *Church Dogmatics* (by Karl Barth)
GNO    Gregorii Nyseni Opera (ed. Werner Jaeger)
*HeyJ*    *Heythrop Journal*
*IJST*    *International Journal of Systematic Theology*
*JLAT*    *Journal of Latin American Theology*
*JRT*    *Journal of Reformed Theology*
*JTS*    *Journal of Theological Studies*
*MTh*    *Modern Theology*
NPNF2    *Nicene and Post-Nicene Fathers*, series 2
*NV*    *Nova et vetera*
PG    Patrologia graeca
*ProEccl*    *Pro Ecclesia*
*SJT*    *Scottish Journal of Theology*
*ST*    *Summa theologiae* (Aquinas)
*StPatr*    *Studia patristica*
*SVTQ*    *St. Vladimir's Theological Quarterly*
*TynBul*    *Tyndale Bulletin*
*VC*    *Vigiliae christianae*
*WTJ*    *Westminster Theological Journal*

# INTRODUCTION

## ISSUES IN THE DOCTRINE OF THE TRINITY

In the opening section of his work *In the Face of Mystery,*[1] the American liberal Mennonite theologian Gordon D. Kaufman distinguishes two genera of systematic theology: "exposition" and "construction." He thinks that historic Christian theology is largely devoted to the former, whereas contemporary scholarship must be concerned with the latter. Classical theologians of the past were for the most part engaged in expounding and making sense of doctrine and dogma by appealing to authoritative documents such as the Bible, creeds, and confessions. That way of doing theology is no longer tenable. In its place, he thinks we should conceive of the task of the theologian as one of imaginative construction. We must face up to the fact that all theology is human construction about the divine, which is ultimately mysterious and beyond our ken. Doctrine isn't *merely* the projection onto the clouds of an idealized image of a heavenly Father, which was Ludwig Feuerbach's central claim about Christian thought. But if it is not that, it is at least constructive in the sense of being our account of God, the divine, and the world in which we find ourselves. Revelation is not a category that has a large role to play in this conception of the theological task.

There are lessons to be learnt from Kaufman's account, even if it is sometimes about which roads not to take. For one thing, he is right to emphasize the role imagination plays in constructive theology. He is also right about the importance of admitting our fallibility in formulating our own arguments for particular dogmatic conclusions, and our limited purview. A Methodist theologian cannot claim to see everything clearly, but she can see certain things and may have her theological "vision" corrected by contact with thinkers belonging to other Christian confessions, whose theological interests are rather different. The same is true, *mutatis mutandis,* of those belonging to other traditions, such as Presbyterians, Anglicans, Lutherans, Roman Catholics, Orthodox, Pentecostals, and so

---

1. Gordon D. Kaufman, *In the Face of Mystery: A Constructive Theology* (Cambridge, MA: Harvard University Press, 1993), especially the preface and part 1.

13

on. However, Kaufman's distinction between theology-as-exposition and theology-as-construction is surely a false dichotomy. One can do expositional *and* constructive theology, taking into account the findings of thinkers of the past and of biblical and creedal witnesses, while also attempting to formulate a way of articulating in a contemporary context the faith once delivered to the saints. It is just this balance between retrieval and construction, exposition and reflection, that informs the papers contained within the covers of the present volume and the theme of the conference at which they were originally delivered.

This need for both theological exposition and construction is nowhere clearer than in recent work that has been done on the doctrine of the Trinity. A generation ago it was not uncommon to find textbook discussions of the Eastern versions of the doctrine of the Trinity, which emphasized the distinctness of the divine persons over their unity, and Western versions of the doctrine, which emphasized the unity of the Godhead over the divine persons. Whereas the worry with Eastern doctrines was that they would press too far in the direction of tritheism, the concern faced by Western doctrines was that they would collapse into modalism. With either distinction in the Godhead, one could possibly end up with three gods not one, or with one divine entity wearing three masks, not three divine persons properly conceived.

Such an oversimplification of the complexity of trinitarian doctrine hardly does justice to the events that shaped the dogma as we have it today. Recent work on the development of fourth- and fifth-century Nicene Christianity has shown just how mistaken such a picture really is. Lewis Ayres, one of the contributors to this volume, has been in the forefront of this revisioning of the development of the doctrine of the Trinity.

But the Trinity has also been the rallying cry for a theological program in modern dogmatics after Karl Barth. If we have a right conception of the Trinity, so this story goes, we will be able to unlock all sorts of difficult knots into which particular doctrines have become contorted over the generations. For instance, a right application of the Trinity to a doctrine of creation will help us not to end up with an understanding of the creature-creator relationship that privileges transcendence over immanence, or vice versa. That is, we will be saved from so exalting God (i.e., so emphasizing his transcendence) that we end up with a hidden God who cannot be known by us; we will also be saved from thinking God so condescends to us (i.e., is so immanent in the creation) that the line dividing divinity from the creaturely becomes thin indeed, if not blurred. Here too there are things to commend, and that are instructive.

The Trinitarian Theology Project, if we may call it this, could be thought of as a corrective to the nineteenth-century dereliction of the dogma, epitomized most starkly by Schleiermacher's relegation of the Trinity to an appendix in his monumental work, *The Christian Faith*. Barth placed at the head of his *Church Dogmatics* what his German forbear thought too arcane to be accommodated in the body of his own system of theology. For this recentering of the Trinity in post-Barthian systematic theology we should all be grateful. What is more, this project has been taken forward by a number of creative contemporary theologians whose work has influenced much recent constructive dogmatic theology, such as the Roman Catholic Catherine Mowry LaCugna, the Lutheran theologians, Robert Jenson and Wolfhart Pannenberg, and their Reformed colleagues, Jürgen Moltmann, Colin Gunton, and Thomas Torrance.

Yet the Trinitarian Theology Project has been called into serious question in recent years. Part of this has to do with the reevaluation of the development of the historic doctrine of the Trinity just mentioned. In addition, there is a question about the viability of Trinitarian Theology so conceived. Is it really the case that the whole of the Christian tradition was misguided or mistaken in the way it thought about the Trinity? Have our forbears missed the importance of the doctrine in its application to other areas of Christian theology? Does the doctrine of the Trinity provide a kind of dogmatic panacea by means of which we can cure all sorts of historic theological mistakes? To increasing numbers of scholars today, this seems unlikely. Stephen Holmes and Fred Sanders, two of our other contributors, have been party to this discussion and have made valuable contributions towards a more rounded, and balanced, understanding of the importance of the doctrine of the Trinity and its place in the history of Christian theology.

Alongside these debates within systematic theology has been an increasingly sophisticated literature on the Trinity written by those trained primarily in analytic philosophy, or in conversation with analytic philosophy. This has even generated a new model of the Trinity, named Constitution Trinitarianism.[2] On this view the Trinity is analogous to a block of stone composed of marble. Suppose there is a marble slab fashioned into a pillar

---

2. This has been developed by Michael C. Rea and Jeff Brower, in part based on work by Peter van Inwagen and Peter Geach on the concept of relative identity. See Jeffrey E. Brower and Michael C. Rea, "Material Constitution and the Trinity," *Faith and Philosophy* 22 (2005): 57–76. [Reprinted in Thomas H. McCall and Michael C. Rea, eds. *Philosophical and Theological Essays on the Trinity* (New York: Oxford University Press, 2009), 263–82.]; and idem, "Understanding the Trinity," *Logos: A Journal of Catholic Thought and Culture* 8 (2005): 145–57. For a recent critique of this model, see Dale Tuggy, "Constitution Trinitarianism: An Appraisal," *Philosophy and Theology* 25 (2013): 129–62.

that is also a statue, which has been placed in an ancient temple. On one way of conceiving things, there are three distinct, but co-located entities composed or constituted by the one stone slab, namely, the block of marble, the pillar, and the statue. Nevertheless, all three are constituted from the one marble block. They are identical to the marble; yet they are distinct things. In a similar manner, the persons of the Trinity are distinct, and yet constituted by the one divine substance.[3]

Thomas McCall, another of our contributors, has made an important contribution toward bringing this analytic-philosophical discussion to the attention of systematic theologians.[4] He has also been an advocate of a more moderate and nuanced approach to the so-called social model of the Trinity, that family of trinitarian views that emphasizes the threeness of the divine persons and their community in the Godhead. In his contribution to this volume, he turns his attention from models of the Trinity to the vexed question of the relationship between divine unity and triunity—a central aspect of the so-called "threeness-oneness problem" for the dogma, which has also been an important topic of analytic-theological discussion.

In Christian dogmatics there has been a longstanding debate about whether and to what extent we can predicate anything of the divine nature. If God is ineffable (as many classical, orthodox divines claim), then we can know literally nothing of the divine essence. God's internal life is, as it were, ever beyond our ken, like the cloud that covered Mount Sinai, hiding the divine presence from the Israelites below. What we do know of God is revealed to us in the divine economy (God's work in creation) and in the divine missions (the roles the persons of the Trinity take on in order to accomplish creaturely salvation). The divine processions (the way in which the particular divine persons are eternally individuated as Father, Son, and Spirit) are only comprehensible, on this way of thinking, to the extent that they are revealed to us via the divine economy and missions. We cannot get "behind" the divine economic relations as revealed to us in Scripture to some deity abstracted, as it were, from the trinitarian missions.

---

3. More would need to be said about this model if we were to give a full account of it, especially about its use of the controversial metaphysical doctrine of relative identity. It has also been the subject of some discussion and objection in the literature, a recent summary of which can be found in Dale Tuggy's excellent article "Trinity" in the online *Stanford Encyclopedia of Philosophy*, located at: http://plato.stanford.edu/entries/trinity/#RelIde (accessed 01/16/14).

4. See Thomas H. McCall, *Which Trinity? Whose Monotheism? Philosophical and Systematic Theologians on the Metaphysics of Trinitarian Theology* (Grand Rapids: Eerdmans, 2010), and with Michael C. Rea, eds. *Philosophical and Theological Essays on the Trinity*. See also William Hasker, *Metaphysics and the Tri-Personal God* (Oxford Studies in Analytic Theology; Oxford: Oxford University Press, 2013).

Others are more sanguine about what we can know of God in himself, however. What God reveals of himself in Scripture, what is understood in the creeds and confessions of Christendom, maps onto who God is: he really is as he appears to be in the economy in his processions and missions. As Colin Gunton puts it, "the problem is a relentless concentration on what God is not, on the analogically reached doctrine that God is essentially what the world is not."[5] One of the most important contributions to this concern about what we can know of God *in se* (in himself) and God *pro nobis* (for us, revealed to us) is found in the much-debated "rule" touted by the Roman Catholic theologian Karl Rahner in the mid-twentieth century. We can express it like this:

> Rahner's Rule: the immanent Trinity (that is, God in himself) is identical to the economic Trinity (God revealed to us), and vice versa.

But, as has been pointed out by a number of different scholars, this seems to be either trivially true, or extremely controversial.[6] It is trivially true if what is meant by the axiom is that God as he is revealed to us is identical with God as he is in himself. However, it may also be taken to mean something like, God in himself is identical to God revealed to us in the economy of salvation, and this is how God *must* be; he must be the God who acts in this way. Clearly, this is a much more controversial claim, one that many theologians concerned to uphold a strong doctrine of divine freedom will find unacceptable.

The debates about Rahner's Rule raise in an acute form the worry about the relation between what we can know of God in himself and what we can know of the divine trinitarian life via divine revelation. Karen Kilby is a contemporary lay Roman Catholic theologian, and in her contribution to this volume she takes up some of these concerns with what is often called apophatic rather than cataphatic approaches to the Trinity. (*Apophaticism* has to do with "negative theology," that is, with saying what God is not—he is incorporeal, atemporal, unchangeable, and so on; *cataphaticism* has to do with saying what God is—he is good, he is triune, he is glorious, and so on.)

Related to this issue of the balance between what can and cannot be predicated of God, and whether anything we say about God successfully

---

5. Colin E. Gunton, *Act and Being: Towards a Theology of The Divine Attributes* (Grand Rapids: Eerdmans, 2002), 16.
6. See, e.g., Randal Rauser, "Rahner's Rule: An Emperor without Clothes?" in *IJST* 7.1 (2005): 81–94.

refers to something "in" the divine essence, as it were, is the matter of religious language. Although this does not feature as the subject of discussion in much of what follows, it does do a lot of work behind the scenes. If we think that God is good as you or I are good, then (on one way of thinking about it) God's goodness is just a more perfect, expansive instance of the sort of partial, limited goodness we see in other creatures. However, this approach to divine language, often called the univocal account, is usually treated with suspicion by those theologians for whom apophatic theology plays an important role.

It is a commonplace in much historic discussion of the Trinity to hold something like a metaphysical package of notions regarding the dogma. These include a penchant for an apophatic approach to the divine essence, skepticism about whether religious language actually refers to the divine essence (which is beyond human ken), and an understanding of religious language about God that makes room for both similarity and difference between creaturely attributes and divine ones. This is the analogical approach to religious language. On this way of thinking, divine goodness is both like and unlike creaturely instances of goodness. He is good, as in some limited and partial sense fallen creatures may be good. But his goodness is also significantly different from anything creaturely. This is not only because of the *degree* of divine goodness (being perfectly rather than imperfectly or partially instantiated, as with creatures), but also because God is not one created being among other beings, but something entirely different from any created entity. He cannot be classified as creatures can into natural kinds and species; to attempt to do so would be like comparing apples and oranges—or (perhaps better) like two-dimensional beings living in a world like Flatland trying to comprehend the existence of three-dimensional beings living in a world like our own.[7]

Several of the authors in this volume conceive of the doctrine of the Trinity in this way. One task that faces contemporary systematic theology in light of the flourishing of different approaches to the study of the dogma is where to draw the line between what we can know of the triune God and what is beyond us. Hand waiving in the direction of "mystery" is not an adequate response. Nor is a glib cataphatic theology that dismisses mystery with the same scorn as paradox and contradiction. At least part of the solution to this conundrum depends on the approach to religious lan-

7. See Edwin A. Abbot, *Flatland: A Romance of Many Dimensions* (Oxford: Oxford World Classics, 2006 1884. ).

guage that is taken and the confidence with which theologians can discern what is and is not within the bounds of human understanding, including a coherent understanding of this most central Christian mystery and the God of whom it speaks.

## OVERVIEW OF THE CHAPTERS

Having given an account of some (but by no means all) of the major themes in current systematic accounts of the Trinity, we can turn to consideration of the nine chapters of this symposium. They are organized according to the dynamics of the particular theological tasks they undertake. The introductory chapter by Fred Sanders offers a broad survey of the way the doctrine of the Trinity informs the project of systematic theology at large; it also serves to introduce some of the themes later chapters take up and develop. The next two chapters engage rather energetically in retrieval of theological commitments that were considered central in pre-modern trinitarianism but have been marginalized or rejected outright in modern trinitarianism. As previously mentioned, Thomas McCall attempts to rehabilitate the doctrine of divine simplicity by describing two historical versions of it that are philosophically defensible by modern, analytic standards. Stephen Holmes likewise recalls the patristic arguments for the inseparable external operations of the Trinity and, instead of recoiling from that doctrine as much modern theology has, ventures a constructive argument for drawing even further implications from it.

Lewis Ayres and Karen Kilby are both concerned to discipline theological curiosity. Ayres explores the way our knowledge of the Trinity takes the form of mystery, and while trinitarian theology is not antagonistic to conceptual clarity about its claims, it is primarily oriented toward transformation by participation in the things revealed. Kilby targets a particular set of projects that appeal to a social model of the Trinity as the model for human political activity, subjecting them to a searching critique before offering her own alternative recommendation, an apophatic version of how the Trinity can inform politics.

The next two chapters, by Kendall Soulen and Darren Sumner, seek to describe the relationship between the Father and the Son in the immanent Trinity. Soulen does so by giving careful attention to a neglected topic from biblical theology, that is, the persistence of the divine name as a theological force in the New Testament. He draws surprising doctrinal conclusions from the Father's giving of the divine name to the Son and applies these insights to recent theological controversies. Sumner launches even more directly into some of these recent controversies, especially the disputed question of how to interpret Karl Barth on the subordination of the Son.

The final two chapters turn toward some practical implications of trinitarian theology. Kyle Strobel recovers Jonathan Edwards's theology of beauty and the trinitarian contours of the beatific vision, in order to show that the contemplation of the Trinity is itself a transformative practice. Finally, Jason Sexton reports on a vast range of missional movements in the global church that are best understood as outworkings of a trinitarian theology of missions that results in baptism in the name of the Father, Son, and Holy Spirit.

We hope that these essays may contribute to the project of revitalizing the study of the dogma of the Trinity and the advancing of a properly trinitarian theology *ad maiorem dei gloriam*.

*Oliver D. Crisp and Fred Sanders, February 2014*

CHAPTER 1

# WHAT TRINITARIAN THEOLOGY IS FOR

*Placing the Doctrine of the Trinity in Christian Theology and Life*

FRED SANDERS

THE CHURCH OF ST. SERVATIUS in Siegburg, Germany, has a treasure room full of medieval art and relics. Among the artifacts is a portable altar crafted around the year 1160 by the workshop of Eilbertus of Cologne (see next page).[1] Eilbertus was a master craftsman of Romanesque metalwork and enamel decoration, a sturdy artistic medium that withstands the centuries with minimal fading or decay. The colors remain brilliant after nearly a millennium. But Eilbertus was also a skillful iconographer, whose fluency with the symbolism of Christian art equipped him to construct dense and elaborate visual arguments. Consider the top of the altar box. Ranged in bands along the top and bottom of it are the twelve "apostles of the Lord," labeled *apostoli domini*. Running down the right border are three ways of depicting Christ's victory over death: at the bottom is the post-resurrection appearance to Mary Magdalene in the garden, at the center is the "empty tomb" (*sepulchru domini*) with sleeping soldiers and the three women seeking the Lord among the dead, where he is not to be found, and at the top is the "ascension of Christ" (*ascensio Christi*).

---

1. This object is held by the treasury of the Catholic church of St. Servatius in Siegburg, Germany. Contact info for the church's treasury is: www.servatius-siegburg.de/kirchen-einrichtungen/einrichtungen/schatzkammer. Photo credit: Foto Marburg/Art Resource, NY.

The event of the resurrection itself is not directly portrayed, of course, but Eilbertus juxtaposes three images of the resurrection's consequences: the presence of the Lord to his people, the absence of the Lord from the tomb, and the ascension of the Lord by which he is now both present to us (spiritually) and absent from us (bodily) until his return. If a picture is worth a thousand words, three pictures placed together in significant visual proximity are not increased simply by addition of ideas, but rather by a remarkable multiplication of meaning.

But it is the left border that showcases Eilbertus as the iconographic and doctrinal master that he is. In the middle is the crucifixion of Jesus, where the Son of God is flanked by his mother Mary and John the evangelist, as well as by the moon weeping and the sun hiding his face. At the foot of the cross, from the feet of the Savior runs the blood of the crucified, and as it runs down the hill of the Skull, it crosses a rectilinear panel border in which is inscribed *passio Christi* ("the passion of Christ"). The blood runs out of its own frame and into an adjoining visual space, a space in which Adam (clearly labeled *Adam*, which is Latin for ... "Adam") is rising from a sepulcher. Adam's arms are outstretched in a gesture of reception, but they also set up a powerful visual echo of the outstretched arms of Jesus. Adam's tomb and its lid are arranged perpendicular to each other, so that Adam's body is framed by an understated cruciform shape of the same blue and green colored rectangles as Christ's.

Eilbertus is making another visual argument here: where the two crosses cross, salvation takes place. Because the second Adam bends his head and looks down from his death, the first Adam raises his head and looks up from his. Eilbertus is offering an invitation here: above are the everlasting arms, outstretched but unbent, as linear and straight as panel borders or the beams of the cross, while below the salvation is received with appropriate passivity into the bent arms of the father of the race of humanity. Redemption is accomplished and applied, and at long last an answer is given to God's first interrogative: "Adam, where are you?"

But even this is not the peak or extent of Eilbertus' iconographic teaching. For that master stroke we have to look not below the cross but above it. In another pictorial space, framed by both a square and a circle, is God the Father flanked by angels. It doesn't look much like God the Father. It looks instead exactly like Jesus, right down to the cross inscribed in the halo. Pity the iconographer who has to represent the first person of the Trinity visually. As a general rule, the Father should not be portrayed: even in the churches that use icons in worship, stand-alone images of the Father are marginal, aberrant, noncanonical. Do you portray him as an elderly man with a flowing white beard, as if he were modeled on Moses or even perhaps Zeus? Eilbertus has taken the imperfect but safe route and depicted the Father christomorphically. Since Christ told his disciples "Anyone who has seen me has seen the Father" (John 14:9), it stands to reason that if an artist decides to show the Father, he should show him looking like what we have seen in the face of Jesus.

Representing God the Father visually is a problem not even Eilbertus can solve, and even though other options might be worse, this christomorphic Father is nevertheless a rather regrettable solution. But if you avert your eyes from that difficult figure, you will notice the dove of the Holy Spirit ascending from Christ on the cross. The dove imagery is, of course, not found at the end of the Gospels ascending from Golgotha, but rather at the beginning of the Gospels, descending at the Jordan, onto the scene of the baptism of Christ. Eilbertus has moved the symbol here to provide a visual cue for something like Heb 9:14, where we are told that "Christ … through the eternal Spirit offered himself unblemished to God." Just as the blood broke the bottom border, the dove breaks this upper border, crossing over from the Son to the Father. The dove also breaks the crucial word, the label that makes sense of it all: *trinitas* ("Trinity").

It's a little word, but it changes everything. Simply by juxtaposing the death of Christ with a visual evocation of God in heaven, Eilbertus indicates that what happened once upon a time in Jerusalem, a thousand years before Romanesque enamels and two thousand years before the internet, is not simply an occurrence in world history but an event that breaks in from above, or behind, or beyond it—an event in which God has made himself known and taken decisive divine action. But by adding the word *trinitas*, the artist has turned scribe and has proclaimed that what we see at the cross is in some manner a revelation of who God is. Here God did not just cause salvation from afar, but caused himself to be known as the Father, Son, and Holy Spirit.

Here we cannot press Eilbertus any further, because the diction of enamel and the grammar of metalwork are not precise enough to say what we must go on to say. Eilbertus has reminded us of the essential movement that we must make, has set us on the path that faith seeking understanding must follow: from the history of salvation to the eternal life and unchanging character of God. But it is high time to come to terms with the precise meaning of that movement, and for that task we need not images depicting the truth, but words: first the form of sound doctrine given in the teaching of the apostles, then the interpretive assistance of classical doctrines, and finally the conceptual redescription that characterizes constructive systematic theology in the present. The craft and wisdom of Eilbertus frame the discussion, but we need to have the discussion.

In this chapter I want to characterize not the doctrine of the Trinity itself, but how it functions within systematic theology. The adjective in the phrase "trinitarian theology" is grammatically ambiguous, since it could indicate either a theology that is about the Trinity, or an overall theological system that is shaped and conditioned by the doctrine of the Trinity. The latter sense is what I intend to describe by exploring what the doctrine of the Trinity is for; what follows is an account of the dogmatic function of the doctrine of the Trinity in the overall structure of Christian theology and life. Under the guiding image of Eilbertus, we have already begun the task of considering the events of salvation history against the background of the eternal being of God; the doctrine of the Trinity poses "the question of how salvation history is to be correlated with the divine being in itself," or "to describe the connection between God and the economy of salvation."[2] As it does this, this doctrine provides five services that promote the health and balance of Christian theology as a whole. First, trinitarian theology summarizes the biblical story. Second,

---

2. I have described it this way in "The Trinity," in *The Oxford Handbook of Systematic Theology* (ed. John Webster, Kathryn Tanner, Iain Torrance; Oxford: Oxford University Press, 2007), 35.

it articulates the content of divine self-revelation by specifying what has been revealed. Third, it orders doctrinal discourse. Fourth, it identifies God by the gospel. And fifth, it informs and norms soteriology.

# 1. SUMMARIZING THE BIBLICAL STORY

The easiest angle of approach to the Trinity begins with a straightforward reading of the Gospels as rather obviously the story of three special characters: Jesus Christ; the Father, who sent him and who is constantly present in his conversation and actions; and then, rather less clearly, the Holy Spirit, who seems simultaneously to precede Christ, accompany Christ, and follow Christ. There are many other characters in the story, but these three stand out as the central agents on whom everything turns. The actions of these three are concerted, coordinated, and sometimes conjoined so that sometimes they can scarcely be distinguished; at other times they stand in a kind of opposition to each other. As for the salvation they bring, it is not three salvations but one complex event happening in three ways, or (as it sometimes seems) one project undertaken by three agents. The New Testament epistles, each in their own way, all look back on and explain this threefold story, adding more layers of analysis and insight but not altering the fundamental shape of what happened in the life of Jesus.

We could summarize this threefold shape of the New Testament story in the formula, "The Father sends the Son and the Holy Spirit." And though we can't take the time to develop it here, we would then have to extend the analysis to include the entire canon, to demonstrate that what happens in the New Testament is a continuation and fulfillment of what happened in the Old. To trace the story line of Scripture, and especially of the Old Testament, as the God of Israel promising to be with his people in a Son of David who is the Son of God, and to pour out his Holy Spirit on all flesh in a surprising fulfillment of the promise to Abraham, is a task for a comprehensive biblical theology, but it can be undertaken while remaining in the mode of mere description, rather than moving to the more contentious field of systematic construction. In that case, giving a particular kind of interpretive priority to the New Testament because of its position at the end of a process of progressive revelation, the sentence "The Father sends the Son and the Holy Spirit" would be a summary of the entire Bible.

This particular threefold formula is not the only possible summary of the story line of the Bible. Other themes in salvation history could be highlighted. Even other threefold patterns could be discerned: exodus, exile, and resurrection suggests itself. The themes of kingdom or covenant could be pushed to the foreground, or even substituted for the Father, Son, Holy Spirit schema. Much can be gained from investigations that give prominence to these other themes, but what I am describing here is how to read the salvation history witnessed in Scripture in such a way as to reach the doctrine of the Trinity. The reason we would want to do that as Christians is that only the trinitarian reading is actually attempting to read salvation history as the revelation of God's identity in a way that transcends salvation history; such a reading shows not only what God does but who God is. The stories of kingdom or covenant, of exodus, exile, and resurrection, could remain personally undisclosed except insofar as his faithfulness to stand reliably behind his actions suggests something about him. The trinitarian reading of salvation history goes further: it construes the divine *oikonomia* (God's wise ordering of salvation history) to be simultaneously an *oikonomia* of rescue, redemption, and revelation— indeed self-revelation. Salvation history on the trinitarian reading is the locus in which God makes himself known, the theater not only of divine action but also of divine self-communication. A faithful God may stand behind other construals of salvation history, but on the trinitarian reading, God stands not behind but also in his actions, at least in the actions of sending the Son and the Holy Spirit.

There are numerous advantages to beginning in this way. In our age, many Bible-believing Christians have trouble seeing the doctrine of the Trinity in Scripture. They see a verse here and a verse there that help prove the different parts of the doctrine (the deity of Christ, the unity of God, etc.), but they struggle to see the whole package put together in any one place. Granting that the doctrine is not compactly gathered into any one verse (not even Matthew 28:19 or 2 Corinthians 13:13 (13:14 in NIV) are as complete or as detailed as could be wished), it is beneficial to approach the doctrine in a bigger-than-one-verse way.

Follow the whole argument of Galatians 4, for example (in the fullness of time, God sent his Son, and has sent the Spirit of his Son into our hearts, crying "*Abba*, Father"), or 1 Corinthians 2 (in apostolic foolishness we have the mind of Christ and we have the Spirit, who searches the deep things of God), or of Ephesians 1 (we are blessed with every spiritual blessing by the Father, who chose us before the foundation of the world, gave redemption in the blood of the beloved Son, and sealed us with the Spirit of promise), or of the Gospel of John (the Word became flesh, talked endlessly about the Father who sent him, and then gave the Spirit), and the trinitarian profile of God's self-revelation emerges clearly. We have to train our minds to think in bigger sections of Scripture than just a verse here and a verse there—the bigger the better.

To arrive at the biblical doctrine of the Trinity requires three large mental steps. The first step is simply to read the whole Bible, to achieve some initial mastery of the long, main lines of the one story that is the Christian Bible. An interpreter needs to be able to think back and forth along the canon of Scripture, with figures like Abraham and Moses and David and Cyrus standing in their proper places, and with categories like temple and sonship and holiness lighting up the various books as appropriate. This familiarity and fluency with all the constituent parts are prerequisite for further steps.

The second step, though, advances beyond canonical mastery by understanding not just the shape of the biblical text but of God's economy. What is required here is to comprehend the entire Bible as the official, inspired report of the one central thing that God is doing for the world. God has ordered all of these words and events that are recorded in Scripture toward one end. Simply knowing the content of the entire Bible is inadequate, if that content is misinterpreted as a haphazard assemblage of divine stops and starts. These are not disparate Bible stories, but the written witness of the one grand movement in which God disposes all his works and words toward making himself known and present.

The third step is to recognize the economy as a revelation of who God is. This is the largest step of all. Once interpreters have mastered the contents of the Bible and then understood that it presents to us God's well-ordered economy, they still need to come to see that God is making himself known to us in that economy. After all, it is theoretically possible for God to do great things in world history without really giving away his character or disclosing his identity in doing so. This final step on the way to the doctrine of the Trinity is to recognize that God behaved as Father, Son, and Spirit in the economy because he was revealing to us who he eternally is, in himself. The joint sending of the Son and the Holy Spirit was not merely another event in a series of divine actions. It was rather the revelation of God's own identity: the doctrine of the Trinity commits us to affirming that God put himself into the gospel.

This is, I claim, the right way to interpret the Bible, and it is also a rough summary of the traditional way the Bible has been interpreted classically, recognized by the church fathers and the Reformers. We could call it the Christian way. It yields the doctrine of the Trinity, not in scattered verses here and there that tell us a weird doctrine at the margins of the faith, but as the main point.

The New Testament obviously features these three characters: the Father, the Son, and the Holy Spirit. Classically, Christian theology has traced these persons back to an eternal Trinity of God *in se*. Since this threefoldness belongs to what God actually is rather than only being something he freely does, it has been called the ontological Trinity, the essential Trinity, or the Trinity of being. Theologians have also called it the immanent Trinity, because "immanent" means "internal to" itself.

In summary, the most crucial conceptual step that must be taken is the move from the events of the economy of salvation to the eternal life of God. This is the crucial step, and it is a step taken with the fewest explicit and concise expressions: verses. Because of the uniquely integral character of the doctrine of the Trinity, it resists being formulated bit by bit from fragmentary elements of evidence. The atomistic approach can never accomplish or ground the necessary transposition of the biblical evidence from the salvation-history level to the transcendent level of the immanent Trinity. Such a transposition requires first the ability to perceive all of the economic evidence at once, including the intricately structured relations among the three persons. As a coherent body of evidence, then, that economic information can be rightly interpreted as a revelation of God's own life. To make the jump from economy to Trinity, the interpreter must perceive the meaningful form of a threefold divine life circulating around the work of Christ. What psychologists of perception call a gestalt, a recognizably unified coherent form, is what the trinitarian interpreter must identify in the economy. This triune form, once recognized, can then be understood as enacting, among us, the contours of God's own triune life. He is among us what he is in himself: Father, Son, and Holy Spirit.

## 2. ARTICULATING THE CONTENT OF DIVINE SELF-REVELATION

Summarizing the biblical story requires an ascent of thought from the economy to the divine being; this is the distinctive movement of thought that makes possible the doctrine of the Trinity. For the sake of clarity, the question that needs to be posed more explicitly is the question of how much the economic Trinity reveals about God's eternal and essential being. As nineteenth-century Congregationalist theologian R. W. Dale said, the most important question in trinitarian theology is "whether in the Incarnation of our Lord and in the 'coming' of the Spirit and His permanent activity in the Church and in the world there is a revelation of the inner and eternal life of God."[3] In other words, "have we the right to assume that the historic manifestation of God to our race discloses anything of God's own eternal being?"[4] Dale answers yes, as all trinitarians, by definition, do. But trinitarian theologians have developed different opinions about what precisely is revealed. The decisions we make here are the master decisions, affecting everything we say about trinitarian theology's other tasks, namely, to express the material content of the whole doctrine. If we say the right things about divine self-revelation in salvation history, the other tasks will fall more easily into place: doctrinal discourse will be better ordered, God will be identified by the gospel, and our soteriology will be properly informed and normed thereby.

So much good work is to be done at the level of describing salvation history holistically that we might reasonably ask whether it is really necessary to transcend the economy and make claims about the God behind it. Even without angling for a trinitarian conclusion, the answer is yes. If Christian salvation is a real relationship with the true God, some such step is necessary. This is a point that Thomas Torrance made with great force and consistency throughout his work:

> the historical manifestations of God as Father, Son, and Holy Spirit have evangelical and theological significance only as they have a transhistorical and transfinite reference beyond to an ultimate ground in God himself. They cannot be Gospel if their reference breaks off at the finite boundaries of this world of space and time, for as such they would be empty of divine validity and saving significance — they would leave us trapped in some kind of historical positivism. The historical manifestations of the Trinity are Gospel, however, if they are grounded beyond history in the eternal personal distinctions between the Father, the Son, and the Holy Spirit inherent in the Godhead, that is, if the Fatherhood of the Father, the Sonship of the Son, and the Communion of the Spirit belong to the inner life of God and constitute his very Being.[5]

The fact that God makes himself known to us as Father, Son, and Holy Spirit because he is in himself Father, Son, and Holy Spirit is the occasion

---

3. R. W. Dale, *Christian Doctrine: A Series of Discourses* (London: Hodder and Stoughton, 1894), 151.
4. Ibid.
5. T. F. Torrance, *The Christian Doctrine of God: One Being Three Persons* (Edinburgh: T&T Clark, 1996), 6.

for wonder and praise, especially since God did not make this revelation to satisfy our curiosity about the divine, but in order to reconcile and redeem us. God the Father did not tell us he had a Son and a Spirit, but he sent them to be among us. And the Son and Spirit did not come to us in order to transmit information, but to do the work of saving, with the information about their existence and their nature being a necessary accompaniment to their saving presence. Considered from this angle, the correspondence between who God is in himself and who he shows himself to be in the economy of salvation is something we receive with praise, raising our bent arms like Adam. Theology in this mode is doxology, the praise of God.

But considered as a reflective theological movement of thought from below to above, the relationship between the economy and the eternal life of God is an intellectual project whose closest analogues are observation, induction, and the formation of conceptual models. Here theology has to be rigorous, consistent, creative in articulating how the various elements of the biblical witness are to be integrated, and accountable to others. It is all well and good to assert, as Karl Barth does, that "to the involution and convolution of the three modes of being in the essence of God there corresponds exactly their involution and convolution in his work."[6] But the actual work begins when we describe *how* the particular involution and convolution seen in the economic relations among Jesus Christ, his Father, and their Spirit are to be construed as revealing the very life of God. Theology in this mode is not just doxology, but "the praise of God by crafting concepts to turn the mind to the divine splendor."[7]

When we ask, "What does the economy signify about God's eternal life?" we have first the challenge of how to draw such inferences, and second the range of options that emerge in answering the question. First, we will examine the rules and restrictions on the inferences.

Not everything that God does is to be taken as revelatory of what he is. Some of what happens in the economy stays in the economy. Some obvious examples would be aspects of the incarnation that have to do with the Son's appropriating a human nature: If Jesus has brown eyes, should we say that the eternal Son before the foundation of the world had this feature? No. There are other, nonbiological aspects of salvation history that have more to do with the nature of the humanity being saved than the character

6. Karl Barth, *CD* I/1, 374.
7. John Webster, "Life in and of Himself," in *Engaging the Doctrine of God* (ed. Bruce McCormack; Grand Rapids: Baker Academic, 2008), 123.

of the person doing the saving. As we consider aspects of salvation history and what they reveal about the life of God in himself, we should bear in mind certain limitations.

A set of three limitations attaches to the notion of divine self-communication. First, divine self-revelation takes place under the form of some condescension from majesty, such that God in the incarnate Son and outpoured Spirit does not appear in his own proper glory but in a humbled form. As a result, second, it requires accommodation to human terms. As patristic discussion helped to clarify, even the term "sonship" is a term first learned from human relationships before God shows us that it applies analogically to a transcendent reality. The writings of Pseudo-Dionysius are a potent witness to the Christian theological tradition of understanding God's self-revelation as being simultaneously an unveiling of the truth about God and a veiling of the divine being behind revealed concepts and images. Calvin likewise describes God's speech as taking the form of divine "lisping," by which God speaks the truth about himself, but in a manner that is adjusted to be appropriate to our understanding. Calvin is also an eloquent advocate of the third restriction, which is divine reserve: God knows that some truths about divinity would not be beneficial or edifying for us, and so he withholds them from revelation. Anything that God does show or tell us, then, is selected from a larger pool of divine truth, things that are not shown or told for reasons reserved to God's inscrutable wisdom.

Another set of three limitations attach to the fact that the incarnation is the central point of God's self-revelatory presence. First, incarnation means that God is present under conditions of createdness, since the eternal Son of God took to himself a true human nature, which, considered in itself, is creaturely. This means that in the incarnation God appears under the sign of his opposite, or at least by taking a stand on the other side of the creator-creature distinction. Entailed by createdness, second, is the fact that what God makes known here is made known under conditions of temporality and multiplicity, whereby the God who does one continuous eternal act of faithful love must act out that same act repeatedly, in a temporally extended way, to continually manifest who he is in the schema of successive moments. Third, the incarnational focus of divine self-revelation means that the Son of God undertakes his mission as a participation in our fallen human plight, not for his own sake but "for us and for our salvation," as the Nicene Creeds says. This being the case, what we see in Christ is God being himself under conditions that are not his native sphere, so to speak.

Any particular observation we make about God's presence in the Son and the Spirit runs the risk of bouncing off these barriers. These barriers to inference are formidable, but none of them is sufficient to block all real knowledge. In fact, the trinitarian schema is uniquely well suited to pierce these barriers and deliver personal knowledge of God. Consider, for example, the way trinitarianism accounts for how God becomes man: not by deity becoming humanity, nor by God showing up in his majesty and lordship to exert sovereignty in the flesh and demand the worship due him. Instead, on the trinitarian view, the Father sends the Son, and so the divine person of the Son can appear under the sign of his opposite (strength as weakness, lordship as obedience, etc.) while still making known the character of God. Austin Farrer puts it this way:

> God cannot live an identically godlike life in eternity and in a human story. But the divine Son can make an identical response to his Father, whether in the love of the blessed Trinity or in the fulfilment of an earthly ministry. All the conditions of action are different on the two levels; the filial response is one. Above, the appropriate response is a co-operation in sovereignty and an interchange of eternal joys. Then the Son gives back to the Father all that the Father is. Below, in the incarnate life, the appropriate response is an obedience to inspiration, a waiting for direction, an acceptance of suffering, a rectitude of choice, a resistance to temptation, a willingness to die. For such things are the stuff of our existence; and it was in this very stuff that Christ worked out the theme of heavenly sonship, proving himself on earth the very thing he was in heaven; that is, a continuous perfect act of filial love.[8]

As Farrer says, it is impossible to imagine how God would act if God were a creature. To put the question that way is to force ourselves into an unresolved paradox: Would he act like the creator, or like a creature? What action could he take that would show him to be both? When the incarnate God walked on water, was he acting like the creator or the created? None of these questions are the kind of questions the New Testament puts before us. What the apostles want to show is that Jesus was the Son; he came, lived, taught, acted, died, and rose again like the Son of God.

It was the eternal Son, whose personal characteristic is to belong to the Father and receive his identity from the Father, who took on human nature and lived among us. His life as a human being was a new event

---

8. Austin Farrer, "Incarnation," in *The Brink of Mystery* (ed. Charles C. Conti; London: SPCK, 1976), 20.

in history, but he lived out in his human life the exact same sonship that makes him who he is from all eternity as the second person of the Trinity, God the Son. So when he said he was the Son of God, and when he behaved like the Son of God, he was being himself and explaining himself in the new situation of the human existence he had been sent into the world to take up. Notice that Jesus does not merely act out sonship, but also declares it and describes it. I do not want to give the impression that God's self-revelation is a pantomime routine, in which our job is to guess the right words from divine actions in history. No; Jesus as the incarnate Son is eloquent; he tells us he is the Son, and then he behaves as such. God's self-revelation is not charades, but show-and-tell. Our inference is always hermeneutics, always irreducibly textually mediated.

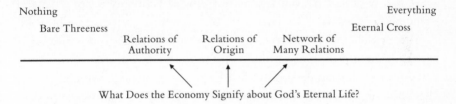

What Does the Economy Signify about God's Eternal Life?

Once we pose the question openly: what do the sendings of the Son and the Holy Spirit signify about the eternal life of God? we need to consider the range of possible inferences from the economy of salvation. Consider the possible answers as ranged on a spectrum with the classic answer at the center: the sending of the Son signifies the eternal relation of generation from the Father, and the sending of the Spirit signifies the eternal relation of the breathing of the Spirit from the Father. Ranging to the left are more minimal positions, and to the right are more maximal positions.

To begin with a glance at the extreme minimalist side, we can see that it is possible to deny that the coming of the Son and Spirit reveal anything whatsoever about the being of God. God shows nothing in the economy; he does something, but shows nothing. The most illuminating light in which to consider unitarian theologies is as the entirely negative answer to the question of what the divine reveals about itself in the history of salvation. Heresies like monarchian modalism, in which the one unipersonal God behaves three ways in his actions toward us, are also best understood as minimalistic answers to our basic question.

But what about the maximalist answer? What if God reveals everything in the history of salvation? This equally radical view on the other end of the spectrum takes all divine action in history and eternalizes it. It is a hard view to maintain because it requires a total rethinking of metaphysics. So Hegel has been the leading spirit, and anglo-American process theology a distant second. The sendings of the Son and Spirit reveal God in this case, but so does everything God does, because the divine nature is actualized fully and only in the history of salvation. In fact, on this view, it is hard to explain why the sendings of the Son and the Spirit should be considered equally important as the comprehensive events of creation and consummation.

The extremes are full of instructive errors, but perhaps the most basic error they share is the assumption that the economy can be interpreted using a general principle of self-revelation. For our purposes, the extremes serve as a warning that our inference from the economy is not a general principle of God-world relatedness, but something we had to be told. Whatever riches of the knowledge of God are revealed in the history of salvation, to approach the history as if it were self-evidently God's self-revelation would run perilously close to positing a general principle about the God-world relationship, a general principle that would itself be under-determined by revelation. Divine revelation is inalienably linked to intention on the part of the revealer, and "unfolds through deeds and words bound together by an inner dynamism," to use the words of Vatican II's *Dei Verbum*. Notice also that the two extremes both give rise to modalism. The nothing option gives us monarchian modalism in which one God does three things, whereas the everything option gives us dynamic modalism, in which the one God becomes three persons by self-actualizing along with creation.

Moving inward from the minimal answer is the position holding that what God has revealed in the economy is that there are three persons. This position refuses to specify further the identity of these three and remains satisfied with bare threeness itself. Relations among the three need not be specified, and the three need not be distinguished from each other. They are, in other words, potentially anonymous and interchangeable, perhaps undistinguished from each other even in themselves, but certainly in their revelation to us. If one sends and the other is sent at the economic level, this is not grounded in any actual relational distinction among them at the level of the eternal or immanent Trinity. Relationships of sending are considered to be not only below the line, but are considered as revealing nothing about what is above the line. Above the line is anonymous three-ness, and below it is free divine action. "Sonship," on this view, can be considered a messianic or salvation-historical characteristic, not attaching to the eternal second person but only taken on as this one takes up his mission and enters the economy.

If the "bare threeness" position is too minimal, the three can be said to be related to each other through eternal relations of authority: the first person sends the second because in eternity they are distinguished by personal characteristics of headship and authority. A Father is ordered over a Son, which is why the Father sends the Son.

The central position on this spectrum is the classic one, maintaining that the missions in the economy of salvation are revelatory of eternal relations of origin. Classic trinitarianism teaches that the Son and the Spirit proceed from the Father by two eternal processions. The sending of the Son, on this view, reveals that Son was always from the Father in a deeper sense than just being sent from the Father: he is eternally begotten. Nicene theology safeguarded this confession by distinguishing between the Son's being begotten by the Father and the world's being created by the Father through the Son. Just as "a man by craft builds a house, but by nature begets a son," reasoned Athanasius, "God brings forth eternally a Son who has his own nature."[9] A parallel argument for the Spirit, that the Pentecostal outpouring is an extension of his eternal procession from the Father (with or without the *filioque*), completes the classic doctrine of the Trinity. On this view, the coming of the Son and the Spirit into our history is an extension of who they have always been. When the Father sends the Son into salvation history, he is extending the relationship of divine sonship from its home in the life of God, down into human history. The relationship of divine sonship has always existed, as part of the very definition of God, but it has existed only within the being of the Trinity. In sending of the Son to us, the Father chose for that line of filial relation to extend out into created reality and human history. Again, a parallel argument for the sending of the Holy Spirit completes the doctrine: at his outpouring, his eternal relationship with the Father and the Son begins to take place among us.

Moving from this classic central position toward the more maximal end of the spectrum, we could argue that relations of origin are not enough, and that the complex relationships that unfold among Father, Son, and Holy Spirit in salvation history must be the manifestations of a corresponding set of eternal relationships in the eternal divine life. On

---

9. Athanasius, *Contra Arianos* 3.62.

this view, not only do missions reveal processions, but economic destinations ("I go to the Father") reveal eternal terminations, and temporal glorifications reveal eternal effusions. Many of these relationships are more obviously reciprocal than relations of origin. The Son comes from the Father, but not vice versa. However, the Son and the Father mutually and reciprocally glorify each other. Aware that he is recommending an innovation, Wolfhart Pannenberg argues that "the nexus of relations between [the persons] is more complex than would appear from the older doctrine of relations of origin ... each is a catalyst of many relations"; indeed, each person is constituted by a "richly-structured nexus of relationship."[10] The crucial thing to note about this view is that it occupies a position from which classic trinitarianism seems too reserved in its affirmation about how much is revealed in the economy of salvation.

Further in the direction of a maximal interpretation of economic revelation is the view that what we have seen in the death of Christ does not stand in paradox to what God is in eternity, but instead stands as the revelation of the very being of God. On this view, Christ's subjection to the conditions of human life, and especially his suffering and death, manifest the truth that God as such suffers. A variety of modern theologies since Moltmann have been drawn to a trinitarian version of theopaschitism.[11] Again, for our purposes here it is only necessary to note how far this view is from the classical tradition in terms of its answer to the question of what is revealed in the economy: proponents of this view believe that more has been revealed than previous theologies have confessed.

This second task of the doctrine of the Trinity, the task of articulating the content of divine self-revelation, is where major doctrinal judgments are rendered. At stake here is the utterly fundamental issue of how we understand God on the basis of self-revelation in word and act. Having surveyed the spectrum of options and indicated how they relate to each other and to the classic formulations of the doctrine, we are prepared for some briefer remarks on the three subordinate tasks of trinitarian theology: ordering doctrinal discourse, identifying the Christian God, and regulating soteriology.

---

10. Wolfhart Pannenberg, *Systematic Theology* (Grand Rapids: Eerdmans, 1991), 1:320.

11. Moltmann's *The Crucified God: The Cross of Christ as the Foundation and Criticism of Christian Theology* (Minneapolis: Fortress, 1974) was already quite far along the path of this sort of "trinitarian theology of the cross" (see 235–49), but *The Trinity and the Kingdom: The Doctrine of God* (Minneapolis: Fortress, 1981) has been most influential.

## 3. TRINITARIAN THEOLOGY ORDERS DOCTRINAL DISCOURSE

Trinitarian theology orders our doctrinal discourse simply by being such a vast doctrine. It is a field that encompasses many other fields of theology, most notably the doctrines of Christology and pneumatology. The health of a doctrine of the Trinity is a good indicator of the overall vigor of a theological system. Christology and pneumatology are each doctrines comprehensive enough to be treated as central and definitive areas; yet they require to be not only fully elaborated in their own right, but correlated with each other. The correlation of Christology and pneumatology with monotheism is not a bad description of the formal structure of trinitarian theology. Other sprawling doctrinal constellations or frameworks, such as the doctrine of revelation or the doctrine of salvation, likewise loom large in theology and are likewise to be subsumed and placed in the matrix of a well-articulated doctrine of the Trinity.

Since theology is primarily about God and secondarily about all things in relation to God, it stands to reason that the doctrine of God ought to occupy a determinative place in an overall doctrinal system. A theological system that takes its bearings from "theology proper" (that is, the doctrine of God) will be centered on, or dependent on, or (to vary the figure of speech again) located within the doctrine of God. When that doctrine of God is elaborated as a doctrine of the Trinity, the implications for the order of the entire system ought to be pronounced. John Webster has put this case sharply: "in an important sense there is only one Christian doctrine, the doctrine of the Holy Trinity in its inward and outward movements."[12] The implications for a rightly ordered theological system are that "whatever other topics are treated derive from the doctrine of God as *principium* and *finis*"; recognition of this is "crucial to questions of proportion and order in systematic theology. No other doctrinal locus can eclipse the doctrine of the Trinity" in its role of shaping theology as a whole.[13] The doctrine of the triune God, in other words, shapes the entire outlook of theology and serves as the matrix for the placement and treatment of all other doctrinal loci.

There are many possible ways of describing the relation of the trinitarian matrix to the other doctrines of systematic theology, especially as it

---

12. John Webster, "Principles of Systematic Theology," in *The Domain of the Word: Scripture and Theological Reason* (London: Bloomsbury/T&T Clark, 2012), 145.
13. Ibid.

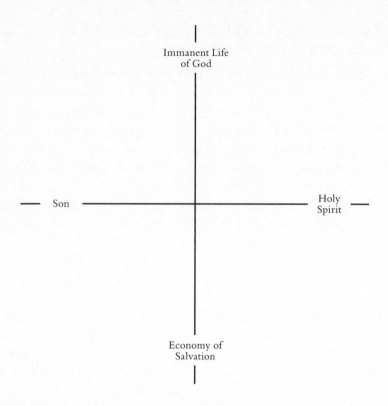

Immanent Life
of God

Son

Holy
Spirit

Economy of
Salvation

forms the background of Christian thought. I have come to prefer a kind of theological Cartesian plane, or the intersection of two axes. Because God has made himself present to us and known to us in the Son and the Spirit, the first axis runs from God's immanent life down to the economy, and the second runs between Son and Spirit. In other words, there is an immanent-economic axis crossed by a Christology-pneumatology axis.

The resulting quadrants establish the field of trinitarian theology, but they do more: they display the way that trinitarian theology orders other doctrinal discourse. The theological dynamics that generate the doctrine of the Trinity are those of God's self-communicating presence on the one hand (vertical axis) and the two missions of the Son and the Holy Spirit on the other (horizontal axis). All Christian doctrines must in one way or another work themselves out in these same tensions, whether each doctrine is rendered explicitly trinitarian or not. Because this way of schematizing the doctrine is an attempt to depict the theological struc-turing forces of trinitarianism rather than to signify the Trinity itself (as triangular diagrams inevitably suggest), it has some helpful peculiarities. Using these quadrants to describe the Trinity, we could talk about the immanent Son and the economic Son, or the immanent Holy Spirit and the economic Holy Spirit. This enables us to discuss the personal identity of the Son and the Holy Spirit at either end of the immanent–economic axis (that is, in the top two quadrants and in the bottom two quadrants, respectively).

## 4. Trinitarian Theology Identifies God by the Gospel

The task of ordering doctrinal discourse follows rather directly from the primary tasks of summarizing the Bible's story line and then articulating the content of divine revelation. Taken together, these three tasks imply a fourth task, one so normative and critical that it must have been accomplished simultaneously with them. The doctrine of the Trinity serves to identify God by the gospel, or to specify the identity of the God of Christian faith. It does so primarily by insisting that God is the author of two central interventions into the course of human history, the incarnation of the Son and the outpouring of the Spirit. These two actions, considered not in isolation but as culminating events, mark God as a particular God. The God who sent a Son and a Holy Spirit, because he always already had a Son and a Holy Spirit to send, must be essentially different from a God who could not and did not self-communicate in this way.

To say this is to treat the doctrine of the Trinity as a kind of name of God, as Robert W. Jenson has argued: "Thus the phrase, 'Father, Son, and Holy Spirit' is simultaneously a very compressed telling of the total narrative by which Scripture identifies God and a personal name for the God so specified."[14] Kendall Soulen's recent book, *The Divine Name(s) and the Holy Trinity*, has championed and recovered the tetragrammaton, the actual revealed name of God, with such vigor that he has made it impossible to speak blithely about the trinitarian formula as the name of God without at the same time recalling the tetragrammaton as the one un-superceded, unrelativized name.[15] But trinitarian doctrine continues to play its crucial role in identifying God by reference to the gospel. Lesslie Newbigin has argued that this function of trinitarianism comes to the fore especially in periods when Christian theology recalls that it cannot take the identity of its God for granted. Various periods of increased awareness of cultural diversity and pluralism have historically brought with them renewed

---

14. Robert W. Jenson, *Systematic Theology* (New York: Oxford University Press, 1997), 1:46.
15. R. Kendall Soulen, *The Divine Name(s) and the Holy Trinity* (Philadelphia: Westminster), 2011.

attention to trinitarian theology: the fourth century, the sixteenth, and the late twentieth.[16]

# 5. TRINITARIAN THEOLOGY INFORMS AND NORMS SOTERIOLOGY

Finally, trinitarian theology plays an indispensable role in orienting the doctrine of salvation. We have already said as much in indicating the trinitarian background of all Christian doctrines, and how they must all be placed on the field of trinitarian discourse. But this function of informing and norming soteriology requires special attention, because it moves us from Christian theology to the Christian life.

For the Trinity to inform and norm soteriology is for the doctrine of the Trinity to give the shape and the material content and to dictate its parameters. The doctrine of salvation needs this sort of outside guidance if it is to maintain its balance between two besetting errors. The errors are of defect and excess, of not enough salvation on the one hand and too much salvation on the other. Trinitarian doctrine holds soteriology to the mean between them.

First, the error of defect: I have in mind a perennial tendency to minimize soteriology, to diminish it to something with no depth of ingression into the life of God. If soteriology is reduced to a lordship and obedience relationship, with forgiveness or sacraments as a way of patching up that relationship when it has been transgressed, then all the richness of the biblical language is flattened out or dumbed down; Christian sonship is merely metaphorical or analogous, and all the apostolic language of temple, courtroom, and family are interpreted as poetic ways of saying that God chooses to forgive or reconcile. A depth is missing here, and it is against this kind of reduction that so many modern trinitarians are reacting, under the slogan of Karl Rahner that many believers are "almost mere monotheists." This minimal soteriology could be underwritten by a unipersonal God—almost by a deistic God, certainly by Allah. Trinitarian theology summons Christian soteriology to go deeper.

But not too deep. For at the opposite extreme is the error of excess. I have in mind here a style of soteriology that obliterates all distinctions between divinity and humanity, leaping over every barrier, beginning

---

16. Lesslie Newbigin, *The Relevance of Trinitarian Doctrine for Today's Mission* (Edinburgh: Edinburgh House Press, for the World Council of Churches Commission on World Mission and Evangelism, 1963), 32.

with that between creator and creature. Think of the Rhineland mystics who boasted of being "Godded with God and Christed with Christ," but also of the way theosis (deification) is celebrated at the popular level, or schemes of ontological participation are championed in a variety of theologies.

When the doctrine of the Trinity is fulfilling its function of informing and norming soteriology, it rules out both extremes. John Calvin reminds us that "God, to keep us sober, speaks sparingly of his essence." And yet the same Calvin, taking his norms from a trinitarian account of the adoption of believers by the Father in the only begotten Son by the Spirit of adoption, celebrates the depth and richness of the fellowship that is ours in Christ. God speaks sparingly of his essence, but lavishly of his Son and of our adopted sonship. A soteriology informed and normed by the doctrine of the Trinity equips us to recognize our intimacy with and our distinction from God in Christ. As Kevin Vanhoozer says, "Only the doctrine of the Trinity adequately accounts for how those who are not God come to share in the fellowship of the Father and the Son through the Spirit."[17] This too is a task of the doctrine of the Trinity, and it follows directly from the major and primary task of correlating the events of salvation history with the divine being in itself.

---

17. Kevin J. Vanhoozer, *The Drama of Doctrine: A Canonical-Linguistic Approach to Christian Theology* (Louisville: Westminster John Knox, 2005), 43–44.

# CHAPTER 2

# TRINITY DOCTRINE, PLAIN AND SIMPLE

## THOMAS H. MCCALL

## I. INTRODUCTION

"Most Christians have not even heard of the doctrine of divine simplicity," observes one recent theological textbook.[1] The authors of this textbook go on to assert that the doctrine of divine simplicity "has been the biggest reason why the Trinity has been presented as an impenetrable mystery of faith ... and why most Christians finally tend toward a unipersonal view of God—typically associated with the Father."[2] They are convinced that the doctrine of divine simplicity does not cohere well with the doctrine of the Trinity; indeed it has "no real biblical basis and has in fact worked to defeat the resources of a full-fledged trinitarianism."[3] My guess is that these theologians are correct in their assessment of the current state of affairs; from my own experience, among many evangelical Protestant Christians at least, there indeed is widespread ignorance. I also think that they speak for many contemporary theologians who *have* encountered the doctrine and have given it some thought—surely many theologians take it to be obvious that the doctrine of divine simplicity is not consistent with the doctrine of the Trinity. The alternatives seem both obvious and stark: either the doctrine of simplicity or the doctrine of the Trinity. The right

---

1. Richard J. Plantinga, Thomas R. Thompson, and Matthew D. Lundberg, *An Introduction to Christian Theology* (Cambridge: Cambridge University Press, 2010), 104.
2. Ibid.
3. Ibid.

choice also seems plainly obvious to most contemporary Christians: go with the doctrine of the Trinity. Christians are supposed to be trinitarians, right? So if the doctrine of divine simplicity clashes with the doctrine of the Trinity, then so much the worse for simplicity doctrine. What is there even to talk about?

But it wasn't always so. The doctrine of divine simplicity—in some version or other—has been a staple ingredient of Christian theology for centuries. At its most basic the denial that God is made up of parts or pieces, it runs from patristic theology (both Greek and Latin) through medieval scholasticism right into the early modern era. Along with the doctrine of the Trinity, it is inscribed in various creeds and confessions (Protestant as well as Roman Catholic). For centuries, Christians have held firmly to belief in both the doctrine of the Trinity and the doctrine of divine simplicity, and they have done so in the face of challenges (challenges to both doctrines and their fittingness for one another). Across the broad Christian tradition, it seems as if the doctrine of simplicity is just *there*, and many times it is used as support for the doctrine of the Trinity. Today, however, there is widespread rejection of the doctrine of divine simplicity—and much of this rejection is based on the assumption that Trinity and simplicity are incompatible.

Before proceeding let me confess that as a Christian, I am committed to the doctrine of the Trinity. So if there is genuine conflict between this doctrine and the doctrine of simplicity, then I'll gladly be a trinitarian. But is there such conflict? Are the two doctrines really incompatible? Here I should make another confession: I find implausible the notion that virtually the entire church was so wrong—and, if the critics are right, so *obviously* wrong, and so obviously and *devastatingly* wrong—about something so central. At any rate, I think this question deserves sustained and rigorous analysis.

I cannot provide all that needed analysis here, but I hope we can make some headway. So this is what I will try to do: I will offer a piece of "retrieval theology."[4] First, I will look at some important patristic and medieval efforts to hold the doctrines together (and to do so in the face of important challenges), and I will relate this work to some important contemporary challenges to the doctrine of divine simplicity (hereafter: DDS). Second, I will use this historical background as I seek to press these

---

4. I borrow the term from John Webster, "Theologies of Retrieval," in *The Oxford Handbook of Systematic Theology* (eds. John Webster, Kathryn Tanner, and Iain Torrance; Oxford: Oxford University Press, 2007), 583–99.

insights into constructive service; here I will develop several accounts of the doctrine of simplicity and relate them to the desiderata of Trinitarian theology. While I readily admit that what I am doing here is more tentative and exploratory than final or definitive, I think we can make some genuine progress. I will show that there is more than one version of the DDS in the tradition,[5] and I will argue that there are at least two versions of the doctrine that are consistent with the doctrine of the Trinity.

# II. YESTERDAY AND TODAY: SOME THEOLOGICAL BACKGROUND

## A. YESTERDAY: TRINITY AND SIMPLICITY IN THE CHRISTIAN TRADITION

Richard A. Muller states that "from the time of the fathers onward, divine simplicity was understood as a support of the doctrine of the Trinity."[6] The theology of Gregory of Nyssa serves as a case in point.[7] Gregory clearly affirms the doctrine (at least some version of it). When speaking of the divine nature, he insists that it does not "possess the good by acquisition, or participate only in the goodness of some good which lies above it: in its own essence it is good ... it is simple [ἁπλή] and uniform [μονοειδής]."[8] For "where a compound is assumed, there the dissolution of that compound must be admitted."[9] God just is "all his attributes always," and "we must remember that God is not a compound; whatever he is is the whole of him."[10] God is "by nature simple, uncompounded, and indivisible."[11]

More specifically, Gregory denies that there are any distinctions in the divine nature "that would divide that divine and transcendent nature within itself by any degrees of intensity or remission, so as to be altered

5. Christopher Stead warns us that "we must not think that simplicity is itself a simple notion"; see "Divine Simplicity as a Problem for Orthodoxy," in *The Making of Orthodoxy: Essays in Honor of Henry Chadwick* (ed. Rowan Williams; Cambridge: Cambridge University Press, 1989), 256.

6. Richard A. Muller, *Post-Reformation Reformed Dogmatics: The Rise and Development of Reformed Orthodoxy, ca. 1520 to ca.1725*; vol. 3: *The Divine Essence and Attributes* (Grand Rapids: Baker Academic, 2003), 276.

7. Andrew Radde-Gallwtiz observes that Gregory uses the DDS against "anti-Nicene Christians like Eunomius, opponents of the Spirit's divinity, and Greek polytheists"; see his *Basil of Caesarea, Gregory of Nyssa, and the Transformation of Divine Simplicity* (Oxford: Oxford University Press, 2009), 212. Interestingly, Stephen R. Holmes sees the DDS employed by Gregory against the Macedonians but not against Eunomius, e.g.,in *The Quest for the Trinity: The Doctrine of God in Scripture, History, and Modernity* (Downers Grove, IL: IVP Academic, 2012), 108. It should be obvious that my interpretation of Nyssa is much closer to that of Radde-Gallwitz.

8. *Against Eunomius*, Book I.22, PG 45:336A; *NPNF2*, 5:61.

9. *Against Eunomius*, Book I.22, PG 45:341A; *NPNF2*, 5:62.

10. *Against Eunomius*, Book I.38, PG 45:433D; *NPNF2*, 5:90.

11. *Against Eunomius*, Book X.4, PG 45:848A; *NPNF2*, 5:226.

from itself by being more or less. Because we firmly believe that it is simple [ἁπλή] and uniform [μονοειδής] ... we see in it no complicity or composition of dissimilars."[12] While it may not seem to us as though "the Good" is the same as "the Wise," "the Mighty," or "the Righteous," yet in God "the thing to which all the attributes point is one; and, when you speak of God, you signify the same whom you understood by the other attributes."[13]

Gregory is deeply convinced of the truth of the doctrine, and he employs it polemically against the theology of the "Eunomians" (or "Neo-Arians").[14] Eunomius of Cyzicus (along with Aetius and others) argued that the Son is "like [the Father] according to will, different according to *ousia*."[15] The Eunomians were convinced that names reveal the essence of things; thus, on Michael E. Butler's terse summary, "*agennetos* = God, *gennetos* = Son."[16] Because names reveal the divine essence, God can be known exhaustively.[17] Ingenerateness is thus the basic and exhaustive definition of God; because "*agennetos* exhaustively defines the essence of God," the "divine essence is absolutely simple and beyond all comparison or analogy."[18] The Son, therefore, is *heteroousios* rather than *homoousios* (or even *homoios*). As Hanson concludes, "in short, for Eunomius generatedness and *ousia* are inseparable, because the Son is generated his *ousia* cannot but be different to the Father."[19] All this entails, of course, that the Son is radically and ontologically subordinate to the Father, with the Holy Spirit subordinate to both Father and Son. As Lewis Ayres puts it, "the Son has a clearly subordinate status; Eunomius assumes

---

12. "On the Holy Spirit," *GNO* III.1, p. 91; *NPNF2*, 5:316.

13. "On the Holy Trinity," *GNO* III.1, p. 8; *NPNF2*, 5:327.

14. For a detailed look at the life and career of Eunomius, see Richard Paul Vaggione, *Eunomius of Cyzicus and the Nicene Revolution* (Oxford: Oxford University Press, 2000). For a mislabeled, somewhat dated, but still helpful account of the theology of "Neo-Arianism," see Thomas Kopacek, *A History of Neo-Arianism* (2 vols.; Cambridge, MA: Philadelphia Patristic Foundation, 1979). For more recent and generally more helpful descriptions, see Michel Barnes, *The Power of God: Δυναμις in Gregory of Nyssa's Trinitarian Theology* (Washington: Catholic University of America Press, 2001); idem, "Eunomius of Cyzicus and Gregory of Nyssa: Two Traditions of Transcendent Causality," *VC* 52 (1998): 59–87; Lewis Ayres, *Nicaea and Its Legacy: An Approach to Fourth-Century Trinitarian Theology* (Oxford: Oxford University Press, 2004), 144–49; and Khaled Anatolios, *Retrieving Nicaea: The Development and Meaning of Trinitarian Doctrine* (Grand Rapids: Baker Academic, 2011), esp. 72–76, 158–94.

15. R. P. C. Hanson, *The Search for the Christian Doctrine of God: The Arian Controversy ca. 318–381 A.D.* (Edinburgh: T&T Clark, 1988), 635.

16. Michael E. Butler, "Neo-Arianism: Its Antecedents and Tenets," *SVTQ* 36 (1992): 370.

17. See Hanson, *Search*, 629; and Graham A. Keith, "Our Knowledge of God: The Relevance of the Debate between Eunomius and the Cappadocians," *TynBul* 41 (1990): 60–88.

18. Butler, "Neo-Arianism," 370.

19. Hanson, *Search*, 626.

that ingenerate defines God in a unique way: God's unity and simplicity imply that ingenerate is the only characteristic of God."[20]

Note that the Eunomians wield the DDS *against* the pro-Nicenes. They are certain that the divine nature is simple, and because it is simple it admits of no distinctions. Obviously, then, there is no room whatsoever for (what the tradition comes to refer to as) *personal* distinctions. God—the high God, that is, the proto-Father—is alone supreme and sovereign, and the divine essence just *is* his ingenerateness. By any reckoning, the Son *is* generated, so it is abundantly clear that the Son does not share the utterly simple divine essence. As Gregory rehearses the view, Eunomius holds that "they say that God is declared to be without generation, that the Godhead is by nature simple, and that which is simple admits of no composition. If, then, God who is declared to be without generation is by his nature without composition, his title of ungenerate must belong to his very nature, and that nature is identical with ungeneracy."[21]

So Eunomius (and the "Neo-Arians") hold that the Son and Spirit are hierarchically ranked, with the Father "on top" as supreme over all while the Son is under him and the Holy Spirit beneath both Father and Son. Thus the divine persons differ from one another "in magnitude and in subordination of their dignities;" they also possess natures that are "foreign and unfamiliar to each other."[22] All this is supported by appeal to the DDS. At the risk of oversimplification, for our purposes his argument may be summarized as follows:

(1) If the DDS is true, then there can be no distinction between ingenerate and generate in the divine nature;[23]
(2) the DDS is true;
(3) therefore, there can be no distinction between ingenerate and generate in the divine nature.

For Eunomius, the conclusion follows directly and is incontrovertible. If we accept the DDS, then the Son and Spirit must be alien to the divine nature of the Father—they are *heteroousios* rather than *homoousios*. And since the truth of the DDS is obvious, the debate is over and Eunomius can claim swift and easy victory.

Or can he? It might seem that the obvious thing to do here would be

---

20. Ayres, *Nicaea*, 147.
21. "Answer to Eunomius's Second Book," *NPNF2*, 5:252.
22. *Against Eunomius*, I.19, PG 45:317D; *NPNF2*, 5:56.
23. E.g., "Answer to Eunomius's Second Book," *NPNF2*, 5:252.

to reject the DDS; indeed, it might seem that denial of (2) is the *only* way forward for the pro-Nicene. But this is not what Gregory does. He does not reject (2). Instead, he rejects (1); here he draws an important distinction between the divine nature (which is simple) and the divine persons who subsist in that nature. As he puts it, "things that are identical on the score of being [οὐσίας] will not all agree equally in definition on the score of personality [ὑποστάσεων]."[24] He continues to hold to the DDS, but he denies that it erases all distinctions. The genuine *personal* distinctions are not distinctions of *nature*. This means that if we interpret Gregory as positing a generic divine essence (as in this context his example of Peter, James, and John might suggest),[25] then we should think of the divine nature as something like the full set of properties that are individually necessary and jointly sufficient for inclusion in the kind-essence divinity.[26] The Father, the Son, and the Holy Spirit all share this essence; they all have it in its entirety. In fact, given the DDS, it couldn't be otherwise, for if the Son (or Spirit) has the divine essence, he couldn't fail to have all divine attributes.

On the other hand, if we take Gregory as a kind of trope theorist (as overall seems more likely as an interpretation of Gregory),[27] then the divine nature is a concrete particular. In this case, the divine persons all repeat it—they all share the numerically identical divine nature three times over. As distinct persons, of course, they repeat it in ways that are appropriate to their personal distinctions; thus they differ in the mode or manner in which each person possesses the divine nature. Either way, Gregory retains the DDS. But either way, his version of the DDS differs significantly from Eunomius's take on the doctrine. For taken either way, Gregory's view needs a genuine distinction between *person* and *nature*.

Gregory does not rest content with a rejection of Eunomius's argument. Instead, he launches a counterattack that also appeals to the DDS. Again risking oversimplification, the relevant elements of his argument may be summarized as:

(4) If the DDS is true, then there can be no gradations of divinity or divisions within the divine nature;

---

24. *Against Eunomius*, I.19, PG 45:320B; *NPNF2*, 5:56.

25. See, e.g., Nathan Jacobs, "On 'Not Three Gods'—Again: Can a Primary-Secondary Substance Reading of *Ousia* and *Hypostasis* Avoid Tritheism?" *MTh* (2008): 331–58; and Johannes Zachhuber, *Human Nature in Gregory of Nyssa* (Leiden: Brill, 2000), and "Once Again: Gregory of Nyssa on Universals," *JTS* 55 (2005): 75–98.

26. E.g., Thomas V. Morris, *The Logic of God Incarnate* (Ithaca, NY: Cornell University Press, 1986).

27. E.g., Richard Cross, "Gregory of Nyssa on Universals," *VC* (2002): 372–410; and William Hasker, *Metaphysics and the Tri-Personal God* (Oxford Studies in Analytic Theology; eds. Michael C. Rea and Oliver D. Crisp; Oxford: Oxford University Press, 2013), esp. 62–67.

(5) the DDS is true;

(6) therefore, there can be no gradations of divinity or divisions within the divine nature.

Given the DDS, Gregory sees trouble for the Eunomians. As he puts it, "it will be clear, upon the very slightest reflection, that this view of the supreme being as simple, however finely they may talk of it, is quite inconsistent with the system they have elaborated."[28] For "simplicity in the case of the Holy Trinity admits of no degrees."[29] He explains further:

> Nothing which possesses wisdom or power or any other good, not as an external gift, but rooted in its nature, can suffer diminution in it; so that if any one says that he detects Beings greater and smaller in the divine nature, he is unconsciously establishing a composite and heterogeneous deity, and thinking of the subject as one thing, and the quality ... as another.[30]

He continues by saying that "if he [i.e., Eunomius] truly conceived of the essence as 'simple and altogether one,' being good in virtue of what it is and not coming to be so by acquisition, he would not have considered greater and lesser in connection with it."[31] Given the DDS, there can be no gradations of divinity. If some person is divine, then that person is fully and completely divine. Given the DDS, being "kinda divine" or "divine-ish" or of a lesser divinity is not even a possibility.

Gregory presses this objection in defense of his Christology.[32] Where Eunomius insists that the Son has inferior qualities and thus deserves less honor, Gregory argues that the DDS makes this impossible. For given the DDS, there "is no greater and smaller in power, or glory, or wisdom, or love, or of any other imaginable good whatever, but the good which the Son has is the Father's also."[33] The Son, if divine, cannot be a created being who is inferior to the Father in power and knowledge. The suggestion that the Father has a higher-quality divinity is unthinkable; "for that which is simple in nature is not parted asunder into contradic-

28. *Against Eunomius*, I.19, PG 45:321B; *NPNF2*, 5:57.
29. *Against Eunomius*, I.19, PG 45:321B; *NPNF2*, 5:57.
30. *Against Eunomius*, I.19, PG 45:321B; *NPNF2*, 5:57.
31. *Against Eunomius*, I.19, PG 45:321C-D; here I adopt the translation of Radde-Gallwitz, *Basil of Caesarea*, 205.
32. Basil Krivocheine says that Gregory employs the DDS "regularly" in theological debate, "Simplicity of the Divine Nature and the Distinctions in God, According to St. Gregory of Nyssa," *SVTQ* 23 (1979): 80.
33. *Against Eunomius*, I.24, PG 45:356B; *NPNF2*, 5:66.

tory attributes."[34] If the Son is "divine," then the Son has the entire set of divine attributes, and he has these attributes maximally.

Gregory argues similarly with respect to the divinity of the Holy Spirit. Again, he denies that there are any distinctions in the divine nature "that would divide that divine and transcendent nature within itself by any degrees of intensity and remission, so as to be altered from itself by being more or less. Because we firmly believe that it is simple, uniform, incomposite, because we see in it no complicity or composition of dissimilars ... we accept by the implication of that very name the perfection in it of every conceivable thing that befits the deity."[35] As divine, the Holy Spirit must be as fully and completely divine as the Father and Son; "simple in every respect equally," there can be no "diminution or essential variation" in the divine nature.[36] Given the DDS, it isn't so much as possible that the Spirit has an inferior level of divinity. Thus "you will find no falling off whatever in dignity, or glory, or omnipotence, such as to constitute him capable of increase by addition, or of diminution by subtraction." For "being wholly and entirely perfect" — as perfect as the Father and Son in virtue of sharing the same nature — "he admits diminution in nothing."[37]

We can summarize Gregory's DDS as follows: it is the absence of any properties that could threaten contradiction or dissolution within the divine essence. It is the "absence of contradiction;" it is the "indivisibility of God."[38] As Krivocheine says, on Gregory's DDS the divine nature is not subject to "internal contradictions;" the divine nature has "no parts, consequently [is not] dissoluable or decomposable."[39] Following the masterful work of Andrew Radde-Gallwitz, we can say that for Gregory, "we are far from holding that divine simplicity entails that God only has a single property or that God has no properties — so far in fact that, in his hands, the doctrine of simplicity actually comes to entail that God has *multiple* properties."[40] How, we might wonder, is this still a doctrine of *simplicity?* Radde-Gallwitz continues to explain that

34. τὸ γὰρ ἁπλοῦν τῇ φύσει πρὸς τὰ ἐναντία τῶν ἰδιωμάτων οὐ διασχίζεται, *Against Eunomius*, X.4, PG 45:847C; *NPNF2*, 5:227.

35. "On the Holy Spirit," *GNO* III.1, p. 91; *NPNF2*, 5:316.

36. "On the Holy Spirit," *GNO* III.1, p. 92; *NPNF2*, 5:317.

37. "On the Holy Spirit," *GNO* III.1, p. 93; *NPNF2*, 5:318.

38. Krivocheine, "Simplicity of the Divine Nature," 91, 93.

39. Ibid., 103.

40. Radde-Gallwitz, *Basil of Caesarea*, 212. Cf. Joseph O'Leary, "Divine Simplicity and the Plurality of Attributes," in *Gregory of Nyssa: Contra Eunomium II, An English Translation with Supporting Studies, Proceedings of the 10ᵗʰ International Colloquium on Gregory of Nyssa* (eds. Lenka Karfikova, Scot Douglas, and Johannes Zachhuber; Leiden: Brill, 2007), 327–28.

because it is the perfect virtues that are reciprocally entailing. And being a perfect virtue is just being a virtue without any admixture of that virtue's opposite. And this way of being unmixed, in turn, is one of Gregory's fundamental ways of describing the state of being simple. So, if God is good and God is simple, then God's goodness is unmixed with its opposite—and, consequently, God is also powerful, just, wise, and so forth.[41]

So Gregory endorses the DDS, but he does not think that this rules out all distinctions. To the contrary, as Krivocheine puts it, for Gregory it is "impossible to speak about the simplicity of the divine nature without referring it to the distinctions which are discernible in God."[42] The Holy Trinity is "consummately perfect and incomprehensibly excellent, yet as containing clear distinctions within itself which reside in the peculiarities of each of the persons [and] differentiated by the unique character of each person."[43] For "when we confess three persons [τρεῖς ὑποστάσεις] we say that there is one goodness [μίαν ἀγαθότητα], and one power [μίαν δύναμιν], and one Godhead [μίαν θεότητα]."[44] The divine nature does not admit of the kinds of distinctions that would divide the persons or that would admit of greater or lesser degrees. To put it crudely, whatever is properly predicated of the divine nature is a sort of unbreakable package. To put it slightly less crudely, the divine attributes are mutually and necessarily coextensive. Are there distinct properties within the divine essence according to Gregory's doctrine? Yes, indeed. Are there "parts" within God? Not at all. While there are genuine distinctions between the divine persons and between the divine essence and the divine persons, such distinctions do not threaten the DDS (on Gregory's version of the doctrine).[45] Nor do they threaten the doctrine of the Trinity—to the contrary, Gregory wields this DDS in support of pro-Nicene trinitarianism.

With this summary in view, we can briefly recapitulate Gregory's argument. As he sees things, it isn't Gregory's view that violates the DDS; it turns out that it is Eunomius's doctrine that does so. For given the DDS, it is unthinkable that the divinity of the Son could be inferior to that of the Father. It simply is not possible for there to be gradations of divinity within the life of the one God. Against Eunomius, Gregory is arguing

---

41. Radde-Gallwitz, *Basil of Caesarea*, 212.
42. Krivocheine, "Simplicity of the Divine Nature," 76. Radde-Gallwitz has convinced me (against such defenders as David Bradshaw and Basil Krivocheine and such detractors as Christopher Stead) that we should not read Gregory as a "proto-Palamite" (cf. *Basil of Caesarea*, 221–24).
43. *Against Eunomius*, PG 45:336B; *NPNF2*, 5:61.
44. "On the Holy Trinity," *GNO* III.1, p. 5; *NPNF2*, 5:326–27.
45. *Against Eunomius*, I.35, PG 45:405B (ὑποστάσιον ἰδιότητα), *NPNF2*, 5:81.

that his position is inherently unstable: he cannot have a Son who is of a lesser divinity and still be a monotheist. The only options are, on the one hand, a doctrine according to which monotheism is secure but the Son is not divine, or, on the other hand, the polytheism that is entailed by the Eunomian doctrine that there are three divine persons who do not share a common divinity.

So for Gregory (as opposed to the Eunomians), the Father does not have A+ divinity, while the Son has A divinity and the Spirit is relegated to A- divinity. There is only one divinity (on pain of polytheism), and either you have it or you don't. If we read Gregory as positing a generic or abstractist account, then this set of mutually entailing divine properties is possessed by Father, Son, and Holy Spirit. The divine nature is thus an "absolutely indivisible unity, not capable of increase by addition or of diminution by subtraction."[46] Each of the persons is divine—*fully* divine. If we interpret Gregory as holding to a concretist account, then the Father, the Son, and the Holy Spirit all share the numerically identical trope of divinity. Again, all are divine—*fully* divine. Given commitment to monotheism and the DDS along with the biblical witness to the distinction and divinity of the persons, it couldn't be otherwise.

Other examples from the tradition can readily be adduced, and in this tradition we can see both varying versions of the DDS and different uses of the doctrine. Bonaventure, for example, devotes considerable and sustained attention to the question "Whether the Trinity Can Exist Together with the Highest Simplicity?"[47] But for our scholastic representative let us turn our attention to the lesser-known account of John Duns Scotus (with a brief look at the more familiar DDS of Thomas Aquinas as background). Famously, Thomas Aquinas (and others) issues a series of denials on account of the DDS: God is not composed of extended parts (God does not have a body), God is not composed of substantial form and form-receiving matter, God is not composed of act and potency, God is not composed of essence and existence, God is not composed of subject and accidents, God is not composed of God-plus-anything-else.[48] God is not, then, made up of parts or pieces more fundamental than God; indeed,

---

46. *Ad Ablabium*, PG 45:120B; *NPNF2*, 5:332.

47. Bonaventure, *Works of Saint Bonaventure III: Disputed Questions on the Mystery of the Trinity* (ed. George Marcil, OFM; introduction and trans. by Zachary Hayes, OFM; New York: Franciscan Institute, 1979), 159–83.

48. *ST* Ia.3. For detailed discussion of Aquinas's DDS, see especially Christopher Hughes, *A Complex Theory of a Simple God: An Investigation in Aquinas' Philosophical Theology* (Ithaca, NY: Cornell University Press, 1989); and Eleonore Stump, *Aquinas* (New York: Routledge, 2003), 92–130; idem, "God's Simplicity," in *The Oxford Handbook of Aquinas* (eds. Eleonore Stump and Brian Davies; Oxford: Oxford University Press, 2012), 135–46.

God is not made up of parts or pieces at all. Other than the real distinctions that are the real relations internal to God's nature, there are no real distinctions. On the contrary, the only distinctions that we can posit are those that we must admit are merely provisional and from our side.

Scotus, however, takes a decidedly different view. He sees conceptual space between "real distinctions" (between independent things) and merely conceptual distinctions; here he locates his controversial "formal distinction." The formal distinction falls short of a real distinction; a formal distinction is not a distinction between different things of the same essence or different things of different essences, nor is it a distinction between separable parts of the same thing. But neither is it a merely conceptual distinction; it isn't something invented by us for our convenience or ease of reference. Instead, the formal distinction is "such that exists between two (or more) formal aspects of the essence of a thing."[49] For Scotus, two entities are formally distinct if the distinction is genuine (that is, it is within the thing itself and not merely rational or mental) but not between two different essences or between separable parts or pieces of the same thing. In other words, two entities are formally distinct if (and only if) they are both really identical and genuinely distinct on account of the distinction within itself.

The key here, once again, is inseparability; separation is logically impossible, it is not even logically possible for the entities in question to be separated and still to exist. So two entities can be formally distinct — that is, genuinely distinct but not really distinct (in the technical sense of "real" in play here) — if they are both really inseparable and genuinely distinct on account of distinctions found in themselves.[50] Scotus employs the formal distinction in several ways: the divine attributes are formally distinct from one another, the divine attributes are formally distinct from the divine essence, and the divine persons are formally — though not "absolutely" — distinct from the divine essence.[51] When it comes to the doctrine of the Trinity, while Scotus will also employ the more traditional language of real distinctions between the divine persons, he holds that the divine persons are "fully real, subsistent entities" who are, in the words of

---

49. Richard A. Muller, *Dictionary of Latin and Greek Theological Terms: Drawn Principally from Protestant Scholastic Theology* (Grand Rapids: Baker, 1985), 93–94. For Duns Scotus's use of this distinction, see *God and Creatures: The Quodlibetal Questions* (trans. with an intro., notes, and glossary by Felix Alluntis and Allan B. Wolter; Princeton: Princeton University Press, 1975), esp. 505–7.

50. This summary draws from Thomas H. McCall and Keith D. Stanglin, *Jacob Arminius: Theologian of Grace* (New York: Oxford University Press, 2012), p. 54.

51. For helpful discussion, see Richard Cross, *Duns Scotus on God* (Aldershot: Ashgate, 2005), 154.

Richard Cross, "necessarily interdependent."[52] Thus the persons are genuinely distinct, and modalism is avoided. But the divine persons are also really—even logically—inseparable, thus polytheism is avoided as well.

To this point we have seen how the DDS relates to the doctrine of the Trinity in two representatives of the Christian tradition. For all their differences—one is, after all, a Greek patristic theologian while the other is the quintessential Latin scholastic—they believe that God is both simple and triune. Moreover, they are convinced that the DDS not only coheres well with the doctrine of the Trinity but indeed provides support to it. But is there promise here? Or is this all nothing more than a big distraction? Are there resources here for a way forward today? Or are these alternatives dead-ends too? To consider such questions, we need to make sure that we are understanding the contemporary worries and criticisms.

## B. *TODAY: CHALLENGES TO THE DOCTRINE OF DIVINE SIMPLICITY*

We can safely say that the venerable doctrine of divine simplicity is somewhat less than wildly popular in contemporary theology. It is confronted with questions and objections from several angles. To mention a few of the most common and most pressing, Alvin Plantinga famously has argued that Aquinas's doctrine faces both a "substantial" objection and a "monumental" objection. The substantial objection is this: "if God is identical with each of his properties, then each of his properties is identical with each of his properties, so that God has but one property. But this seems flatly incompatible with the obvious fact that God has several properties."[53] The monumental objection is this: "if God is identical with each of his properties, then, since each of his properties is a property, he is a property ... but no property could have created the world; no property could be omniscient, or, indeed, know anything at all. If God is a property, then he isn't a person at all but a mere abstract object."[54] Ryan T. Mullins adds an extremely important charge (among others); he alleges that the doctrine of simplicity entails the loss of divine freedom and thus modal collapse. To get the basic idea, his argument may be summarized as:

(7) If the DDS is true, then God cannot be free (in any meaningful or theologically robust sense of freedom);

---

52. Ibid., 154–55.
53. Alvin Plantinga, *Does God Have A Nature?* (Milwaukee: Marquette University Press, 1980), 47.
54. Ibid.

(8) God is free;

(9) Therefore, the DDS is not true.[55]

Because we are most directly interested in the doctrine of the Trinity, I won't have much to say about these criticisms. I think that some of them are based on misunderstandings of the traditional doctrine,[56] some of them do not take sufficient notice of variety within the traditional affirmations (and may be fatal to some versions of the doctrine but not to others), and others can be met head-on.[57] The criticisms deserve serious and sustained engagement, and surely further work remains. Such work would take us too far afield. For present purposes, however, the most important criticism is this: the charge that the doctrine of the Trinity is logically inconsistent with the doctrine of divine simplicity.

## III. TODAY AND TOMORROW: ON BEHALF OF SIMPLE TRINITARIANISM

So how are we to think about these issues? Are the critics right that the doctrine of the Trinity is simply inconsistent with the DDS? Or is the venerable doctrine defensible and believable for trinitarian Christians?

### A. *SIMPLICITY NOT SO SIMPLE: INITIAL STEPS TOWARD CLARITY*

Throughout I've been referring to various versions of the DDS; now it might help to distinguish between three possible formulations of the DDS (I'm sure that there are others, and these might be Chisholmed out further, but this is a start). Often the doctrine is considered only as "Strict Simplicity," which we can summarize as:

> (S-DDS) God is simple in the sense that within God (i) there is no composition whereby God is made up of parts or pieces that are onto-logically prior to or more basic than God; (ii) there is no metaphysical or moral complexity of any kind; (iii) there are no genuine distinctions

55. Ryan T. Mullins, "Simply Impossible: A Case against Divine Simplicity," *JRT* 7 (2013): 181–203. Cf. idem, "Divine Perfection and Creation," *HeyJ* 52 (2011): 1–13. This is a very serious objection, and it deserves serious consideration.

56. E.g., Stump, *Aquinas*, 108–15; Muller, *Post-Reformation Reformed Dogmatics*, 3:40 n.63. Stump argues that "accident" does not mean for Aquinas what the critics of the DDS usually take it to mean; Muller argues that Plantinga does not adequately understand Aquinas's meaning.

57. E.g., Jeffrey E. Brower, "Simplicity and Aseity," in *The Oxford Handbook of Philosophical Theology* (eds. Thomas P. Flint and Michael C. Rea; Oxford: Oxford University Press, 2009), 105–28; and Alexander R. Pruss, "On Two Problems of Divine Simplicity," *Oxford Studies in Philosophy of Religion* (ed. Jonathan L. Knanvig; Oxford: Oxford University Press, 2008), 1:150–67.

within God, and (iv) everything in God is identical (divine properties are identical with one another, and the divine persons are all identical with the divine essence).

Or we might consider the doctrine in a somewhat more nuanced sense. In honor of Scotus, let us refer to this as "Formal Simplicity":

(F-DDS) God is simple in the sense that within God (i) there is no composition whereby God is made up of parts or pieces that are ontologically prior to or more basic than God; (ii) there is no metaphysical complexity that would threaten divine unity or moral complexity of any kind; (iii) there are no genuine distinctions within God other than formal distinctions (recall: inseparability); and (iv) all divine perfections are really identical.

More modestly yet, and taking a cue from Gregory,[58] we might conceive of it as "Generic Simplicity:"

(G-DDS) God is simple in the sense that within God (i) there is no composition whereby God is made up of parts or pieces that are ontologically prior to or more basic than God; (ii) there is no metaphysical complexity that would bring contradiction or moral complexity of any kind; (iii) there are genuine distinctions within the divine nature; and (iv) all essential divine attributes are mutually entailing and coextensive.[59]

## B. GENERIC SIMPLICITY AND THE DOCTRINE OF THE TRINITY

Taking these in reverse order, let's start with Generic Simplicity. Is there anything about this doctrine that would be inconsistent with trinitarian theology? It is not obvious that there is, or indeed that there might be anything problematic here. Consider (i); surely there is nothing here that would contradict any important desiderata of trinitarian theology. The divine persons are not parts or pieces of God, and on no tolerably orthodox doctrine of the Trinity are the divine persons in any sense ontologically prior to God. Since it is not so much as possible that any of the divine persons exist without the others or apart from the divine essence, they are not, strictly speaking, *parts* of God.[60] So far as I can see, (ii) is no threat

---

58. Radde-Gallwitz points out that "Gregory merely asserts the simplicity of the divine nature, rather than adequately responding to Eunomius," and he concludes that a charitable reading sees Gregory's "attempt to reconcile simplicity with trinitarianism as an incomplete task rather than as a logical blunder," *Basil of Caesarea*, 217–18.

59. Cf. Jay Wesley Richards, *The Untamed God: A Philosophical Exploration of Divine Perfection, Simplicity, and Immutability* (Downers Grove, IL: InterVarsity Press, 2003), 217–24.

60. Although William Lane Craig does propose a mereological model of the Trinity, e.g., J. P. Moreland and William Lane Craig, *Philosophical Foundations for a Christian Worldview* (Downers Grove, IL: InterVarsity Press, 2003), 589–95.

at all to the doctrine of the Trinity, and (iii) coheres very well with what the trinitarian theologian should wish to say. Meanwhile, (iv) actually brings support to the trinitarian, as it serves to definitively rule out all versions of Arianism (at least for the monotheist). Maybe G-DDS doesn't really do enough for the trinitarian, and some may protest that it looks like simplicity "on the cheap." Some will think that it really turns out to be an account of divine *unity* rather than simplicity (preferring to reserve the label "simplicity" for more robust versions). And maybe it is rendered moot by essentialism.[61] But it surely looks consistent with the doctrine of the Trinity.

## C. FORMAL SIMPLICITY AND THE DOCTRINE OF THE TRINITY

What about F-DDS? So far as I can see, there is nothing here that would bring the doctrine of the Trinity into conflict with simplicity. On (i), God is not composed or built up out of parts or pieces that are somehow more basic than God. Any traditionally-minded trinitarian can affirm this. According to (ii), there is no metaphysical complexity that would destroy or threaten divine unity as well as no moral ambiguity or complexity within God. Again, the trinitarian—even the social trinitarian—should say this much.

The important element here, so far as I can see, is (iii). According to (iii), the only genuine distinctions are *formal* distinctions. Recalling that, according to the formal distinction, separation is logically impossible; it is not so much as logically possible for the entities in question to be separated and still to exist. Whatever other work the distinction might (or might not) do, it works well indeed for the trinitarian here, for is not this exactly what the trinitarian wants to say? According to classical trinitarian doctrine, the divine persons are genuinely and irreducibly *distinct*. They are also, on classical accounts, ontologically and logically *inseparable*. So it appears that F-DDS coheres well with the doctrine of the Trinity. Indeed, it offers an account of irreducible distinction-within-inseparability. Far from being antithetical to (or even in tension with) the doctrine of the Trinity, it actually supports the doctrine. Of course this doctrine of simplicity itself is not without critics (both traditional and contemporary), and it may be that the common criticisms will turn out to be fatal. My point

---

61. I am grateful to Oliver Crisp's Beard for pressing me on this point (uncomfortable though the encounter was).

here is rather modest: it is only that F-DDS is a version of the DDS that coheres well with the doctrine of the Trinity.

## D. STRICT SIMPLICITY AND THE DOCTRINE OF THE TRINITY

What about "Strict Simplicity?" I fear that this version of the doctrine truly may be inconsistent with trinitarian theology. If there are no distinctions within God, then the divine persons cannot be distinct. But if the divine persons cannot be distinct, then we do not have any doctrine of the Trinity.

Some traditional statements of the doctrine affirm real distinctions between the divine persons but deny all other distinctions. On some statements of "simple trinitarianism," the Father is said to be identical to the divine essence, the Son is said to be identical to the divine essence, and the Holy Spirit is said to be identical to the divine essence—while, of course (and on pain of modalism) the divine persons are not identical to one another. The immediate—and immediately damning—problem is obvious on standard accounts of identity. Identity, as an equivalence relation that satisfies "Leibniz's Law" of the Indiscernibility of Identicals, is reflexive, symmetrical, and transitive. Transitivity is crucial. As William Hasker explains, "if A is identical with B, and B with C, then A is identical with C."[62] But then the claims that the Father is identical with the divine essence and the Son is identical with the divine essence just entail that the Father is identical to the Son. The doctrine of the Trinity gives us

(10) the Father is not identical to the Son.

Meanwhile, some versions of the DDS give us both

(11) the Father is identical to the divine essence;[63] and
(12) the Son is identical to the divine essence.

Given the fact that identity is symmetrical and transitive,

(13) the Father is identical to the Son

is strictly entailed by the conjunction of (11) and (12). But (13) is the direct and explicit denial of (10), and as such it is in direct contradiction to orthodox trinitarianism. This entailment is heretical, of course, but it follows inexorably from the identity of both the Father and the Son with the divine

---

62. William Hasker, *Metaphysics and the Tri-Personal God* (Oxford Studies in Analytic Theology; ed. Michael C. Rea and Oliver D. Crisp; Oxford: Oxford University Press, 2013), 59.
63. Cf. Thomas Aquinas, *ST* I, q.39.1.

essence. If the divine persons are all identical with the divine essence, then (on the argument from (10) to (13)) the divine persons will be identical with one another. Such a doctrine seems hopeless for trinitarian theology.

In a recent article, James Dolezal remonstrates in defense of S-DDS (or something close to it). He sees that there is some problem in the neighborhood, for he says that the claim that "there can be real identity between the essence, which is one, and the divine persons, which are three," surely "seems to contravene the law of identity."[64] So far as I can see, his defense amounts to an appeal to an analogical (rather than uni-vocal) account of religious language. But it isn't obvious to me that this appeal can do enough work to address the concern. For even if we deny that the notion of "person" is univocal and allow for the traditional kinds of qualified differences between human persons and divine persons, we nonetheless are left with the argument. Nothing about this argument (from (10) to (13)) depends on a univocal account of personhood, nor does it assume that the divine persons are "modern individuals." For *whatever* they are, if the Father is identical to the divine essence, which is also identical with the Son, then the Father and the Son are identical. Moreover, even Dolezal's defense (here following Turretin) appeals to what can only appear to be differences in properties between the essence and the persons: the essence is absolute and communicable, while the persons are relative and incommunicable.[65] But if the divine essence has the properties *being communicable* and *being non-relative*, while the persons have the properties *being incommunicable* and *being relative,* then they clearly have different properties. And if the divine essence and the divine persons have different properties (presumably of necessity), then they are not really identical after all.

In summary, I fear that I cannot see a way forward for S-DDS.[66] This is not to say that there could be no way forward. It is possible that my theological myopia is the only real problem here. Perhaps an appeal to

---

64. James E. Dolezal, "Trinity, Simplicity and the Status of God's Personal Relations," *IJST* 15 (2013): 10.

65. Ibid., 17.

66. The extent to which the version I'm calling S-DDS actually reflects most tradition-based (Latin) versions of the doctrine is an open question. I readily grant that Thomas Aquinas and oth-ers sometimes say things that sound much like it, but Aquinas also insists that the divine persons are really distinct (e.g., *ST* Ia.28.3, resp.). Muller argues that both defenders (e.g., William Mann) and critics (e.g., Plantinga) of the DDS often mistakenly assume S-DDS (or something like it); see Muller, *Post-Reformation Reformed Dogmatics,* 3:40–41. See, e.g., William Mann, "Simplicity and Immutability in God," in *The Concept of God* (ed. Thomas V. Morris; Oxford: Oxford University Press, 1987), 253–67.

numerical sameness without identity can help here, or maybe there are other ways forward.[67] Any such possibility warrants further consideration. Nonetheless, it should be clear that the challenges look daunting.

# IV. CONCLUSION

Much of the Christian tradition has taken the doctrines of the Trinity and divine simplicity to be coherent and indeed true. The situation is very different today. The doctrine of divine simplicity faces many questions, challenges, and objections. It is charged with denying that there are any genuine distinctions in God, with reducing God to a property, and with entailing modal collapse and thus (among other problems) the loss of divine aseity. I realize that I have done nothing to advance the discussion of these important issues, nor have I offered any analysis of the factors that might motivate the doctrine. My own view—and here I part company with some of my historically respectful theological colleagues—is that these questions deserve responses and the challenges deserve careful consideration. We cannot simply brush off the concerns of the critics with hand-waving dismissals about historical (mis)understanding. To the contrary, I also think—and here I part company with some of my colleagues in analytic theology—that the case against the doctrine of simplicity has not yet been shown to be decisive. Surely there is more work to be done.

What I hope to have done here is something rather modest: I hope to have reopened conversation about the relation of the DDS to the doctrine of the Trinity. So far as I can see, this conversation should remain open. For there are at least two versions of the doctrine of simplicity that appear to cohere well with trinitarian theology. Indeed, for major theologians in the Christian tradition, the DDS offered help to the trinitarian Christian. Perhaps the contemporary theologian who wishes to embrace classical orthodoxy and remain a monotheist may learn from this tradition. If I can encourage this conversation, this exercise has been a success.

---

67. Relative Identity strikes me as the most promising way forward.

CHAPTER 3

# TRINITARIAN ACTION AND INSEPARABLE OPERATIONS
## Some Historical and Dogmatic Reflections

STEPHEN R. HOLMES

THE ANCIENT LATIN SLOGAN *opera trinitatis ad extra sunt indivisa* has not been universally popular recently. Indeed, it has been held up by some systematicians as a lapidary summary of everything Augustine and the Latins got wrong in their misappropriation of Greek trinitarian theology. It, or at least the doctrine it summarises, has fared better in patristic scholarship, however; recent study on the fourth-century debates, led by Michel Barnes and Lewis Ayres, has stressed repeatedly and, to my mind, simply convincingly not just that pro-Nicene theologians universally held to the inseparability of divine operations, but that this principle was key to the logic of pro-Nicene theology, providing (along with the related commitment to divine simplicity) one of its central bulwarks against the charge of tritheism.

In this paper I will first sketch this argument with regard to two representative pro-Nicene theologians, Gregory of Nyssa and Gregory of Nazianzus. This will largely be repetition of already established scholarship, but will be helpful in bringing clarity over the shape—and variety—of pro-Nicene claims concerning inseparable operations. I will then explore two issues that the doctrine raises: the relationship of the relationships of origin to the doctrine of inseparable operations, and the relationship of the economic missions of the Son and the Spirit to that doctrine. I explore these as systematic questions, looking to demonstrate the coherence of the various doctrines; in this I draw gratefully on the tradition, of course, but I am not primarily trying to expound the thought of any particular theologian or school. Rather, given the narratives about trinitarian theology that have predominated in systematic discussions in recent decades, I think certain doctrinal themes, including the inseparability of divine operations, stand in need in our context of retrieval and re-presentation to be rendered comprehensible and plausible in our culture. This is my prospectus; let us begin the exposition by turning to the Cappadocian Fathers.

# 1. THE DOCTRINE OF INSEPARABLE OPERATIONS IN THE FOURTH CENTURY

Barnes has argued in a number of essays that the crucial distinction between pro-Nicene and Eunomian theology in the third quarter of the fourth century was a differing understanding of divine operations — classed sometimes as causality,[1] sometimes as *dunamis* or power.[2] He characterises Gregory of Nyssa's core argument as a syllogism:

> The Father and the Son have the same power.
> Whatever has the same power has the same nature.
> Ergo, the Father and the Son have the same nature.[3]

To be clear, the point about possession of "the same power" here is not equality, but identity. For Barnes, the move from earlier "Nicene" theologies to later "Pro-Nicene" theologies comes in the move from the older "X from X" arguments, and specifically from the — perfectly biblical — claim that the Son is the power of the Father, to more nuanced claims that the Father and the Son share one and the same power. This distinction depends on the fact that "power" had two parallel traditional uses in pre-Nicene theology: on the one hand, God can be spoken of as

---

1. Michel Barnes, "Eunomius of Cyzicus and Gregory of Nyssa: Two Traditions of Transcendent Causality," *VC* 52 (1998): 59–87.
2. Michel Barnes, "'One Nature, One Power': Consensus Doctrine in Pro-Nicene Polemic," in *Historica, Theologica et Philosophica, Critica et Philologica* (ed. Elizabeth A. Livingstone; StPatr 29; Louvain: Peeters, 1997), 205–23.
3. Ibid., 219.

power—so Tertullian, for example, can use phrases such as "one power, one substance" to assert the unity of Father, Son, and Spirit; on the other hand, the Son can be spoken of as the Father's power. This second use is then developed by claiming that the Father is never impotent, never without his power, and so the Son must be coeternal with the Father. (An argument with which Augustine found fault, of course.)

A standard development of these two lines, made popular by Origen and then found in other terms in the creed, speaks of the relationship of the Son to the Father in "X from X" language: in the creed, "God of God, light of light, true God of true God"; here, "power from power." The unity of power in this slogan is most naturally understood, if there is no further qualification, as a unity of equality. This is clear the common pre-360 language of the Son as "image": the exact image of the Father is equal to, but other than, the Father.

Later pro-Nicene theology, exemplified for Barnes by Gregory of Nyssa, moves beyond this. Although Gregory against Eunomius will be his crucial example, Barnes finds the earliest examples of the new position in Latin writers of the 350s who find language to oppose extreme Homoian theology by reaching back behind Nicaea to the anti-modalist tradition of Hippolytus and Tertullian. Phoebadius and Hilary of Poitiers are both cited arguing that Father and Son have the same nature because they have the same power—not equality, but identity. To take a crude analogy, the point is not that I am as wealthy as my wife (equality) but that we have a joint bank account, so our wealth is simply identical. Later Ambrose in the West, and Gregory in the East, will make the same assertion; Barnes sums up with the claim "Gregory's argument for the unity of the Trinity uses the unity between φύσις and δύναμις as the fundamental proof for the unity between divine nature and the divine persons and between the Father and the Son."[4]

Now, without some background in ancient philosophy this language of "power"—still more Barnes's other example of "productive cause"— might be opaque. The import of it can helpfully be seen, however, in a well-known text, Gregory's On "Not Three Gods." I will sketch Gregory's argument in this well-known, and oft-anthologised, text; although it is not the most important text for his trinitarianism, it does illustrate my points here well and has the great benefit of familiarity to many readers. Ablabius has offered Gregory an analogy: we say that Peter, James, and

---

4. Ibid.

John share a common nature, humanity, but we happily call them three men; why do we then not call Father, Son, and Spirit three gods even though they share the common divine nature? Gregory offers two arguments in response: one concerning the indivisibility of natures, which even if true is not really to the point, in that it would leave us with the same unity between Peter, James, and John as we find between Father, Son, and Spirit; I thus take it, with most modern readers—Stead is the significant exception[5]—that the second argument, which concerns unity of action, is the heart of the case made.

Gregory insists, in common with every pro-Nicene theologian, that we cannot know or name the divine essence—if this point is conceded, Eunomianism seems to be the only option. All our names for deity, therefore, refer to divine operations (at one point Gregory offers a rather implausible etymology of θεότης, "Godhead," as being derived from θέα, "seeing," and so referring to God as "the all-seeing One," a name that references an operation). Given that Gregory wants to insist that all our names for deity apply indifferently to Father, Son, and Holy Spirit alike, he therefore argues that the divine operations are indifferently the operations of Father, Son, and Spirit. Unity of power and unity of action/operations are, in Gregory's view, mutually entailed, just as unity of power and unity of essence are: there is one divine operative power, so, on the one hand, God is one, and, on the other, divine operations are inseparable.

His famous analogies of three cooks preparing the same meal are in fact offered as disanalogies: this is not what the divine life is like. Three cooks perform three separate actions toward the same end; Father, Son, and Spirit together perform one single action. There are no analogies for this that are useful; elsewhere Gregory will, like Augustine later, speculate about psychological analogies that, as with Augustine, attempt to show not the personality of God, but this triune single action, but Gregory—again, like Augustine—is well aware of the limitations of such moves.

Gregory of Nazianzus is important in the story also: on the one hand, his famous "theological orations," preached in Constantinople in the months before the Council convened, show a reaffirmation of similar points to Nyssan; on the other, a recent essay by Verna Harrison[6] argues

---

5. G. Christopher Stead, "Why Not Three Gods?" in *Studien zu Gregor von Nyssa und der Christlichen Spätantike* (ed. H. R. Drobner and Christoph Klock; Leiden: Brill, 1990), 149–63.

6. Verna E. F. Harrison, "Illumined from All Sides by the Trinity: Neglected Themes in Gregory's Trinitarian Theology," in *Re-Reading Gregory of Nazianzus: Essays on History, Theology, and Culture* (ed. Christopher A. Beeley; Washington, DC: Catholic University of America Press, 2012), 13–30.

that he has in fact a distinctive position, which may allow some of the recently claimed distinctions between West and East to be maintained.

The fifth theological oration (*Or.* 31) illustrates both these points helpfully—although again of course the proof, as opposed to illustration, of either must rely on a broader reading than I can offer here. To illustrate, first, the role of unity of power in Nazianzen's thought, consider his summary statement of his doctrine:

> We have one God, because there is a single Godhead. Though there are three objects of belief, they derive from a single whole and have reference to it.... They are not sundered in will or divided in power. You cannot find there any of the properties of things divisible ... the Godhead exists undivided in things divided. It is as if there were a single intermingling of light, which existed in three mutually connected Suns.[7]

The image of light is, of course, an ancient one, owing something at least to Ps 36:9: "With you is the fountain of light; in your light we see light," a text regularly used to demonstrate the unity of Father and Son in the patristic period. Gregory references the text elsewhere in this oration (*Or.* 31:3), and Theodoret quotes Athanasius as suggesting that the line "light of light" in the creed of Nicaea results from the citation of this text during the council.[8] Although the text is regularly invoked, Gregory's particular use here is interesting, however: he has moved away from the traditional image (which he does consider elsewhere) of the sun, its rays, and its light to an image of three suns—stressing the equality of Father, Son, and Spirit (and at least implying, contra Zizioulas for instance, that the Son and the Spirit are autotheotic, but that is an argument for another day). The three suns are "mutually connected"—every created image needs to be strained to breaking point (and, here, some way beyond) to serve even remotely adequately as an analogy for the divine life—and their light is one; notice that Gregory deliberately qualifies "intermingled" with "single" to make the point that there is one operation here.[9]

Gregory continues to stress the point: "each of the Trinity is an entire unity as much with himself as with the partnership, by identity of being and power" (*Or.* 31:16). Unity of power implies unity of identity and unity of essence. The Cappadocian doctrine—in Nazianzen as much as

---

7. *Or.* 31. 14, translation from St. Gregory of Nazianzus, *The Five Theological Orations and Two Letters to Cledonius* (Crestwood, NY: St Vladimir's Seminary Press, 2002), 127.

8. Theodoret, *Hist. eccl.* 1.7.

9. The Greek is μία τοῦ φωτὸς σύγκρασις.

in Nyssan—is that confessing unity of operations is the crucial, perhaps the only, defense against the accusation of tritheism.

Alongside this recognition, however, these quotations illustrate Harrison's suggestion of a distinctive theme within Nazianzen's theology. She proposes that there is a characteristic rhetorical move in his various *Orations*,[10] a repeated employment of antithesis to hold together two truths that are apparently in tension. With regard to the Trinity, there is, perhaps unsurprisingly, a regular antithesis between unity and plurality. A fine example of this occurs in *Or.* 39: "... they are divided undividedly, if I may speak thus, and united in division. For the divinity is one in three, and the three are one, in whom the divinity is, or, to speak more precisely, who are the divinity."[11] This delight in rhetorical antithesis is certainly a feature of Gregory's preaching; the question is whether it implies a distinctive theology.

Harrison argues that it does, specifically on the point I have been considering. She speaks of "distinct yet collaborative activities of the divine persons"[12]—a denial of the claim of inseparable operation—and then suggests that this distinctive theology, mediated through the regular liturgical reading of Gregory's homilies in the Eastern church, is adequate to establish the claim that there is a distinctively Eastern trinitarianism, which has recently been rediscovered by the West; are these claims supported by the evidence?

I fear the answer must be no, in both cases. On the first, the only textual evidence she presents for separated operations is the quotation I have already cited from *Or.* 31. She places emphasis on the word translated in my citation "intermingling"—she prefers "commingling," but I am not sure there is much at stake in that translation difference. The Greek word is σύγκρασις, which she identifies as a technical Stoic term that "refers specifically to a kind of mixture in which the things blended—in this case, the *activities* of the three divine persons, named as light—each retain their own identity and properties. This kind of blending," she continues, "contrasts with a fusion in which the distinct identity and properties of each are lost."[13]

I note first that the contrast drawn from Stoic philosophy here is not to the point: I see nowhere a claim that the "distinct identities" of Father,

---

10. She counsels, rightly, against focusing too heavily on the "Theological Orations," suggesting that these are essentially polemic, and that Gregory's other sermons, particularly his festal sermons, are better sources for his positive doctrine. Accepting all this, as with Nyssan I reference the most familiar text for purposes of illustration.

11. Quoted in Harrison, "Illumined from All Sides," 18.

12. Ibid., 22.

13. Ibid., 21.

Son, and Spirit are lost in their unity of operation (the "distinct ... properties" are moot, since Gregory, of course, affirms that there are no distinct properties of the persons, save only the relationships of origin). Rather, the question on the table is whether there is one single divine operation or three separate divine operations. Even Harrison's own description of the meaning of the technical Stoic term suggests that there is only one — she speaks of a "blending" resulting in a "mixture."

Elsewhere, it seems to me that Harrison's citations make it clear that Gregory was committed to unity of power and so unity of operation; her concern about the triune nature of this single power/operation is important, and something I will come back to, but for now let me survey the evidence for unity. As her title ("Illumined from All Sides ...") makes clear, Harrison is concerned about a powerful image from Gregory in which in contemplation we are caught up in, surrounded by, the light of the Trinity. She describes Gregory's narration of this as an endless movement, his "gaze" shifting "between God as one and the three persons"; she immediately acknowledges, however, that "Gregory uses a περί compound to speak of the hypostases as three lights surrounding him, adding that together they constitute one undivided light."[14] She concludes this discussion of mystical vision with the summary comment, "When he says 'but one light,' this statement is juxtaposed antithetically to the statements about threeness that precede it and must not be understood as negating or superseding them."[15] Again, the positive point, that we must not lose the specifically trinitarian character of the single power/being/light of God, is well taken, but it cannot be read, as Harrison clearly acknowledges, as a denial of the singleness of those divine realities.

We find the same result when we move away from mystical vision to classical theological claims. Harrison cites the third theological oration as follows:

> Monarchy [in God] is what we value, yet not a monarchy restricted to one person ... but held together by equality of nature, agreement of will, identity of movement, and convergence to the one from whom they came — all of which is impossible for created nature. So though there is distinction in number, there is no division of the essence.[16]

The monarchy — an absolutely central theological term — and the movement here are unequivocally asserted to be single; I take it that the

---

14. Ibid., 20, citing Gregory, Or. 23:11.
15. Harrison, "Illumined from All Sides," 21.
16. Gregory, Or. 29:2, cited in Harrison, "Illumined from All Sides," 23.

terms in the repetition "equality of nature, agreement of will, identity of movement" are to be taken as synonymous, and that Gregory here—as he does elsewhere—asserts singleness of "essence" and "will" also. If Harrison's only concern is to insist that the single essence, operation, will, light, and life of God is triune, then of course she is right, but it is difficult to see that this point is unique to Nazianzen.

The essay begins by suggesting that, in focusing on Nyssan, Barnes—and indeed Ayres—have inaccurately minimised the distinction between East and West, and that a focus on Nazianzen would correct that inaccuracy; unfortunately, the distinctions being sought are, I believe, phrased unhappily: inseparability of operation can coexist with specifically, and ordered, triune action. Harrison offers a helpful reminder of the distinctive shape of triune action, which will become important for my reflections before the end of this paper (which is why I have given her arguments so much time); this does not, however, in any way suggest the basic doctrine of a single divine power, or of the inseparability of divine works, stands in need of amendment.

## 2. INSEPARABLE OPERATIONS AND THE RELATIONS OF ORIGIN

So, I turn to the first of my two systematic investigations, concerning the relations of origin. The theology I have sketched so far insists that there is one divine essence, and so one divine power, and so one divine operation; how, under this rubric, do we make sense of the claims that the Father begets the Son and that the Spirit proceeds from the Father and the Son?

Now, it may be that the right answer here is, "we don't!" The ancient slogan with which I began insists only that the external operations of the Trinity are inseparable, precisely because, I presume, there was an unwillingness to ask the speculative question concerning the eternal divine life. The immanent life of the Godhead, insofar as we can speak of it at all, is characterised by two eternal events (whatever that means): the eternal generation of the Son and the eternal procession of the Spirit. This leads quickly to the five notions, the only five things that, according to Thomas Aquinas, we can actually know to be true of the eternal divine life: the Father is ingenerate; the Father generates the Son; the Son is generated by the Father; the Father and the Son spirate the Spirit; and the Spirit proceeds from the Father and the Son. Perhaps the wise theologian confesses all this to be true and then stops and refuses to speculate how any of this relates to the single power of the Trinity and the inseparability of the divine operations; certainly this seems to have been the general patristic answer.

Contemporary systematicians, however, face questions in articulating the doctrine of the Trinity that the Fathers never faced, and so perhaps they do need to face questions they never framed or chose to pass over as too speculative. In particular, the pervasive post-Rahnerian predilection for identifying the eternal life of God with the gospel history, even if it is rejected, creates a particular intensity around the question of how economy and eternity relate. The two systematic problems I have identified are both, I suggest, raised to prominence by this context.

This first problem is real, if we are to avoid the error that Harrison warned against in her explorations of Nazianzen. We must not move from a recognition of the three distinct eternal divine hypostases to an account of the economy that is undifferentiated and that speaks simply of the work of God. If recent theology and spirituality has been guilty of that—it was Rahner's weighty charge, of course—then recent theology and spirituality has been inadequately trinitarian. (This only I will concede to Rahner.) Further, this question of divine activity does seem to me to be where this problem bites most seriously; many of the problems raised against classical trinitarianism can be answered easily and quickly by an appeal to Christology, if only we are attentive to classical Christology; this one cannot. We find ourselves required, on the one hand, to insist on a single divine operation—as a condition, as I have shown, for not lapsing into tritheism; the monarchy of God is what is at stake here—and, on the other hand, to confess at least two diverse operations—generation and procession—that are not just appropriated but actually divided up between the three Persons. I think in the contemporary context I have sketched, it is appropriate to find this unsatisfactory and not to rest content with a suggestion of impenetrable mystery.

I do not think, however, that the resources to answer this question are available in fourth-century trinitarianism; I am no great expert on the period, and would be happy to be told otherwise, but for now this is how it looks to me. Thomas, already cited, gives us the clearest way through. At the heart of Thomas's doctrine is the claim that the three Persons are subsistent relations, and here I think is a clue to how to solve our first systematic problem.

Thomas's reasons for teaching that the Persons are subsistent relations bear examination. He is aware, of course, of the problems of terminology

that were noted explicitly by Augustine:[17] simply put, straightforward etymology would translate both *ousia* and *hypostasis* as *substantia* in Latin, and
so the Greek distinction between the two appears unavailable. The Latins
had their own vocabulary, *substantia* and *persona*, developed by Tertullian,
but mapping the two vocabularies together was at least nontrivial; indeed,
by Thomas's time, several definitions of what *persona* actually meant were
available: Boethius had offered the classic version, but he had derived his
definition from reflecting on the subdivisions of Aristotelian categories,
not from trinitarian dogma, and it did not easily correspond; as a result,
Richard of St. Victor had offered an alternative definition more adequate,
so he thought, to trinitarian doctrine. Thomas is aware of all this debate
and negotiates it carefully; in his view Boethius's definition is the right
one, but it needs some degree of redefinition to make it serviceable for
trinitarian use.[18]

All of this is to say that Thomas was aware of a need to adequately
narrate the being of Father, Son, and Spirit, and he was actively engaged
in reflecting on this question. His account of the persons as subsistent relations no doubt owes something to this reflection—and indeed to similar
reflection that his teacher Albertus Magnus and other medieval theologians had undertaken. The primary question in this tradition of reflection
was, does the word *person* most properly reference the essence of each of
the Three, or the relation, the distinctive character? Thomas rejects the
former fairly quickly: necessarily, the essence of the divine Persons is just
the divine essence, and so this option leads to a collapsing of the Persons
into the *ousia*. Most medieval theologians attempted a middle way, holding that the term referred to both essence and relation, but to whatever
extent "essence" is invoked, the same problem occurs: *persona* means to
some degree the same as *substantia*. Thomas therefore insists that *person*
means just the relation, the peculiar property of each of the Three—
unbegottenness, begottenness, and procession.

He is able to make this move only because of his earlier analysis of the
nature of the triune relations. Following the line proposed variously by
Gregory of Nazianzus, Augustine, and Boethius, *relation* is a metaphysical
term that refers to a genuine distinction in a simple essence that does not,
however, introduce division and so compromise simplicity. The eternal
generation of the Son by the Father is an account of how the unrepeatable

---

17. *De Trin.* 5.9.
18. Giles Emery gives a helpful summary of this background: *The Trinitarian Theology of Thomas Aquinas* (trans. Francesca A. Murphy; Oxford: Oxford University Press, 2007), 110–14.

divine essence is related to itself. The relations are real, but the essence remains simple and so, crudely speaking, one.

This account presumes for its coherence, I think, Thomas's account of perichoresis, an idea that was not developed in the fourth century, which may be a reason why the logic Thomas proposes was not worked out earlier. He insists on the complete mutual indwelling of the Three: commenting on John's gospel, Thomas asserts:

> In material things, what comes forth from another is no longer in it, since it comes forth from it by a separation from it in essence or in space. But in God, coming forth does not arise in this way. The Son came forth eternally from the Father in such a way that the Son is still in the Father from all eternity. And when he comes forth, he is in him, in such a way that he is always coming forth and always in him.[19]

On the basis of this mutual indwelling, we can see that the relations of origin can be considered self-relations of the single divine essence.

The last part of the jigsaw here is Thomas's fundamental account of God as *actus purus* ("pure act"). The claim is once again connected with the nexus of divine perfections that mark out the uniqueness of the Godhead. Here the initial point is the logical claim that metaphysical perfection excludes potentiality because to fulfill any imagined potentiality in the divine life would make God better, and a claim that God is perfect excludes the possibility of God becoming better. Given this, we may assert that there is no activity proper to God that is not always eternally fulfilled by God: God is pure act, without any unfulfilled potentiality.

The point for our purposes is the dynamism here proposed as being native to the divine life. (As an aside, one of the repeated complaints against so-called "classical theism" in the twentieth century was that it proposed a unacceptably static view of deity;[20] it may be that this is demonstrable, perhaps with particular reference to certain debased forms of the tradition—the neo-Thomism of a Garrigou-Lagrange, for example—but at the level of assertion, where it usually operates as far as I can see, it is a complaint so wrong-headed as to be almost incredible; Thomas asserts that God is a verb, eternal action without any external stable actor; his God cannot be classed as too static.) What is this eternal action that God is? The conclusion is (I think) mine, not Thomas's, but it seems necessary: it is

---

19. In *Ioan.* 16:28 (no. 2161) the translation is from ibid., 307.

20. The point is endemic, but see (*e.g.*) Colin E. Gunton, *Becoming and Being: The Doctrine of God in Charles Hartshorne and Karl Barth* (London: SCM Press, 2001[2]) or Sang Hyun Lee, *The Philosophical Theology of Jonathan Edwards* (Princeton: Princeton U.P., 2000[2]).

the single, simple, unrepeatable, eternal generation-of-the-Son-and-pro-cession-of-the-Spirit. We must here speak hesitantly and reverently, but I think we may with good reason say that this happening *is* the divine life.

The point of all this derivation is as follows: my first systematic question was how the eternal generation of the Son and the eternal procession of the Spirit related to the single divine operation claimed as necessary by Cappadocian trinitarianism; we are now, I suggest, in a position to propose an answer to that question; my answer, not that of either of the Gregorys or of Thomas, although I hope I have shown that I am trying to stand in continuity with their various theologies: the one eternal divine operation just *is* the generation of the Son and the procession of the Spirit.

Just to clear up the one obvious question: I take it, as I think Thomas must have done, that the eternal divine relations are a single simple event, although we cannot speak of that event without speaking of two different processions. I suspect indeed that if we think hard enough, we will discover that the reason it is dogmatically necessary to say *filioque* is that it protects this character of the two processions as a single and simple eternal movement—but that is definitely an argument for another day. Let me turn instead to my second systematic investigation, the relationship of inseparable divine operations to the particular economic missions of the Son and the Spirit.

# 3. INSEPARABLE OPERATIONS AND THE DIVINE MISSIONS

The systematic problem here is easy to state: if all divine operations are inseparably works of the whole Trinity, how do we parse such obviously true claims as "God the Son was incarnate of the Virgin Mary" or "the Holy Spirit was poured out at Pentecost"? Within the tradition we have the doctrine of appropriation, but that clearly is of little use here: it makes some sort of sense to say that creation is a work of the whole Trinity that can nonetheless be appropriated to the Father, but to say that incarnation is a work of the whole Trinity that can be appropriated to the Son appears much more difficult—indeed, just wrong.

The point in the patristic tradition at which this problem became most obvious was probably the run-up to the fifth ecumenical council. A formula had been proposed, which incidentally has been regularly quoted, and just as regularly misunderstood, in recent theology: "One of the

Trinity suffered in the flesh."[21] The problem with this formula in the eyes of the Fathers—Boethius was much involved, if I may have him as a church father—was not any squeamishness about divine suffering; Christological claims about the impassible suffering of the Son had been commonplace since at least Cyril of Alexandria.[22] No, the problem was whether it could possibly be meaningful to speak of "one of the Trinity" doing anything—the extent to which contemporary dogmatics has found the question of suffering generative or problematic, but has simply ignored the question of divine action, is perhaps a sober illustration of how distant from the concerns of the writers we cite we have sometimes become. That said, the formula seems unarguable, and indeed something similar enough was declared orthodox at the Council;[23] how can it be squared with a commitment to the inseparability of divine operations?

Thomas is again helpful in putting the conditions in place for a possible solution. First, he proposes a link between the relationships of origin and the economy. Emery suggests that formulae such as "the temporal procession of creatures drives from the eternal procession of persons" can be found nearly twenty times in the corpus.[24] This is not, as I read it, a suggestion that it belonged to God's nature to create—Thomas had issues around the eternity of creation, but they come elsewhere; rather, it is an insistence that, given the contingent fact of creation, it was inevitable that this God, who is Father, Son, and Spirit, would create as Father, Son, and Spirit, and not in some different way.

What does this look like? To again quote Emery, who is helpful on this point: "The three persons act in the same action, but each of them performs this act in the distinct mode of his personal relation.... The Father acts as source of the Son and Spirit, the Son acts as Word of the Father, the Holy Spirit acts as Love and Gift of the Father and the Son. We are not in the milieu of appropriations, but solidly within that of the persons' *properties*."[25] The situation here described is, of course, utterly unimaginable—but that does not make it wrong; the incapacity of our imaginations, variously or collectively, is not evidence on which to build a theological argument. We have no concept, and no capacity to imag-

---

21. For a sympathetic overview of the history, see Patrick T. R. Gray, *The Defense of Chalcedon in the East, 451–553* (Leiden: Brill, 1979), 451–553.

22. See on this point J. Warren Smith, "Suffering Impassibly: Christ's Passion in Cyril of Alexandria's Soteriology," *ProEccl* 11 (2002): 463–83.

23. "If anyone does not confess that our Lord Jesus Christ who was crucified in the flesh is true God and the Lord of Glory and one of the Holy Trinity: let him be anathema" (*Cap.* 10 of the Second Council of Constantinople, 553).

24. So Emery, *Trinitarian Theology*, p. 343.

25. Ibid., 355.

ine, what a single action inseparably performed by three agents might be like—which is just to say that God remains beyond our conceptual grasp, a thesis that should not elicit surprise.

Gregory of Nazianzus's image of the intermingled light of three conjoined suns might begin to give us some tiny element of purchase, however: it is possible for us to imagine three lights shining creating one light, which is one light, but in which the particular properties of the three lights are in some sense preserved. We must insist that the analogy is weak, the more so more we consider the physical nature of light, where in fact each photon could in theory be traced back to one or another of the sources; but, for all its inexactness, it is the best image I have come across in the literature.

This analogy tells us something of the nature of economic action, but it does not help us with our current problem: How do we parse "God the Son became incarnate" or "one of the Trinity suffered in the flesh" under the rubric of inseparable operations? If we return to the broader concept of missions, we may quickly draw some points out that might begin to point toward a solution. This account of divine action being shaped according to the relations of origin does give us some grasp of why there is a mission of the Son and a mission of the Spirit, but no mission of the Father: Son and Spirit have a movement from an origin in their eternal being, and so their sending corresponds to their eternal relation of origin—this is Augustine.[26] This also, I propose—and as far as I am aware I now move again into my own analysis, which however I maintain is congruent with the tradition—helps us to solve the problem we face.

I have suggested, following Thomas, that inseparable divine operations are nonetheless patterned after the triune relations of origin. I have also noted that the economic missions of the Son and the Spirit make sense because their sending corresponds to their relations of origin. These two ideas together suggest that we might be able to make sense of the missions if we consider them not as discrete works, but as particular aspects of broader divine operations. It can, that is, make sense to confess "one of the Trinity suffered in the flesh" if that claim is understood as a partial and incomplete narration of a broader divine operation that includes also proper works of the Father and the Holy Spirit.

There is not space to work this idea out fully here, but let me make a comment or two that might serve to render it more plausible. It is surely not just possible, but necessary, to locate the incarnation or passion as part of a wider divine work: God's purpose was not to suffer, but to save.

---

26. Augustine, *De Trin.* 2–4.

Incarnation, even, is a means to an end, not the end in itself. To borrow Basil's ordering, we might accept, putting the point extremely crudely and schematically, that the single work of salvation was initiated by the Father, carried forth by the mission—and the passion—of the Son, and is being brought to perfection by the mission of the Spirit. In saying this, however, we have to remain committed to the notion that this is one single activity, an inseparable operation. What from our perspective looks like several discrete activities is one single inseparable work in divine intention and execution, and so the particularity of the divine missions may be maintained without compromising the claim of inseparable operations.

## 4. BY WAY OF CONCLUSION

I have been unapologetically speculative in this paper; in closing I might perhaps explain why. I recently wrote a book on the history of trinitarian doctrine; in several warm reviews, for which I am grateful, the same point was made that the book is merely historical—well, yes—and that I now need to write a constructive book on the doctrine. Initially when pressed in public, I resisted this rather flippantly by saying that I had nothing to add to the traditional statements of the doctrine found in, say, Aquinas, and certainly had no hope of improving on them, and so there was nothing for me to do constructively.

More recently, however, I have begun to imagine what a more constructive essay might look like. My, presently tentative, conclusions are that it would involve two things. On the one hand, it would involve taking doctrines—such as the inseparability of divine operations—that are attested in the tradition, but that have not been the focus of extensive recent dogmatic reflection, and engaging in a work of recovery, showing why these doctrines need to be taken seriously and negotiated, even by those who wish to reject them. On the other hand, I have been reflecting that there are certain seemingly speculative questions—such as the relationship of the inseparable divine works to the eternal relations of origin, or to the missions of the Son and the Spirit—that serve to focus those points of classical Christian dogma that contemporary historical/ cultural/ecclesiastical situations render difficult, offensive, or strange. So this admittedly speculative and sketchy paper has been a first attempt to test out my theories of what constructive systematic theology in the area of trinitarian doctrine might need to look like today.

CHAPTER 4

# THE TRINITY AND POLITICS
## An Apophatic Approach

KAREN KILBY

## INTRODUCTION

"The Trinity is our social program." So Miroslav Volf, an alumnus and former professor of Fuller Theological Seminary, entitled a 1998 paper in *Modern Theology*.[1] Volf, who was also a student of Jürgen Moltmann and is currently a professor at Yale, finds a place on most people's list of social trinitarians; indeed he works with a breadth and sophistication that make it plausible to look to him as one of the most substantial and serious proponents of the approach.

Volf's use of this phrase as a title, it should be said, is a little more complex than it might first seem. "The Trinity is our social program" is a quotation from the nineteenth-century Russian thinker Nicholas Fedorov (originally Nikolai Fyodorovich Fyodorov, but Volf uses an Anglicised version of the name), and nearly the first thing Volf does in the essay is to distance himself from Fedorov: "No arguments need to be wasted on showing that Fedorov's proposal is specious and his vision chimerical."[2] These are surprisingly strong words, but not so surprising when one learns that the Russian thinker proposed that not only immortal life but also

---

1. Miroslav Volf, "'The Trinity Is Our Social Program': The Doctrine of the Trinity and the Shape of Social Engagement," *MTh* 14 (1998): 403–23.
2. Ibid, 403.

the resurrection of the dead were to be achieved through scientific progress. Whatever his excesses, however, he was, according to Volf, onto something. Even if Fedorov's own social program was manifestly mistaken, and even if his slogan needs to be hedged around and used with great care, still Volf does in fact make the slogan his own.

One can see why he would want to. To say the "the Trinity is our social program" is to capture, in a pithy and powerful way, a significant part of the appeal of social trinitarianism. The attractiveness of social models of the Trinity has not just been that they make the obscure clear, but even more that they make what had seemed arcane relevant and practical. The doctrine of the Trinity is not a point of difficulty deep in the technical bowels of theology, but something useful, applicable, motivating—it provides us with a social program. Right at the heart and centre of the Christian faith, we can say, is something with deep and wide practical application.

Social trinitarianism has been criticised on a number of fronts, and it has been criticised, it seems to me, to great effect.[3] But I am not persuaded that all of these attacks have made it go away. If one wants to dislodge an approach that has gained a wide grip on the theological imagination of a generation, criticism alone may not be enough. Something like this is, I take it, one of the premises of this conference: a more positive and constructive alternative is needed. To this I would add that it is necessary to get some sense of the appeal, the pull, of social trinitarianism, to understand its power. I think much of this power is captured precisely in the phrase "The Trinity is our social program."

My own view is that the proper alternative to the promotion of a social model of the Trinity is not the promotion of some *other* model of the Trinity—with perhaps even more impressive social and political consequences—but rather a certain asceticism as regards models, deriving from a shift in our understanding of what the proper task of theology with regard to the Trinity is. The Christian life is lived *in the midst* of the

---

3. The historical work of Michel René Barnes, Lewis Ayres, and others has been significant here. Stephen Holmes's recent *The Holy Trinity: Understanding God's Life* (Milton Keynes: Paternoster, 2012) serves both as a historical introduction to the doctrine and a decisive critique of claims by social trinitarians to be retrieving the tradition. From a more conceptual angle, Kathryn Tanner's "Trinity" chapter in *Blackwell Companion to Political Theology* (ed. Peter Scott and William T. Cavanaugh; Oxford: Blackwell, 2003), 319–332, develops a forceful criticism of social trinitarianism, at least insofar as it is put to work for practical purposes.

It might be argued that the kind of social trinitarianism discussed by analytic theologians is largely untouched by these critiques. Historical rootedness—a thick connection to tradition—carries less weight in this school of thought, and the concern for relevance and practical import is less marked.

Trinity, drawn by the Spirit into the movement of the Son toward the Father, and this is also where Christian thought is most fundamentally situated. We do not find ourselves in a position, then, I think, to view the Trinity as though from a distance and to develop an intellectually satisfying model of it.

If we call this—which I will expand on further in due course—an apophatic trinitarianism, then what I want to explore in this essay is where such an apophatic trinitarianism stands in relation to politics, in relation to having, to use Volf's language, a social program. If one's approach to the Trinity is all about *mystery*, about what we cannot know, what we do not understand, and of which we cannot form a satisfactory grasp, is it bound to lack the appeal and the relevance of the social trinitarians and their social programs? Will we have to say that theology, or at least trinitarian theology, caught up with policing the boundaries of its own unknowing, can have no relevance to political struggle and political reform? Will an apophatic trinitarianism be part of an inward looking, politically neutral, perhaps even escapist approach to theology? Must it encourage the church into passivity and disengagement, and therefore, by default, an implicit support of the status quo? These are the questions I hope to explore in this paper.

I will begin, however, with a little more on Volf, because he offers an unusually careful and qualified exploration of the practical consequences of the doctrine of the Trinity, conceived according to a social model.

## VOLF AND THE SOCIAL PROGRAM

As we have seen, nearly the first thing Volf does in his paper is to distance himself from the thinker from whom he derives its title. In fact he locates his own position by setting up a contrast between Nicholas Fedorov on the one hand and Ted Peters on the other. Each is taken to represent an extreme position: Fedorov attempts "to imitate the Triune God in blatant disregard for the fact that we are not God";[4] Peters insists absolutely on creaturely *difference* from God. But we do not have to accept these as the only alternatives: between "copying God in all respects" (so seemingly Fedorov) and "not copying God at all" (so seemingly Peters) lies the wide open space of human responsibility that consists in "copying God in *some* respects."[5] We need neither say that the Trinity is in every regard and

---

4. Volf, "'The Trinity Is Our Social Program,'" 404–5.
5. Ibid., 405.

entirely a model for human community, nor rule this out altogether; the real question, according to Volf, is "in which respects and to what extent [the Trinity should serve as a model for human community]."[6]

Human community *should* be modeled on the Trinity, then, but, a little more concretely, we should be aware of two kinds of limit to this modeling. There is an intrinsic limitation deriving from our creatureliness, which means that trinitarian concepts can only *analogously* be applied to human community; and there is a contingent limitation deriving from the fallen and historical character of our current lives.[7]

Volf's social trinitarianism is marked, in fact, by multiple layers of caution and qualification. We have seen two so far: first, his distancing himself from his own slogan, or at least from the unfettered enthusiasm he sees for it in Fedorov; and second, his insistence on the limits of the way the Trinity can model human community. In a third stage, Volf presents us with a methodological consequence from this limitation: trinitarian theology must work from below as well as from above. It is not a one-way matter of reading off from the triune God a pattern of human community: the "conceptual construction of correspondences," he writes, "must go back and forth on a two way street," taking into account our created and sinful nature as well as the Trinity as an ideal model.[8] So we cannot pretend to read off a social program *directly* from the Trinity: we have to acknowledge the process is more complicated than that.

Volf introduces two further qualifications. First, he actually prefers "social vision" to Fedorov's "social program." This is because the doctrine of the Trinity "does not constitute ... a plan or system of action" but gives us "the contours of the ultimate normative end toward which all social programs should strive."[9] He acknowledges that "the road from the doctrine of the Trinity to proposals about global or national social arrangements is long, torturous, and fraught with danger," and so keeps his focus on "the character of social agents and their relations" rather than "the issue of social structures";[10] the focus, in other words, is to be on how to think of people in relation to one another rather than how to think of, say, neo-liberalism or socialism or globalisation.

---

6. Ibid.
7. Volf does not, in this essay at least, distinguish particularly carefully between temporality and sin, i.e., between being fallen and being historical.
8. "By describing God in whose image human beings are created and redeemed, the doctrine of the Trinity names the reality which human communities *ought* to image. By describing human beings as distinct from God, the doctrines of creation and of sin inform the way in which human communities *can* image the Triune God, now in history and then in eternity" (ibid., 405–6).
9. Ibid., 406.
10. Ibid.

The final qualification arises from Volf's commitment to working with *both* immanent *and* economic Trinities, and indeed to focusing more heavily on the economic, "build[ing] mainly on the narrative of the Triune God's engagement with the world."[11] If proposals about the nature of human community drawn from reflection on the immanent Trinity are not somehow related to or situated within a discussion of the "narrative of divine self-donation" (i.e., the economic Trinity), he suggests, these proposals will be "underdetermined," "too formal," "overly diffuse generalities," even "theologically empty."[12]

Volf's own constructive proposals, then, are offered in two main sections, the first drawing from reflections on the immanent Trinity, and the second, as he presents it at least, rooted in the economic Trinity. In fact, however, really in only the first of these sections does Volf sounds like a social trinitarian. The focus of the second section is not on relations within the Trinity—whether immanent or economic—but on God's relation to the fallen, sinful world and what we should learn from this for *our* relations to the world. This part of the essay might more easily be understood if it were entitled "the cross is our social program." This is not to say that Volf here becomes somehow *untrinitarian*. What he sets out in this part of his essay is a perfectly reasonable example of Christian theology, and so it naturally has a trinitarian dimension. But one can no longer really say that he is principally focused on the *doctrine* of the Trinity at this stage.

So let us turn to the first of the sections that I have mentioned, which starts from the immanent Trinity. Here, after briefly affirming allegiance to an egalitarian rather than a hierarchical understanding of the Trinity, Volf sets out to develop an understanding of identity from the concept of perichoresis. Perichoresis teaches us that the divine persons are "personally interior to one another," but that their "interpenetration presupposes their distinctions."[13] What this means for identity is exemplified by Jesus' capacity to say, in the Gospel of John, "my teaching is not my own. It comes from the one who sent me" (John 7:16). The interplay of the "my" and "not mine" here suggests the two corresponding principles, that "identity is not self-enclosed" and that "identity is non-reducible."[14]

It is interesting to consider the detail with which Volf expands on these principles. In relation to identity as "not self-enclosed," he writes of the

---

11. Ibid., 407.
12. Ibid., 412.
13. Ibid., 409.
14. Ibid., 410.

boundaries of the self as "porous and shifting," of the self as "in a state of flux stemming from 'incursions' of the other into the self and of the self into the other"; and he speaks of how the self is shaped in various ways by the other, including "by re-examining itself when the other closes his or her doors and challenging the other by knocking at the doors."[15] In relation to the nonreducibility of identity, he writes about "the need for boundary maintenance—a certain kind of assertion of the self in the presence of the other." He also writes that "since negotiation of identities is always conflictual, non-assertiveness of the self in the presence of the other puts the self in danger either of dissolving into the other or being smothered by the other." And so "to ward off [the] dangers [of obliteration of the self], we must attend to the boundaries of identities by enforcing rules that protect identities and by providing environments that nurture them."[16]

Volf's presentation of the self in relation to the other is, it seems to me, appealing. It can be a useful way to think about one's own sense of self, for instance, as it slips and slithers around in relation to interactions with spouse, friends, colleagues, parents, children, even people met at a conference. It's helpful both to face the reality of the instability of one's own sense of self, the way my sense of who I am is very much dependent on day-to-day reactions from others I meet. And it is helpful to remember that one is not *just* these incursions, that I need to, and that I do, assert and defend myself at times. It is commendable, furthermore, that Volf notices the tension between his two principles, and acknowledges that he has no algorithm to specify how to handle this tension: "How does one know," he asks "when to close the boundaries of the self in order to stabilize one's identity and when to open them in order to enrich it?" His answer is that no answer can be given in advance, that everything depends on the particular cases, that one must "seek supple wisdom rather than stable rules."[17]

It may be that the patterns of thought Volf lays out can also be useful in thinking through various kinds of group identity—this at least ought to be expected from the way he introduces the theme of identity itself into the article, pointing as he does to the importance of identity *politics* in our time. Perhaps something about being a woman over against men, or being straight and encountering gay people, is captured by this dialectic of the incursion of the other into the self and the need for boundary maintenance—although one might wonder whether the balanced symmetry of his language of self and other is helpful in some of these cases.

---

15. Ibid.
16. Ibid.
17. Ibid., 411.

Nevertheless, on the whole his supple and evocative language of self and other is appealing and to a large extent plausible. What is not so plausible is that it is supposed to be derived from an understanding of the immanent Trinity. Can one really get from the concept of perichoresis and the biblical portrayal of Jesus in relation to Father and Spirit, to this general understanding of the self's identity? If the sheer quantity and detail of what Volf can find to derive from perichoresis does not give pause, then some of his phrases should. In what sense can we say that from the trinitarian perichoresis we learn of identity as a matter of *flux*, of *shifting* boundaries, of *incursions* of self into other, of the proper response to the other "closing doors," of the danger of dissolving or being smothered by the other? All the overtones contained in this language of change, of threat and of loss, are simply antithetical to the way trinitarian relations have traditionally been understood.

But perhaps this is just an expression of Volf's "two way street," of his conviction that in developing correspondences between Trinity and human sociality one needs to work from below as well as above, from the facts of our creatureliness, historicity, and sinfulness as well as from the ideal provided by the triune God? Perhaps. It's striking, though, that for all the methodological self-consciousness that is manifest in other parts of the essay, Volf here, in the discussion of the significance of perichoresis for understandings of identity, gives no hint or signal that he is beginning to introduce considerations drawn from finitude and sin into his discussion of the meaning for identity of perichoresis. The transition is unmarked. On the other hand, it's also striking that everything that gives this discussion of identity, of the self/other relation, its richness, plausibility, and interest, is introduced precisely when considerations drawn from limitation, historicity, and fallenness quietly find their way into the discussion — precisely when Volf leaves behind anything that could possibly apply to or be derived from the Trinity.[18]

I have spent some effort exploring Volf's essay because it is instructive to examine a social trinitarian who proceeds — on the whole — with such care, with such an alertness to the dangers and possible difficulties of the project. In fact, one might ask why, given this awareness, Volf continues at all to espouse a kind of social trinitarianism. If he realizes the limitations of modeling creaturely, historical, and sinful human relations

---

18. Kathryn Tanner succinctly suggests that the danger of a strategy like Volf's is that "the Trinity fails to do any work" ("Trinity," 327).

on eternal, perfect, divine relations; if he realizes the dangers of abstraction and theological emptiness that loom over general deductions about human relations deriving from the inner-trinitarian life; if he thinks that the primary weight must be given to the *narrative* of the divine engagement with the world—why then does he not simply abandon the project of gaining political wisdom from the examination of inner-divine relations?

Is the answer simply biographical? Is it that, while Volf is alert to the difficulties involved in this kind of project, he finds himself already too enmeshed in it, given his history of working in an ecumenical context on communion ecclesiologies, and given that he is a student of Moltmann? Perhaps. Certainly none of the indications Volf gives in the paper itself for why we must "copy God to some extent" could be considered inescapable arguments pushing us towards a social trinitarian project: he mentions that we are made in the image of God (something which can be, and has been, taken in all kinds of ways), that we are made for communion with the Trinity and that Jesus commands his disciples to "be perfect ... as your heavenly Father is perfect."[19]

## THE APPEAL OF SOCIAL TRINITARIANISM

Perhaps, then, we could look for an explanation of Volf's espousal of social trinitarianism simply in intellectual biography, but as I've suggested I think it is also important to be aware of the appeal, of the attraction, in social trinitarianism. And this is very much present, in spite of all the qualifications, in Volf's paper. There are two dimensions to this appeal. One is what I have already indicated: the very ability to announce "the Trinity is our social program" (or even "social vision") is somehow deeply pleasing. It is satisfying because it implies that theology really does have something *special* to contribute, something definite and distinctive and practical to show for all its labours. "The Trinity is our social program" suggests, on the one hand, that theology has something distinctive to say as against mere secular thought,[20] its own unique trove of ideas to source social and politi-

---

19. Volf, "'The Trinity Is Our Social Program,'" 404. It is rather striking that Volf doesn't seem to notice the *particularities* of this injunction to copy—he simply substitutes "*God*" for "*Father*" in glossing the gospel text, and then weaves the result into his general discussion of modeling ourselves on the *Trinity*.

20. Also, of course, as against Jewish and Muslim thought. For most social trinitarians, however, Christian self-assertion over against Jewish and Muslim thought is closer to an unintended consequence than a deliberate goal.

cal theory. On the other hand, it also carries the suggestion—maybe less consciously—that the theologian has something distinctive to say by contrast with ordinary Christians. After all, most believers who haven't been exposed to formal theological study might think to look for their guidance on social vision from the Ten Commandments, the prophets, proverbs, the sayings of Jesus, their understanding of the love of God and of the nature of Christian discipleship, even natural law and their own intuitions, but they wouldn't think to look, I suppose, to the nature of inner-trinitarian relations. So if they enroll on courses of systematic and practical theology, they'll have something new to take home—they'll have gained something quite concrete. We theologians can justify our salaries.

The second dimension of the appeal has to do with the nature of some of the technical trinitarian concepts themselves and the kinds of reflection to which they lend themselves. Kathryn Tanner suggests that the trinitarian concepts just happen to be well adapted to the kinds of political questions that currently preoccupy us, and this explains why the Trinity is in recent years such a popular site of political theology.[21] This is right, I think, but not the whole story. There is also the enticement of having such an elusive, even paradoxical concept to work with; something like perichoresis, a notion that we don't really understand, has, precisely *because* it is paradoxical, elusive, and not really understood, a distinct flexibility. It is not hard to weave into it our best insights about the complexities of human identity, relationship, community. It lends itself, one could say, to conceptual play. Nearly *any* understanding I hold of self and other, individual and group, person and community, could be spun as perichoretic.

It is at this point, of course, that the attractiveness of social trinitarianism is also closely bound up with what can be most problematic in it. For all his care, caution, and qualifications, when Volf begins to reflect on perichoresis, he seems to become enthralled with the intellectual possibilities of the concept, with the richness of thought it allows him to discover in trinitarian theology. Careful distinctions among the sources of our knowledge and cautious attention to the ways in which God is *not* like us disappear under the force of the speculative and dialectical attractions of the notion of perichoresis. Or to put it another way, the project of discovering in trinitarian relations the way we humans should relate seems able to bear interesting fruit precisely at that moment when the caution, the attentiveness to limits, slips away.

---

21. Tanner, "Trinity," 319–20.

Volf offers what looks at first like a sober, restrained form of social trinitarianism, one that, rather than unthinkingly assuming that the Trinity should serve as a model for human community, will instead carefully consider "in which respects and to what extent" it should do so. But a closer look at Volf's work suggests, I think, that what we in fact need is not a restrained and careful version of this business of finding in the Trinity a model for human community, but a different approach to trinitarian theology altogether.

## TRINITY AND POLITICS: AN ALTERNATIVE APPROACH

I've suggested above that I don't think the different approach should involve locating some key concept that can replace community, some *alternative* master idea that we can suppose is at the heart of the doctrine of the Trinity. I think it is perfectly possible to say that the proper stance of Christian theology in face of the doctrine of the Trinity is non-comprehension, not knowing, not being in possession of a unifying grasp, idea, or model. It is perfectly possible to say, that is, that the doctrine of the Trinity should intensify rather than diminish our sense of the unknowability of God, that it presents us with a pattern we cannot understand, rather than with a specific set of insights and concepts on which we can draw.[22] If this is the case, then rather than searching for the right model for understanding the Trinity, we should perhaps be seeking to resist our own penchant for making models.

"What then is the point of the Trinity?" one might ask. If it so thoroughly defeats us intellectually, in what sense can it make any difference to affirm faith in the doctrine of the Trinity? In what sense can it be significant for Christianity? Can something that so radically transcends our understanding have anything to do with us?

One way to answer this question is to consider that perhaps we cannot understand the Trinity, the three-in-oneness of God, not because it is so far from us, but because it is so near. We are caught up in the Trinity. The Christian life is a life of being brought into the Trinity—not a contemplation from a distance or a mimicry at a distance, but a genuine incorporation, a being taken up by the Spirit into the movement of the

---

22. These ideas are developed more fully in Karen Kilby, "Is an Apophatic Trinitarianism Possible?" *IJST* 12 (2010): 65–77.

Son from and to the Father.[23] Perhaps we are too much in the midst of the Trinity—too close, too involved, in other words—to be able to form an overarching conceptualization.

From this perspective, in fact, the business of attempting to construct models of the Trinity can come under suspicion of idolatry. Is there not something problematic in imagining that I can lay aside my actual position in relation to Father, Son, and Holy Spirit in order to play around with ideas of triangles or three leaf clovers or psychological or social models and gain some sort of a grasp on a concept of the Trinity, as though Father, Son, and Spirit can become a kind of intellectual object over which I dispose? Maybe the language of idolatry is too inflammatory. But at least it seems that one can become involved in a kind of intellectual dabbling, a game of intellectual construction, that has little intrinsic link to the life of faith.

But of course, if one has no model of the Trinity, then one has no model which one can apply to society, whether in the wholehearted and uninhibited manner of some social trinitarians or in the more cautious and selective manner of Volf. And so one seems to have cut off the possibility of a politically relevant theology of the Trinity.

One response to this objection might be simply to grant that not every element in Christian theology need have equally immediate practical relevance. We could perhaps borrow an image from the philosopher Willard van Orman Quine and think of Christian belief on analogy with a spider's web, where, though everything is interconnected, only some parts come into contact with the realm of the practical, of the ethical, of politics.[24] Perhaps we could say, then, that the doctrine of the Trinity plays its role somewhere in the interior of the web. It is necessary to the whole; it is

---

23. My language of incorporation here is not of course distinctive in contemporary theology. Similarities to Kathryn Tanner's position are discussed in note 25 below. Cf. also Sarah Coakley's trinitarian writings—most recently *God, Sexuality and the Self* (Cambridge: Cambridge University Press, 2013)—for a sustained reflection on the importance of our incorporation into the Trinity for theology. I am not inclined to give the absolutely decisive place in trinitarian theology to either sexuality or "deep" contemplative prayer that Coakley does, although I think that each of them can and should be given a trinitarian framing, and that one can learn well from Coakley how to do this.

24. This is, it should be said, a fairly free adaptation of Quine's image. It is not only that the web here becomes an image for the structure of Christian belief rather than scientific thought, but that what is imagined to be at the web's *edge* is practice, whereas for Quine it is (empircally construed) experience. See W. V. O. Quine, "Two Dogmas of Empiricism," *The Philosophical Review* 60 (1951): 20–43.

For a related use of Quine's web metaphor, cf. Paul Murray, "Discerning the Dynamics of Doctrinal Development: A Post-Foundationalist Perspective," in *Faithful Reading: New Essays in Theology in Honour of Fergus Kerr* (ed. Simon Oliver, Karen Kilby, and Tom O'Loughlin; London: Continuum, 2012), 193–220.

linked to other beliefs in various ways, supporting them and being supported by them. But it is not really close to the edge where the action takes place, and so it cannot be burdened with the expectation of giving rise directly to social, ethical, or political wisdom.

But a problem with this approach is that it would involve imagining the doctrine of the Trinity as a particular *fragment* of the totality of Christian belief, a localised node, a delimitable bit, and this is not quite right. It is safer to suppose, I think, that the entire pattern of Christian belief is trinitarian than that it contains one particular element that is the Trinity. If we are to use something like Quine's metaphor, the Trinity is better imagined as something about the structure of the whole web, and the quality of each of its strands, than as a particular point in the web.

Still, the notion that not every element of Christian theology needs to come into *direct* contact with our thinking about social programs and politics seems to me to have a certain plausibility, and I would think that some likely candidates for this kind of non-frontline role are in fact the technical concepts that have emerged *within* trinitarian theology — concepts such as persons, relations, processions, and perichoresis. We need these — or similar — concepts. They have a function, helping to hold patterns of belief in place and to articulate in brief form the rejection of heresies. But we shouldn't put them under pressure to further justify their existence by supplying direct dollops of social or political wisdom. They are, we might say, backroom workers who should be allowed to remain in their backrooms. This is something that Barth and Rahner implicitly recognized when each, in coming up with a replacement term for "Persons," gave us what are, from a rhetorical point of view, utterly uninspiring suggestions ("modes of subsistence," "ways of being").

So we do not have, on my view, a model of the Trinity that can serve as a model for society, nor should we look to highly specific concepts that have emerged in the tradition to provide us with tidy packets of practical or political insight. But I would like to propose that there are nevertheless two dimensions in which an apophatic trinitarianism has potential political significance. The two dimensions correspond to the two aspects of the approach I have been recommending: a resistance to the project of constructing trinitarian models on the one hand, and an emphasis on our incorporation into the Trinity on the other.

First of all, then, what is the political significance of resistance to the construction of models? If one cultivates an awareness of the ungraspability of God, the impossibility of finding an image or model or integrating vision of the Trinity—if one cultivates the capacity to live with questions to which we have no answers—might this be correlated, not with a particular political commitment to one form of socioeconomic system or another, to one social vision or another, but with a resistance to an absolute confidence in any system and social vision? Economic and political regimes do, after all, tend to take on a sacred aura, to demand unconditional commitment, to imagine themselves as the end and goal of history. If Christians are schooled, by the doctrine of the Trinity as well as in other ways, to know that God is not within our grasp, that we possess no concept or overaching understanding of that which is highest, then we are in a sense schooled into a suspicion of systems that present themselves with a kind of sacred, all-encompassing necessity. Might we not imagine that an important political contribution of Christian thinking about God be, then, not that it provides us with something like a shortcut to formulating a distinct alternative of our own, but that it helps call in question, helps relativize, all such systems we might find ourselves enticed by? Might there not be a correspondence, in other words, between a resistance to idolatry in relation to God, and a resistance to ideology in relation to political systems?[25]

Let me now turn to the second side of what I take to be the political potential of the approach that I am advocating. The unknowability of the Trinity, I've suggested, need not just be conceived as the result of some sort of unfathomable distance between us and God, but also as a result of our involvement in the Trinity, its closeness to us, our incorporation into it. Now, if the whole of the Christian life can be thought of in terms of incorporation into the Trinity, it follows that social and political dimensions of the Christian life also have this quality. That is to say, every dimension of our life in community, with others, in society, in politics, is somehow also connected to our life lived toward the Father, with the Son, in the Spirit.[26]

---

25. The cautious phrasing here is deliberate. Kathryn Tanner has argued persuasively in *The Politics of God* (Minneapolis: Augsburg Fortress, 1992) that a variety of political programs can be correlated with any one way of believing in God, and I think the point also holds in the apophatic case. So I am suggesting a possible political correlate of an apophatic emphasis, but not claiming that it is the *only* possible one.

26. My position here is very close to the one set out by Tanner in her "Trinity" article in the *Blackwell Companion to Political Theology*. She suggests that participation in the Trinity, rather than modeling ourselves on it, is the key to thinking about its significance for politics: "Humans do not attain the heights of trinitarian relations by reproducing them, but by being incorporated into them as the very creatures they are" (329). Two differences between what are, structurally, similar positions, are worth mentioning. First, Tanner lays less emphasis on unknowing than I have. Second, she fills out the notion of "incorporation into the Trinity" with a slightly different, and more christocentric, emphasis than I will do below. While I am not inclined to disagree with anything she proposes, I fear that her account is open to being taken as a *denial* of political significance to the doctrine of the Trinity: everything of political import seems to lie in Christology alone.

That this formula sounds rather general and not informative should come as no surprise. I've suggested the Trinity is not best thought of as a localised element within the structure of Christian thought, one little bit from which to get some nice ideas, but as structuring and characterising the whole. So if one talks about its political significance in general terms, one has to expect to say something formal. Furthermore, concepts of "the social" or "the political" are themselves general and can be taken in many ways.

## TRINITY AND POLITICS: AN EXAMPLE

To make the discussion a little more concrete, it may be useful to focus on a particular dimension of political existence and a particular context, and try to sketch at least one *example* of what an incorporative, rather than a mimetic, trinitarian political orientation might look like. As the context, let me take the nonpoor parts of the relatively rich world, a context that includes myself and, it is likely, a considerable portion of my readers. As a particular dimension of "the political," let me take the question of Christian political engagement considered in the limited sense of the struggle for justice.

I will presume in what follows that the Christian commitment does in fact include a commitment to work, as individuals and communities, for justice and for the alleviation of suffering in the societies in which Christians find themselves. I will presume that this may involve working for structural change to one degree or another. Neither of these views is universally held among Christians, but neither of them can be thought of as representing a particularly eccentric or minority perspective.

Now it might seem that I have already begun to paint myself into a corner. I am using words like "society" and "justice," suggesting that I need to know what these things are, and I have talked about the possibility of working for structural change, suggesting that I need to understand how society is and ought to be structured; yet earlier I suggested that the doctrine of the Trinity, rather than giving us a social or political vision, causes us to relativise, to call into question, to distance ourselves from all the available possibilities. But in fact I don't think this is such a problem. It seems to me that even in the absence of a comprehensive sociopolitical ideology, derived from the Trinity or anywhere else, it is perfectly possible to look around and see that there are many things that are not as they ought to be, that there are features of the world around us crying out for change, and that it is possible to do something about them.

My reading of our context, in fact, is that the biggest impediment to proper political engagement is not the lack of a comprehensive analysis of social reality, or the lack of a utopian vision of the ideal society and politics toward which we ought to move; it is rather a lack of a willingness to really look around us and take what we see into account.[27] My hypothesis, that is to say, is that many of us in the context on which I am focused, the nonpoor in the rich world, live with a knowledge that we mostly want to suppress, a knowledge that the circles of comfort and stability in which we move do not really reflect to us the true story of the world. To look at the conditions of life and the suffering of those in absolute poverty, unable to feed and educate their children properly, or at the suffering of those who are mentally ill, or of those who are trafficked, or of those caught in the asylum system of a country like Britain, or the criminal justice system of a country like America, is something that in my judgment we who live in comfort often simply do not want to do. This brokenness and monumental injustice and suffering are part of the reality of the world, but it is hard to look at it. What Jon Sobrino calls "honesty with the real" is not easy.[28] It is a little too disturbing. We sense that it will unsettle us, call us into question, that to look and to keep looking and act in a way that is in keeping with what we see might destabilize our existence.

Now, it would be silly to suggest that political engagement is a theory-free zone, requiring neither social analysis nor a vision of human flourishing. Clearly it requires elements of both, and the imperfections and limitations in one's analysis and one's vision will have practical consequences. But, first of all, the absolutely *generalized* kinds of vision one might hope to derive from just the right concept of the Trinity are not the intellectual tools most required in this kind of political engagement. Second, while it is true that incomplete or imperfect sociopolitical analysis will hinder efforts to work for justice and alleviate suffering, it seems to me that what *most significantly* inhibits proper political engagement, the *key* sticking point, is not a lack of analysis but a lack of this honesty with or fidelity to the real, a lack in our willingness to look at and really take seriously the world around us. Indeed I think that often we do not fail to

---

27. I sketched a similar reading of our context and a similar reflection on the doctrine of the Trinity in relation to this context in "Trinity, Tradition and Politics," in *Recent Developments in Trinitarian Theology: An International Symposium* (ed. Christoph Chalamet and Mark Vial; Minneapolis: Fortress, forthcoming).

28. Sobrino introduces this concept, together with "fidelity to the real," in his article "Spirituality and the Following Jesus," in *Mysterium Liberationis: Fundamental Concepts of Liberation Theology* (ed. Ignacio Ellacuria and Jon Sobrino; Maryknoll, NY: Orbis, 1993), 677–701.

engage because we lack the right analysis, but we lack the analysis because we are not willing to engage.

This point is worth illustrating. Suppose I hear a piece on the radio about the plight of trafficked women in Britain. I am, perhaps, unsettled and troubled to think of such misery and oppression going on near where I live. What should I do about it? I don't know. I don't really understand what global forces of capitalism and crime contribute to trafficking, and I don't know what role faulty legislation or policing play, or what reform might be necessary, or where if anywhere pressure could be applied to bring it about, or what organisations ought to be supported in working on this problem. So I go about my daily tasks, and I listen to other items on the radio. But whatever I tell myself in this situation, my ignorance is not really what blocks me from engagement—it is much more truly understood as the result of disengagement. I don't look away and do nothing, then, because of a lack of understanding of what to do—even if that is how it seems—but I lack an understanding of what to do because I have opted to look away and do nothing.

Let's suppose, anyway, that this is the case. What does it have to do with the Trinity, one might ask? Well, it is not too hard to imagine that it has something to do with Jesus. Whatever temptation we might have to tell ourselves that the way to relate to God is by rising directly above the sufferings and injustices and particularities of this world, putting them out of mind—any such temptation is thwarted by the pattern of Jesus' life, incarnate and engaged as it is in a particular political moment, responsive to the injustices and sufferings of a distinct time and place. Perhaps not everyone would agree with this reading of the Gospels, but again I don't think that it is an eccentric or minority reading.

It's not clear, of course, that we can abstract from the life and teaching of Jesus a tidy political program and then apply it at will in any other time and place, but if Jesus is understood as the Word of God spoken into creation, then this speaking, it seems, takes place in the midst of things, in the midst of the messy, suffering, conflicted reality that is the world—this is how and where we have to listen for God. If Jesus is understood as the fundamental pattern of human response to God, this response, too, takes place in the midst of things, through and not apart from the engagement with the messy, suffering, conflicted reality that is the world.

This focus on the Word Incarnate, considered on its own, however, leaves us with two problems. First, if there is no concrete program to be transferred from his time to ours, how do we know in *particular* what to do? And there is the deeper problem on which I have already dwelt, the danger that we don't necessarily *want* to know, don't want to be disturbed and destabilized from a comfortable, secure existence. Where can we find the strength, the commitment, to genuinely confront the demands of justice and love, wrapped up as most of us are in our own secure cocoons, caught in a position of both knowing and not wanting to know of the suffering and injustice that stalk our world?

Each of these questions can, in fact, lead to reflection on the role of the Spirit. It is a classic Christian affirmation that the Holy Spirit incorporates us, in our variety and difference, into Christ, and this is significant for the first question. Trinitarian faith legitimates a certain trust, as Christians seek to engage with the social and political demands of their time, drawing on all the resources, theological and nontheological, that they can, that the Spirit may be at work aligning them with and incorporating them into Christ's own relation to the world. If we have no algorithm for a transition from Christ's engagement to the one required of the contemporary church and contemporary Christians, there can nevertheless be a kind of confidence that this is a gap that the Spirit can bridge.

As regards the reluctance, the disinclination to really see what is before us, we can again be led to reflection on the Spirit, although by way first of a reflection on *sin*. For surely this evasion of the real is a dimension of the sin of the rich world. Indeed, what I have tried to suggest is that it is a sphere in which sin has a particularly strong grip, so strong that it can be hard to see how to escape, how as individuals or communities we could be really willing to look at the real when to do so would so discomfort and destabilize us. But it is part of the fundamental grammar of the Christian faith that where we know there is sin, we must also trust in and look for the reality of grace, the movement of the Holy Spirit. For if it is a basic Christian conviction that the Holy Spirit is at work in the world, in the church, and in individuals, freeing and making new things possible, it is a fundamental Christian requirement to attend to, to listen for, the promptings of the Spirit. So in the realm of the political, faith in the Holy Spirit means not needing to remain simply trapped and frozen, caught between a half-suppressed awareness of the injustices and oppression of the world on the one hand and one's own fear of confronting them on the other; the individual or community is rather in a position, first, to acknowledge the sin of their own situation, and second, to seek out and attend to the movements of the Holy Spirit that, on one level or another, allow a new fidelity to the real.

So I have said something of the Son and the Spirit, but what of the Father? At this point I think it may be useful to consider the almost inevitable frustration of political engagement. NGOs may tell their supporters that they *can* end hunger, make poverty history, eradicate debt, and so on, but Christians who engage with any of these things must do so in the knowledge that in all likelihood they won't end hunger or make poverty history or usher in a new age of justice. At best political efforts may contribute to some partial success, and they may utterly fail. What can make ongoing, sustained engagement possible under these conditions? One strategy might be to ignore the complexity and ambiguity of the world and attend only to a limited problem where there is hope of seeing full success—but this would once again be a kind of escapism. But what if the whole of our engagement in the world is itself—and is lived as and understood as—part of an orientation and a movement toward a horizon that transcends the world, toward the Father who is the source and goal of all?

In brief, then, one can conceive of political engagement as the Spirit moving within us, working to overcome our selfish blindness, seeking to unite us with Jesus, whose own engagement with the world and "fidelity to the real" is at the same time always also his pointing beyond the world to the Father. Or at least we can say, that is *one example* of how one can bring the Trinity and politics together.

I asked above whether an apophatic trinitarianism could in any way match the appeal of the social trinitarians, with their ability to say "the Trinity is our social program," and whether an apophatic trinitarianism was bound to be apolitical, encouraging the church into passivity, disengagement, and escapism. We are now in a position to give at least a provisional answer to these questions.

To the first question—can an apophatic trinitariansim match the appeal of social trinitarians—the answer may well have to be "no." There is, it must be acknowledged, something elusive about the incorporative approach to thinking about politics that I have been sketching; it cannot provide a particular difference, a particular policy, a particular political proposal, that could trace its pedigree to the doctrine of the Trinity. And there is a certain intellectual asceticism required. Maybe we would like to have in our grasp special concepts about God that give us a special basis for our political thought, but this is a desire that on my account has to be resisted. So it is undoubtedly difficult to compete with the appeal of social trinitarianism.

But does this mean that the upshot is, on a political level, passivity, disengagement, and escapism? I don't think so. Disengagement and escapism are certainly powerful temptations for Christians, I've been trying to suggest, at least in some contexts. But highly generalised social and political proposals that can be derived from thinking about how we may "copy" the Trinity don't help to counter these temptations. In fact, one might see such highly generalised proposals as themselves another form of escapism. It's not difficult to play around with ideas of perfection. It *is* difficult to really look at and think about long term, massive suffering, particularly if I have to wonder, as anyone in the so-called first world does, about, say, third world poverty, whether I am somehow implicated in and responsible for this suffering. The doctrine of the Trinity doesn't in my opinion give us a blueprint for remaking society. But in reminding us of our true situation—disciples of Jesus, in whom the grace of the Spirit is constantly at work, in the midst of the world on a journey to the transcendent Father—it can do something to overcome our fear, passivity, and escapism, to make engagement more possible in the first place, and to help sustain this engagement in the face of our imperfection and failure.

CHAPTER 5

# "AS WE ARE ONE"
## Thinking into the Mystery[1]

### LEWIS AYRES

"My prayer is not for them alone. I pray also for those who will believe in me through their message, that all of them may be one, Father, just as you are in me and I am in you. May they also be in us so that the world may believe that you have sent me." (John 17:20–21)

"Faith is not a light which scatters all our darkness,
but a lamp which guides our steps in the night
and suffices for the journey." (*Lumen Fidei*, 57)

## I. INTRODUCTION
Trinitarian theology has a long, complex history and has stimulated some of the most philosophically deep and beautiful reflection in Western thought. The essays in this volume give some sense of that depth and beauty. But even as we find ourselves drawn into the fascinating conceptual structures and details of that tradition, we should not neglect to take a breath and remember where we begin and, I want to emphasize, to where we should constantly return. The language of trinitarian theology

---

1. This paper draws on two of my Pentecost Lectures offered to the Benedictine community of Pluscarden Abbey in Scotland during 2012. A later version was then delivered to the September 2013 conference "Beholding the Wonder of Trinitarian Relations" at the Southern Baptist Theological Seminary in Louisville, Kentucky. I would like to thank my hosts on both occasions—Dom Anselm Atkinson and Dr. Bruce Ware—and those in these two communities who provided such good conversation. I would also like to thank Oliver Crisp and Fred Sanders for the wonderfully organized conference at Fuller Seminary at which the final version was read and the participants for their excellent questions and conversation.

begins in the Scriptures, language and life of Israel, and then in the earliest Christians' use of that Scripture, language and life as a resource for understanding what God had done and was doing in Christ. Classical trinitarian theology arose as a reflection on the Scriptures that those earliest Christians recognized and in the light of their own life in Christ.[2] Even if one believes that the formulae and language of the church's trinitarian faith are a gift enabling an ever truer comprehension of the Father who sent his Son and Spirit—as I do—we should not forget that these formulae and this language should also stimulate and shape our reading of the Scriptures.[3]

In this essay I have two goals. The first is to suggest some ways in which we may read our Scriptures in the light of classical trinitarian belief, both as part of our attempts to understand the Trinity itself, and to think about how trinitarian faith undergirds the whole complex of Christian faith. There are many ways of so doing, both in the sense that there are many ways in which one might construct such a reading and in the sense that there is a legitimate variety of trinitarian perspectives that one might creatively use. My own reading is the product of my own attention to the Scriptures, but it is also deeply informed by my research on patristic theology, and specifically Augustine. That it is so informed, however, should not make it seem somehow less "scriptural"![4] My second goal—and if the first provides something of the essay's form, this second provides some key features of its content—is to reflect on the interrelationship between how we imagine the divine unity and how we reflect on Christ's invitation for us to think about ways in which our existence may reflect that divine unity and indwelling.

## II. Seeing and Not Seeing

We must to spend a little time thinking about the character of Scripture's talk about God and about the modes of thinking to which it seems to invite us. What I have to say will probably make more sense at the end of

---

2. The best introduction to this process is provided by Robert Wilken, *The Spirit of Early Christian Thought: Seeking the Face of God* (New Haven CT: Yale University Press, 2005).

3. For an excellent introduction to classical Catholic trinitarian theology, see Gilles Emery, *The Trinity: An Introduction to Catholic Doctrine on the Triune God* (trans. Matthew Levering; Washington, DC: Catholic University of America Press, 2011).

4. There are many complex questions here about the character of appropriate biblical interpretation. On the one hand, I have no intention of indicating via the form of my argument that I think there is no place for a close historical interrogation of the texts I explore; on the other hand, I do think that exegesis—in its different legitimate modes—is essential to the task of expounding Christian doctrines. I attempt to give a fuller view of how I negotiate some of these problems in my "The Word Answering the Word: Opening the Space of Catholic Biblical Interpretation" in *Theological Theology: Essays in Honor of John B. Webster* (ed. R. David Nelson, Darren Sarisky, and Justin Stratis; London: Bloomsbury, forthcoming).

my paper than at the beginning, but saying something at this point will be helpful.

The first eighteen verses of John's gospel seem to tell a clear story. The Word who is also Life and Light is with God. John the Baptist was sent to witness to the light, and soon after, the light to which he had borne witness came into the world. Many did not recognize him for the light that he was, but those who did knew that this man was the Son of God, the Word, and they saw his glory. The story seems to be one of revelation: "No one has ever seen God, but the one and only Son, who is himself God and is in closest relationship to the Father, has made him known." The language of the Word becoming flesh seems to have as one of its main implications the Word becoming visible and known. But the language of visibility and invisibility is actually used here in a far more complex manner.

These few verses of John's gospel parallel statements about the Word being made visible with statements that the Word was and remains curiously unseen. The Word came and yet was already here; the Word came and yet his own people did not receive him. What, then, does it mean to emphasize that the Word shines and cannot be extinguished? A clue is offered when verse 14 emphasizes that "we have *seen* his glory," but who are we? Well, verses 11–12 are clear that although "his own … did not receive him," to those who did so receive and believe, to these he has given "the right [power] to become the children of God." The "we" mentioned in verse 14 seems to be those who have believed: only these can be said to have seen. The seeing that is, then, possible, is not the seeing we understand when we speak of all those with sight seeing that the sun rises or falls; this is a seeing that follows on from belief, and it is only ever analogous to the "seeing" of which we so easily speak.

The paradoxes and ambiguities of this seeing in faith are explored throughout John's gospel. To take just one example, call to mind John 14. Chapter 13 focuses on Jesus's washing of his disciples' feet. But the chapter is framed by an emphasis on Jesus doing this because he knew the time had come for him to depart from the world. The theme is announced at the beginning of the chapter and ends with Peter asking, "Lord, where are you going?" (13:36). The answer he receives is that Peter cannot yet follow. It is this exchange that introduces chapter 14. Christ calls us not to be troubled, to calm our anxiety, and to have faith that while he will go where we cannot yet, he *will* return for us. But Christ does not only speak of a future bodily return at some distant point; in the middle of chapter

13 he speaks of sending the Spirit to lead us in love, and he speaks of our continuing to live because Christ *continues* to dwell in us. Here we have it again: going, hiding, and yet being present.

This theme recurs throughout this chapter. Thomas asks his Lord, "How can we know the way [to where you are going]?" (14:5). Jesus answers by saying, first, that he *is* "the way and the truth and the life," and then immediately adding, "If you really knew me, you will know my Father as well" (14:7). When Philip, unsatisfied, pursues the point by saying, "Lord, show us the Father and that will be enough for us," Jesus repeats his point: "Don't you know me Philip, even after I have been among you such a long time? Anyone who has seen me has seen the Father.... Don't you believe that I am in the Father, and the Father is in me?" (14:9–10). The true seeing that Christ recommends to Philip is a seeing-in-faith. Christ draws Philip to question his seeing in aid of a deeper seeing and knowing; that which is visible must now be known as a guide to that which lies within and beyond the visible. That which lies beyond and within is known to us through faith, and that faith has a clear content. To see Christ we must see him as the Word made flesh, as the Son of God who comes from his Father, as the one in whom the Father dwells and who dwells in the Father. Knowledge of the Trinity—although we will need to think about what we mean by knowledge here—is at the heart of the Christian's grasp of who Jesus is.

In just a few verses Christ explains that he will come to anyone who loves him and will "show myself to him" (14:21). Once again the text pushes us to ask what it means for Christ to "show" himself when our seeing of him fails and he himself has also gone away. The answer Christ gives is simply that the Father and the Son will come and be in the one who loves. The manifestation of which Christ speaks, then, does not occur so much *to* someone but *in* them.

The character of our "seeing" of Christ thus should be shaped by the complexities of trying to know ourselves as indwelt by Father, Son, and Spirit. Jesus says to Philip in that wonderful Johannine irony, not only "If you really know me, you will know my Father as well," but also "From now on, you do know him and have seen him." Central to the task of understanding Scripture's speech about God is the task of understanding what is before us although we fail to see it, attention to why this is so, attention to how we may reform our vision so that we do see. We do not just "see" God in us; rather, the Johannine Christ calls us to consider in more complex ways the very task of seeing and understanding God. In the first place, we may recognize that the central task in any "seeing" of God is the reformation of the heart. In the second place, we must attend ever more closely to what it means for the existence of Father, Son, and Spirit to be unlike objects in the world. As we reflect on how it can be that the divine life indwells us, this truth (and the mysteriousness of God) is driven ever more deeply into our awareness. Then, in the third place, we must not fail to see that if Father, Son, and Spirit indwell us as individuals and as members of Christ's body, we must divert our gaze also to the fruits of that indwelling, to the love of God shown in the body of Christ in the world.

This, then, is the character of the revealed Word: the paradox that what is made visible reveals and points toward the invisible. God's revelation takes the form of an invitation into mystery. But that invitation is always in part an invitation to understand ourselves anew, to understand that Christ reveals the Father as the one who is in the Son, as the Son is in the Father — Christ reveals the mystery of the divine life — only to tell us that we have been indwelt by that life already, which thus gives a new character to our search for God.

## III. PATTERNS OF NAMING

The language of faith, then, draws us toward the mystery of God and to the mystery of God's presence in and to the Christian. But, within our search to know the divine life that is already in us, what can we say about the relationships of Father, Son, and Spirit? I want to begin by thinking a little about the manner in which Scripture speaks of those relationships. Allow me to turn to Romans 8, a text not normally noted as the important trinitarian witness that it is. Let me look, first, at something on the surface of the text, and then try to penetrate its depths a little more. Paul's language here is, I take it, no accident — and even if we believe it to be so, we should hold that the Spirit's presentation of it to us as canonical is not. And yet, that language is complex in the way that it speaks of three characters or actors in the story of our salvation. The theme of the chapter is announced at the beginning: through sending the Son for sin, and through enabling us to live in Christ, God has done what the law could not. Two themes are thus intertwined: God's action in sending his Son and the character of life in Christ. Both of these themes are described in the same language, a language I think we can term "paradoxical."

Romans 8:11 reads: "If the Spirit of him who raised Jesus from the dead is living in you, he who raised Christ from the dead will also give life to your mortal bodies because of his Spirit who lives in you." How many characters are named here? There is one who raised Jesus, and there is also the Spirit of him who raised Jesus. If we look through the chapter as a whole we find this Spirit named sometimes as the "Spirit of," and thus we might be tempted to understand it as a periphrastic expression, "the Spirit of Christ" being equivalent to "Christ's spirit." And yet, elsewhere in this chapter the Spirit is also presented as a distinct actor: the Spirit is that which leads some of us to be children of God; to live according to the Spirit is to set one's mind on the things of the Spirit.

The picture is even more complex when we note that the Spirit is also named in the same chapter as "the Spirit of God" or "the Spirit of him who raised Jesus from the dead," and as "the Spirit of Christ." This ambiguity in the Spirit's status is seen even more clearly when we bring into the conversation Gal 4:6: "Because you are his sons, God sent the Spirit of his Son into our hearts, the Spirit who calls out, 'Abba, Father.'" Here it is God or the Father who sends his Son's Spirit into our hearts. The final ambiguity is that, going back to Romans 8, verse 10 speaks not of the Spirit of Christ being in us, but simply Christ. In the same way, at Gal 2:20, Paul famously asserts that "I no longer live, but Christ lives in me."

Thus, Romans 8 presents us with a paradox and an invitation. The paradox is that there seem to be three actors, each of whom plays a role in bringing the Christian to new life, often in overlapping ways. Some basic ordering of these agents is clear enough: God or Father appears to order the actions of Son and Spirit, but Son and Spirit act with a power that we think of as divine—the power to give life to the dead, for example. One of the most fundamental questions the text poses to us concerns how we speak of the Father's self-gift to Son and Spirit and what it means for our understanding of the divine life that Son and Spirit possess the full reality of divine power.[5] Throughout Romans 8, the text also plays with us. The relationship between Son and Spirit remains unclear, the same actions are accorded to both, and the relationship between the two is not codified but performed for us.

We might seek to dissolve these paradoxes by claiming simply that Paul himself did not clearly differentiate Son and Spirit, and that the linguistic

---

5. There is a long and complex debate in the fourth century about how we should understand Father, Son, and Spirit as each possessing the fullness of divine power and as being one power through their inseparable action. See for introduction Lewis Ayres, *Nicaea and Its Legacy: An Approach to Fourth Century Trinitarian Theology* (Oxford: Oxford University Press, 2004), 280–84 (and index for references to discussion of the theme in particular theologians); Michel R. Barnes, "'One Nature, One Power': Consensus Doctrine in Pro-Nicene Polemic," in *Historica, Theologica et Philosophica, Critica et Philologica* (ed. Elizabeth A. Livingstone; StPatr 29; Louvain: Peeters, 1997), 205–23.

complexity I have identified resulted from his confusion. In the first place, I am not convinced even as a historian that this explanation accounts for the evidence before us. But, in the second place, I think that we do not only read Scripture by attempting to uncover Paul's intentions—we have this text given us through the Spirit, and its complexities are an invitation to us. In the third place, the invitations any one passage of Scripture puts before us become even more complex when we remember that we read a canon of texts together: the patterns that I have drawn out of this one text are then both complexified (because we see so many different vocabularies and nuances: the Son, for example, is also Word and Wisdom and Power and Light and Image and Glory and the Only-begotten), and they are rendered all the more central (because we see just how often they may be read from the text).

It is from reflecting on these invitations, reflecting on them in the light of our encounter with Christ and his Spirit, that doctrinal statements were borne. But these doctrinal terms and statements should be understood not only as summaries of biblical narratives, as rules for Christian speech (although these are two of the tasks they perform), but also as ways of stimulating our return to the matrices of terms and passages that they guard and organize. Working hard at what we mean when we say that Father, Son, and Spirit are of one "nature" is certainly good. Clarity in and care about our language should surely be valued by those to whom God has given minds. But, as I have indicated, I believe that such arguments should always be viewed as also parasitic and as gateways back to the terms and statements and passages that stimulated their appearance. Remembering that our formulae are signposts back to particular patchworks of texts, to particular configurations of scriptural invitations, may help to order all our speech and thinking appropriately toward God, toward a place where rational investigation must draw us only toward mystery. Doctrinal formulae enable articulation of what is revealed in rational terms, and they enable a certain clarity about and defense of what is revealed; but this does not mean that the divine mystery is a fog to be cleared, and the same formulae may also shape our ever deeper entry into that as it is revealed through the text of Scripture.

# IV. THE HOLY SPIRIT WHO HAS BEEN GIVEN TO US

And so back to my question: What do all these invitations allow us to say about the divine life? There are many paths that we might take to answer this question, but let us for a few minutes follow just one—a path of reflection on the Spirit that opens to us some of the fundamental mysteries of the divine relationships.[6]

As may be obvious, if you want to talk about the Son or the Father, not only do you have a lot of scriptural discussion of what Father and Son *do*, but you also have a great deal of material that discusses who they *are*. Thus, the Son is Word, Wisdom, Power; he is the image of God's substance. Sometimes we find lists of terms that seem to tell us mostly about the Son's role in our salvation. The Son is, for example, "the way and the truth and the life." But, still, each of these titles requires our reflection and thought, and each may help us learn a little more about him.

When we try to find the same sort of material about the Spirit, we find ourselves in some difficulty. John 4:24 tells us simply that "God is spirit," and it is possible to take a great many of the New Testament's references to "Spirit" to be simply references to Father or Son as divine. At the same time we find a lot of descriptions of what the Spirit does in the world, but none of these seem immediately to tell us who the Spirit is. Thus, for example, we know through Luke and Acts that the Spirit is at work. Above all, the Spirit makes it possible for people to understand God's will and for them to prophecy by "filling" them. Just a few examples: close to the beginning of the gospel Zechariah is filled with the Holy Spirit and prophesies, telling all who can hear that John will "go on before the Lord to prepare the way for him" (Luke 1:67–80). When Joseph and Mary bring the infant Jesus to the temple, they encounter Simeon, to whom it was revealed "by the Holy Spirit that he would not die before he had seen the Lord's Messiah" (2:26). Simeon goes to the temple "moved by the Spirit" (2:27) and prophesies when he encounters the infant.

When we look on into the book of Acts we continue to find the Spirit leading, instructing, and filling. Thus, in Acts 1:2, 7–8, Jesus has taught "through the Holy Spirit," telling the disciples that they will be baptized with the Spirit and will receive from the Spirit the power to witness to Christ "to the ends of the earth." In Acts 2, it is by being filled with the Holy Spirit that the apostles speak and are heard in many languages. All of these texts enable us to speak ever more clearly about one of the Spirit's key roles and to see that the Spirit is different from Father and Son; but

---

6. My emphasis on offering an account of the Spirit inspired by Augustine's as a fundamental point of departure is intended also to be a recommendation of his account (though it is only fair to note also some influence from Didymus the Blind's *On The Holy Spirit*). For discussion of Augustine himself, see Lewis Ayres, *Augustine and the Trinity* (Cambridge: Cambridge University Press, 2010), chap. 10.

what do they enable us to say about the Spirit's nature and the Spirit's relationship to Son and Father?

Well, turn again to Romans. There we saw the Holy Spirit as that which is both distinct and given, and that which is the Spirit of the Father and the Spirit of Christ. How else is the Spirit of Father and Son named? Romans 5:5 says that "God's love has been poured out into our hearts through the Holy Spirit, who has been given to us." At the very least this text points us toward the idea that the Spirit is the one who gives us God's love, but there may be more here—hidden in a question the text poses. The sentence actually breaks into two parallel halves: "God's love has been poured out into our hearts" and "the Holy Spirit has been given to us." Is the Spirit the love that is given and is that then the fount of love for God in our hearts?

We know that this Spirit gives life—we see that here and in other Pauline texts that speak of the Spirit as simply "life-giving"—and we know that through the giving of this Spirit we become lovers of God and of each other. We see it also in the community of those who received the Spirit in Acts: filled with the Spirit they are "one in heart and mind" (Acts 4:32). Moreover, not only does the New Testament call God Spirit (John 4:24), but we know from 1 John 4:8 that "God is love." The Spirit is God's own Spirit, Christ's Spirit, and the Spirit who is love drawing us into a communion of love. From the character of the Spirit's mission do we learn of his eternal character? Theologians have for centuries believed so. Thus, when we seek to speak about the unity of Father and Son, a unity that can also be narrated as their sharing the same Spirit, we can say that the divine being is a communion brought about from eternity through the Father's sharing of his being, his Spirit, his love with the Son, and the Son's possessing as his own life the Spirit, who also shares the fullness of divinity, who himself gives life and blows where he chooses. The divine life and unity thus may be understood as an act brought about from eternity by the Father's generation of the Son and spiration of the Spirit. We must of necessity give this act an order, a sequence, and yet we must also recognize that doing so should evoke of us a qualification or another story in which we insist that there is no time here; this is simply how God determines to be from eternity.[7]

Follow two steps. First, I have suggested elsewhere that Augustine comes to view the divine persons as identical with the intra-divine acts

---

7. Here I have begun to tread gently onto the turf that Steve Holmes explores in his paper. I largely agree with his account, except that I think one can already find in Augustine the seeds of the account he seeks.

that Scripture predicates of them. The Son *is* a seeing of the Father—this is how we should read John 5:19. But the Son does not come to be a seeing of the Father subsequent to his generation; he is generated as a seeing of the Father. The Son is the Father's Word, the Father speaking (as it were), but this is not a subsequent action—as if the Father thought *and then* decided to express what he had thought in a distinct Word. No, the Father from eternity speaks his Word and Wisdom. Speaking this Word and Wisdom is how the Father determines from eternity to be.[8]

Second, Augustine speaks of the Spirit being as a love who makes many into one. Here Augustine sees Acts 4:32's account of the Spirit's drawing the apostles together so that they are "one heart and mind" as enabling us to speak a little further about how the Spirit is love. Dramatically and yet hesitantly Augustine suggests that the Spirit from eternity is breathed as the one who makes Father, Son, and Spirit one. The Father generates the Son from eternity as one who loves the Father; he loves with the Father's Spirit who is also his own Spirit, who is also the Spirit who possesses the fullness of divine knowledge and will. The act of breathing the Spirit is thus one with the generation of the Son; it is through the breathing of the Spirit that there is from eternity the divine communion. The act that is God is the act of generation and spiration. This account is certainly inchoate in Augustine—but it is there.

But once we begin to speak like this, we are inexorably drawn to confess that while we can and should base our speaking about the divine life in a personalist language of individual agents acting, this language is gradually rendered more and more opaque to our minds as we see the ways in which we must also talk of the persons "in" each other. The language that we thought we could grasp is seen to point toward a reality beyond the temporal and the spatial. It does so, to make the point again, because of the character of the divine love and unity. There is certainly a task here for the speculative reason, and yet there is also a need for that reason to recognize when the target of its gaze has receded beyond sight.[9]

Allow me here to venture a comment in this light on the sort of enterprise represented by Tom McCall's paper in this volume. Tom offers a

---

8. Ayres, *Augustine and the Trinity*, chap. 9.

9. Not surprisingly, I have a number of problems with the family of perspectives grouped under the phrase "social trinitarianism." Many versions of it fail for me most importantly because they are simply inattentive to the principles classical trinitarian theology. But one substantive point may be made on the basis of my exploration here. If I am right about the necessary combination of personalist and non-personalist language at the heart of classical trinitarianism, then some who are tempted to give in to the seductions of a "social trinitarian" perspective *as opposed to* a classical perspective must rethink the character of the opposition they think exists.

sophisticated and historically sensitive analytical account of the range of accounts of divine simplicity that one can find in patristic and medieval theology. He does so in order to isolate one that does not fall foul of those fairly common modern critiques of divine simplicity, which argue that the irreducibility of the persons (for example) shows the illogicality of arguing *simpliciter* that all things in God are identical. I salute his historical sensitivity, but I wonder if he—like a significant number of those who attempt to use analytical philosophical tools in this way—has paid sufficient attention to the way in which the language of divine simplicity is actually used in patristic theology (I make no claim here about medieval debates). For all late fourth- and early fifth-century pro-Nicene theologians I know who attempt some account of the divine unity as simple, it is important to end and surround our attempts to speak of the character and pattern of divine existence with confession of our failure to grasp the uniqueness of that existence.

Augustine, for example, seems to articulate a rather direct version of simplicity as identity, and he uses that notion as the context within which we should understand the divine act or acts I described above. And yet, as I have noted elsewhere, Augustine links his notion of simplicity as identity to an account—Neo-Pythagorean in origin—of divine unity as uniquely preceding and being the source of number. From this language and for theological reasons, he draws the assumption that while God calls us to reach out with our speculative reason, God also may be known as exceeding our attempts to use concepts univocally of him. The rules of identity and non-identity that we know are, in a way unknown to us, exceeded by the divine life. Thus one of the most fundamental functions of Augustine's account of divine unity and simplicity is to serve in the trenches of our re-formation as an intellectual guerilla fighter against the pride that so easily affects that reason as it reaches toward the source of all rationality.[10]

# V. THE STILL POINT

Exploring how the Scriptures speak to us about the Trinity is to follow a path that leads us from statements making use of temporal and material imagery, statements that we initially seem to grasp fairly easily, toward a recognition that such language points us toward a reality of mutual indwelling that escapes our mental grasp. The road leads, in another terminology, toward a "still point" whose beauty we can sense and whose

---

10. Ayres, *Augustine and the Trinity,* chap. 8.

necessity we can imagine, but which always alludes our intellectual grasp in this life. The language I use here comes from the first of T. S. Eliot's "Four Quartets." Eliot uses this language to describe the true experience of beauty and time possible in the memory that has been schooled in the garden of earthly beauty and which has come to see—as far as we can— the nature of time's movement. As we see the true beauty that is possible in the temporal world we inhabit, we recognize that the turning of the world draws us toward and stems from a point where all our categories are transcended. Thus, by analogy, as we come to grasp something of the divine indwelling and unity that is the divine life, we are seeing what shines within all the many different scriptural discussions of the various divine relations, within and between the various different terminologies used for Father, Son, and Spirit. *Within* here is an important word; we do not move beyond that language, we discover that to which it points. Eliot writes:

> At the still point of the turning world. Neither flesh nor fleshless ...
> And do not call it fixity,
> Where past and future are gathered.
> Neither movement from nor towards,
> Neither ascent nor decline.
> Except for the point, the still point, there would be no dance, and
>     there is only the dance.
> I can only say, there we have been: but I cannot say where.[11]

The movement of the intellect toward awareness of this still point for the intellect contemplating Scripture's speech about the divine life and unity is not, however, a movement toward a point at which we realize the futility of all our thought. It is *not* a movement that convinces us trinitarian theology is merely a fiction. It is, in fact, a movement that may shape the heart and the imagination toward an ever-deeper recognition of ways in which the trinitarian life lies within each of the actions Scripture attributes to Father, Son, and Spirit. Each of those titles and actions that Scripture attributes to Father, Son, and Spirit eventually draws us by a particular path toward this same still point. This is a movement in knowing and loving that the Spirit intends for us to follow as far as we may; this is a movement into knowing and into mystery that is intended when God addresses us in his Word.

---

11. Excerpt from "Burnt Norton," from T. S. Eliot, *The Four Quartets* (New York: Houghton Mifflin Harcourt, 1936; renewed 1964). Reprinted by permission of Houghton Mifflin Harcourt Publishing Company. All rights reserved. Also permission granded © T. S. Eliot Estate by Faber and Faber Ltd.

As a further example of how important it is that we embrace this conceptual movement toward the still point of the divine nature, consider for a moment the Nicene insistence that Father, Son, and Spirit are of one will. For many advocates of recent "social" accounts of the Trinity, the one divine will is obviously opposed to there being three wills. To assume such an opposition is, I suggest, to miss the journey toward the still point taken by those Nicenes who most deeply reflect on this language.

Take, for example, an argument found in Basil of Caesarea.[12] The Son truly exists as a distinct divine individual and hence he must will, and he must have the power to accomplish what he wills. Father and Son each must will, and they must each will from eternity and accomplish what they will. But any question concerning the Son's life, the Son's mode of existence is inseparable from his relationship to the Father. Basil draws a parallel: just as Scripture tells us that the Son draws his being from the Father, so we are told that the Son comes to do the Father's will, that he speaks the words that have been spoken to him (John 12:50; 14:24). But, says Basil, it would not be fitting to think that the Son's acting at the command of the Father involved any lack of power or self-determination on his part. We know, however, that the Father shows all things to the Son. Thus, Basil suggests, the Father shares his will with the Son eternally in the same way—the Son is a spotless mirror of the divine being, goodness, and will. Thus, from eternity, the Son's will is fully his own, and yet also the Father's; there is one divine will shared by the Father, fully possessed by the Son in communion with the Father. There is no opposition between one or three wills here. Basil's argument is, in part, an attempt to bend our speech slowly toward a still point where, because of the divine unity that has arisen through the Father's gift, our conceptual resources are exhausted and must end in adoration.

In his recent apostolic exhortation *Lumen fidei*, Pope Francis wrote succinctly: "faith is not a light which scatters all our darkness, but a lamp which guides our steps in the night and suffices for the journey."[13] This statement offers us helpful resources for thinking about the character of Scripture's speech about God and for thinking about the dignity, reach, and darkness of the gift that is theological speculation. The language of

---

12. My argument here paraphrases *On the Holy Spirit* 18.20.51ff. For an excellent new translation see St. Basil the Great, *On the Holy Spirit* (trans. Stephen Hildebrand; Yonkers NY: St. Vladimir's Seminary Press, 2011), 87ff.

13. Paragraph 57. The text may be accessed at www.vatican.va/holy_father/francesco/encyclicals/documents/papa-francesco_20130629_enciclica-lumen-fidei_en.html.

faith—the language of Scripture—illuminates, enabling the human mind to understand and move toward its true object, God, and to understand the character of our world, its brokenness, redemption, origin, and destiny.

But this light also illuminates a darkness that lies ahead of us and surrounds us, for it shows to us the limits of our knowledge—or better, it begins to initiate us into those limits, and if we rest on the language of faith, we can be drawn ever more deeply into this darkness. Learning to love not only the illumination but also the darkness is, I suggest, essential if we are to see both what faith is and the importance of decentering our search for knowledge into a search for greater awareness of our own failure and our need for grace. The language of faith, then, is a lamp that draws us through and into a darkness—but we can trust that the illumination it provides is sufficient for the journey! Christian apophaticism is a divine gift, a work of the Spirit reforming the mind, purifying the mind; but it is a gift that is founded on the fact that God has given us to share in his own knowledge, in his own Wisdom; it is a gift found on the gift of true speech about the divine.

## VI. The Father and the Divine Life

Now that we have spoken a little of the divine life, I want us to think about the role of the Father—illuminating the divine unity from a different angle. I do this so that we can begin to think not only toward the divine unity, toward the still point at which our theological reason fails, but also from that unity toward our own lives. We can turn first to the relationship between the Father and the Son. The Son has come not to do his own will. The incarnate Christ is a model for us of humility before his heavenly Father, and even the eternal Word and Son depends on the Father. One of the most interesting texts in this regard is John 5:19–29. Jesus' discourse here culminates a chapter in which he has healed on the Sabbath and been accused of making himself equal to God by naming God as his Father. In response to this critique—which is given by the narrator, not put into the actual dialogue—Jesus relates his mission to the will of the Father.

I would like to point to two themes woven through his enigmatic words. First, Jesus tells us that "the Son can do nothing by himself; he can only do what he sees the Father doing" (John 5:19). The verse parallels famous words found later in this chapter and virtually repeated in the next: "I have come down from heaven not to do my [own] will but to do the will of him who sent me" (6:38), and I certainly think that we must take from them the principle that the incarnate Son's humility before the Father reveals something about what it means for the Son to be eternally who he is. The Son in eternity looks toward the Father, knows the Father, and in the words of 5:19, does "whatever the Father does."[14]

But note, second, the emphasis throughout this passage on what the Son does and what he is able to do. The Father shows the Son *all* that he does, and the Son is able to do those things. The Father raises the dead, the Son raises the dead. Indeed, it is not even that the Son raises *because* he acts with the Father's power; he gives life "to whom he is pleased to give it" (John 5:21). Verse 26 tells us that as the Father has life *in himself,* so he has granted the Son to have life *in himself.* The gift the Father gives to the Son is one not of loaned authority or power, but of being in himself one who can give life. Both Son and Spirit are "life-giving."

Complement these texts with the perspective found in the first verses of John's gospel. God's Word is with God, but with God in a manner that enables the equivalent statement "and ... was God." This gnomic phrasing has, of course, invited a library of speculation, but let me note only that it conveys a mystery to us. The Word is with God—and thus a distinct reality—in such a way that we can also say "and the Word was God" (John 1:1). There is no hint here that we should read this as "and was a lesser not fully divine being," or as meaning "but not, of course, having the full power of the Father." The Word simply "was God." And yet, verse 3 tells us that it was "through" this Word that "all things were made." How? Well, part of an answer should surely point to the next sentence: "In him was life." The Son and Word is the one through whom all things are created, the one who follows the will of the Father—the one who embodies obedience. Yet the Word or Son does so because the Father has given all to him, given him *in himself* the power to give life and to restore life.

This mystery points us, I think, toward the language of loving gift if we are to understand the relationship of the two: the Father holds back nothing from the Son—and I mean this in a deep ontological sense; all that the Father is he gives to the Son. The Son's love for the Father is one of endless conformity in will, endless exercise of the nature and power he has received—but what we may also describe as the endless exercise of

---

14. I have already mentioned this text and noted my own discussion of Augustine's interpretation. In the same discussion, I offer a survey of prior patristic exegesis (*Augustine and the Trinity,* 233–40).

his *own* will. At this point our notions of "ownness" and "authority" are stretched almost to breaking; they are stretched toward the still point of which I have spoken.

We can then certainly speak of an order among the trinitarian persons. It is the Father who generates the Son and breathes forth the Spirit. Yet, Scripture invites us to reflect until our minds fail on the reality of the gift or gifts that constitute the divine life. We are invited, I suggest, to ask what it means for the Father to be the Father by meditating on the Father's giving of his own Spirit so that the Son is fully divine, fully his own divine agent. The Father acts from eternity to give rise to a communion of Father with a Son and a Spirit in which these latter two owe all to the Father but also possess all. We are also invited to reflect on the divine fatherhood by noting how "Father" and "Son" are also God and Word, the Son being the Father's own eternal speaking of what he is and what is to be. God from eternity determines that he will be God with his Word and Spirit, defined as the Father who shares all with his Son in the Spirit as an eternally generative, loving communion.

# VII. "NOT A LIGHT ... BUT A LAMP"

Meditating on the communion that constitutes the divine life is in itself a good. When God is all in all, the just will be eternally entranced by the inexhaustible vision of God, and so beginning to think about that vision now is part and parcel of training us toward heaven. Thus when we ask the question, "What is the doctrine of the Trinity for?" while we should certainly answer that this doctrine orders all others, we should also say that this doctrine is drawn from Scripture through the Spirit's work as an initial glimpse of that which will be our sight in eternity. In other words, this doctrine describes and reshapes our vision of all toward that which truly is. But how should we draw parallels and analogies between the divine life and our own Christian lives?

One common move in recent trinitarian theology has to been to argue for fairly direct links between accounts of the inner life of God and aspects of human relationships: just as the life of God is X, so should we be. This move is found in distinct forms. Thus we have, for example, the liberal Protestant argument that "the Trinity is our Social Program"; we have the more conservative Protestant linking of the relations between Father and Son with the relationships of men and women; we have the Catholic movements of *communio* ecclesiology and some recent versions of what has become known as "the theology of the body."[15] Now, each one of these receives *some* warrant in the Scriptures, and so my goal in this last section is not to favor or criticize any one of them, but to make a suggestion about all in the light of my argument so far.

There are obviously enough many dangers when we draw parallels between the divine life and ours. Most obviously we may simply claim too much. The divine life is unique, occurs under conditions that are not ours, and always recedes from our grasp even as it draws our minds and hearts. But such a dismissal is not sufficient: Christ himself calls us to the task at John 17:20–21 and, as I have tried to argue, the darkness attendant on Christian faith does not *prevent* our speech but rather gives a particular cast to an enterprise that is commanded of us. Thus, we must ask ourselves what mode of analogical reasoning *is* appropriate for us when we consider texts that invite us to parallel the divine life and our own. I do not have a simple and clear answer to my own question. But I do want to offer three sets of related observations toward an answer.

First, I do not think there is much use in our imagining for ourselves a comprehensible model of the divine life in abstract or formal terms, and then arguing that our lives should also be ordered to mirror such a model. Thus, we might imagine for ourselves a highly personalist model of three persons in loving relationship and say that our community should also exhibit loving relationships. Such a mode of thinking may involve our projecting onto the divine life models of relationship that we favor and then, in a (perhaps unconscious) sleight of hand, calling for those models to be promoted among us. In this sleight of hand there are many difficulties. One of the most important is that our conceptions of the divine life have become too far removed from the mass of scriptural references and images and complexities that we should call to mind when Christ says "as we are one." What we know of the divine life is constituted by a dense field of statements and allusions, and the whole task of producing a model is deeply problematic.

---

15. And, for Catholic theologians, the suggestive words of *Gaudium et Spes* paragraph 24 provide a further authoritative push: "...the Lord Jesus, when He prayed to the Father, 'that all may be one... as we are one' (John 17:21–22) opened up vistas closed to human reason, for He implied a certain likeness between the union of the divine Persons, and the unity of God's sons in truth and charity. This likeness reveals that man, who is the only creature on earth which God willed for itself, cannot fully find himself except through a sincere gift of himself" (the text is available at: www.vatican.va/archive/hist_councils/ii_vatican_council/documents/vat-ii_cons_19651207_gaudium-et-spes_en.html). In another context I hope to reflect on the styles of trinitarian thought that stretch from this text, through the teaching of John Paul II and on to the recent accounts of Cardinals Scola and Ouellet.

Another difficulty is that thinking about the relationship between the divine life and ours *as if* we were dealing with two distinct and separated realities is a mistake. The divine unity that we seek to emulate or the love that the persons show to each other is already here among us and in us. If we are baptized we are in Christ, we have received Christ's Spirit and the Father also. Somehow the life of the church must already show us what we so easily take to be conceived only in an act of the imagination reaching up into the heavens. We are already in and being shaped by the life toward which we reach; and we are in it a particular point in the drama of salvation, and we are in it through being drawn into Christ's body. Rather than focusing on the life of God and constructing a model that may be eschatological, we must attend to the conditions of life and relationship that befit the fallen who are now being redeemed in Christ.

To explore a little further what I am trying to say here, let me offer a second set of observations. It is, I suggest, also a mistake to think about the relationship between the divine life and ours without recognizing that we, now, are always only growing toward the unity that Christ tells us will be ours. The analogies we offer should always be offered in faith and to form hope and love. They are always analogies to aid the journey. Thus, I suspect we must draw such analogies with the intention that they *always* illuminate our failure and our need. We both fail to undertake that to which Christ commands us if we are to manifest him to the world, and we fail to recognize that the unity we seek to exhibit is already at work within us. Our need is to accept the slow reformation of mind and heart through grace that is constantly offered us. Or, as I said above, our need is to recognize that the life of the church that is ours is a life in which the divine life is already at work. Resting in this body and attending to the ways in which God acts among us through Son and Spirit is the context in which our most important learning occurs. It is here that the intellect is humbled, and in being humbled it soars.[16]

My third set of observations concerns the content of the analogies we *can* draw between aspects of the divine life and our own. If I am right about the importance of turning to the different range of scriptural

---

16. Although I construe what we should and what we cannot say about the Trinity differently from Karen Kilby, readers will note a number of common themes between my brief comments here and her own helpful final reflections on ways in which we should reflect in the light of our trinitarian theology. The final pages of Karen's chapter are by no means exhaustive, but they do indicate the importance of our seeking a complex range of ways on which to reflect on the relationship between our communion and the divine, and specifically in the light of our particular place in the divine economy.

passages that draw us toward such analogies and then of meditating on them, what may we say about the overall character of such analogies? Is there a primary focus to the analogies Scripture draws us toward? Yes, I think there is. In each case that I can think of, Scripture invites us to meditate on the priority of love as the constitutive feature of what it is to be a divine person in relationship. Whether we attend to the unity of Father and Son, to the manner in which the Father shows all to the Son, or to the complex parallels between the Spirit as the love of God and the gift that draws us into unity, in every case the reality that we are drawn to contemplate is that of an eternally self-giving love.

But note that this love is something we can only move toward contemplating because each of the divine three *is* this love from eternity and from the Father's gift. This love will always escape our grasp. We should be, I suggest, wary of describing the content of particular divine relationships in order to make our analogies too clear, too fixed; doing so might hide from our minds and hearts the manner in which our expectations are always transcended by the depth of the mutual gift that constitutes the divine unity. Nevertheless, when we attend to these relationships well, we see that we are drawn into them, that they ground our lives as created beings and as Christians. Thus we may perhaps find ourselves not simply imagining the life of God "out there" and wondering how we should emulate that which seems impossibly different. We must also be drawn to reflect on how the Christian life reveals (and hides) the process of our being drawn into one as Father and Son (and Spirit) are one.

When we think about the relationship between the one that Father, Son, and Spirit are, and the one we seek to be, I suggest that the main focus of our attention should not be the overall likeness (and lack of likeness) between God as three and one, and us as multiple and unitary—whether we consider ourselves as families, as churches, or as human communities of whatever scope. Rather, our main focus should be the character of the individual and multiple interrelationships between the divine three. The manner in which the divine love is performed by Father as eternally giving all that he is, by the Son eternally receiving and eternally being the giver of life, by the Spirit as drawing us into unity as the body of Christ, the different ways in which the divine love is performed here provide us with a matrix of points of departure for our meditation and prayer. Attention to any of the ways in which the life of divine love is performed draws us—I hope—first, constantly toward a confession of our own failure to act in love and hence in unity, and, second, constantly toward recognition of our need to rest on the work of grace within us. In this last recognition we come to what I think is at the very heart of that to which Christ calls us in John 17—the unity that we are called to exhibit is a unity into which we are *already* being drawn and reformed.

In this paper I have followed a path toward a notion of divine unity and then back out toward our process of reflection on ourselves as imaging the divine life. My account has revolved around insistence that the divine unity is an incomprehensible act of communion established from eternity by the Father. Indeed, I hope that it was reasonably clear that I see a close link between recognizing how and why the divine unity exceeds our grasp and the particular style of analogical reflection that I argue is most appropriate. At every stage, though, my account has been accompanied by a vision of theological speech as a process of speculative reflection on God's written Word that is drawn from us by God's work. In focusing attention on this speculative process, I have sought, first, to challenge us to think about what mode of argument is the necessary or most appropriate context for good theological thinking. But, in second place, I hope I am also heard as calling us to reflect on the "failure" of our speculative gaze. Reaching a point in our reflections at which the divine life seems to have receded before our grasp is not to reach a point of failure. In part, it is not because along the way toward that still point, paths and parameters for further thought will have been sketched and stimulated. But in the largest part, this is not failure, because this is to follow the path into the divine mystery that God's Word himself opened up for us as he spoke through his person and through the writers of Scripture.

# CHAPTER 6

# "THE NAME ABOVE EVERY NAME"

## The Eternal Identity of the Second Person of the Trinity and the Covenant of Grace

### R. KENDALL SOULEN

> "It is only when one knows the unutterability of the name of God that one can utter the name of Jesus Christ."
>
> —*Dietrich Bonhoeffer*

## 1. JUST SUPPOSE

Suppose that instead of there being just one most appropriate way of naming the persons of the Trinity, there were actually three. Each way of naming the Trinity told the truth, the whole truth, and nothing but the truth, but each did so with a vocabulary that tended to place the whole mystery of the Trinity and of salvation in the light of one person in particular.

Suppose furthermore that one of these three ways of naming—say, the one with a special affinity for the first person—became largely invisible to Christians on account of the church's ancient alienation from the Jewish people. What, in that case, might be the consequences for the doctrine of the Trinity?

One answer might be, "Not much." After all, the church would still have two other ways of naming the persons of the Trinity, and these together would more than ensure the basic soundness of Christian worship and reflection.

On the other hand, perhaps the consequences would be more worrisome after all, at least in certain respects. Perhaps problems would arise from time to time that would be hard to solve in terms of the familiar patterns of naming alone. The church's relationship to the Jewish people might be an example. But perhaps the absence of the neglected pattern of naming the persons of the Trinity would prove consequential in other areas of faith and practice too.

As you no doubt guess, the scenario I just sketched is one that I myself think is true. I think Holy Writ gifts the church with three equally basic ways of naming the Trinity, that Christians have often been color-blind to one of these, and that this has created problems for Christian theology that can be resolved by becoming more sensitive to the neglected pattern.

I wish I had time to persuade you of all that—but I don't.[1] What I can do, however, is suggest the relevance of my thesis for one hotly debated issue in contemporary theology. The controversy I have in mind concerns the relationship between Trinity and election: Is the Trinity "complete in itself from all eternity and apart from God's determination to become incarnate in Jesus Christ, or is it constituted by the eternal decision of election?"[2] The question arises in two contexts. First, what was Karl Barth's view of the matter, and second, what should be a Christian's view of the matter, regardless of what Barth thought?

As is well known, formidable theologians have lined up on both sides of these questions, and the battle has been intense. My own view of the matter is quickly stated. I believe that the Trinity is eternally complete in itself apart from God's eternal election of grace in Jesus Christ. I believe that this is so, both in the writing and intention of Karl Barth and according to the merits of the case.

At the same time, I think that proponents of the opposite view, such as Bruce McCormack, are on to something crucially important in this debate. In his doctrine of election, Karl Barth was trying to wring the ambiguity out of how Christians think about the eternal Trinity as the subject of election. As I see it, theologians such as McCormack are champions of this worthy Barthian impulse. The thing is, there is another and

---

1. I discuss the thesis at length in my book *The Divine Name(s) and the Holy Trinity, vol. 1: Distinguishing the Voices* (Louisville: Westminster/John Knox, 2011).

2. Michael Dempsey, ed. *Trinity and Election in Contemporary Theology* (Grand Rapids: Eerdmans, 2011), 1. The book provides an excellent introduction to and anthology of relevant literature.

better way of achieving what Barth was after. Rather than make the Trinity dependent on the covenant of grace, as McCormack proposes, we should instead reclaim a neglected scriptural pattern of naming the persons of the Trinity, a pattern whose special charism lies in expressing the incomparable uniqueness of the triune God—in time and in eternity.

But I'm getting ahead of myself. Let me back up and introduce our three patterns of naming the persons of the Trinity, before focusing more closely on the neglected pattern.

## 2. THREE PATTERNS OF NAMING THE PERSONS OF THE TRINITY

Sacred Scripture, I suggest, gives us three equally important ways of naming the persons of the Holy Trinity. Each is rooted in the Old Testament, comes to full flower in the New, and is evident in Jesus Christ's own characteristic ways of speaking about himself, the Spirit, and the God to whom he prays.

One way Jesus speaks about these three is by means of kinship terms. He address the one to whom he prays as "Father," an address that entails a corresponding way of identifying Jesus himself, as "Son." The terms also suggest a related way of thinking about the Spirit, as the Spirit of this particular kinship relation, of the Father and the Son.

Another way Jesus typically speaks of God, himself, and the Spirit is by means of a variety of common nouns drawn from everyday life and thought. We see this pattern of speech exemplified by Jesus' parables of the kingdom of God and by the wisdom hymns of the epistles and the Gospel of John, where Jesus (to speak only of him) is called "Word," "Image," "Reflection," "Imprint," and so on. Saints and theologians have further developed this pattern of naming the Trinity by a countless host of ternaries, such "God, Word, and Wisdom" (Irenaeus); "Sun, Ray, Apex" (Tertullian); "Lover, Beloved, Love," and "Unity, Equality, Connection" (Augustine); "Rose, Blossom, Fragrance" (John of Damascus); and so on.

The third and final way Jesus speaks about God is less familiar than the previous two, in large part because of this curiosity: it revolves around a word that Jesus never says. That word, of course, is the Tetragrammaton. The Tetragrammaton is neither a kinship term like "Father," nor a common noun like "God" or "King." It is a personal proper name, constituted by the four Hebrew letters *yod, heh, vav,* and *heh* (יהוה; hence Tetragrammaton). From remotest antiquity to the present day, this name is the most sacred term for God known to Jews, by a wide stretch. This is not because the name has a particularly remarkable meaning, or indeed any certain meaning at all. The famous "I am" of Exod 3:14 is an elucidating pun on the Tetragrammaton, not the Tetragrammaton itself. Rather, the Tetragrammaton's significance resides in the simple fact that it refers exclusively to the God of biblical attestation. Unlike appellative names and titles such as God, King, Father, which apply to many besides the one true God, the Tetragrammaton applies to God alone. It is the only personal proper name of the biblically attested God, and it refers to none but him.

Significantly, the Bible knows of no point in time or beyond it when "the LORD" (a common surrogate for the name) became the bearer of the personal proper name *yod heh vav heh*. The LORD becomes "the God of Israel" through a gracious act of election. He becomes the Creator by deciding to create. But the Bible never suggests that the LORD ever *becomes* the LORD. Of course, this is not evident from the word *Lord* itself, which much rather implies a contingent relationship of superior to inferior into which God enters at some point in time. But that is just the point: LORD is a surrogate for the divine name, not the name itself. Here the elucidating pun of Exod 3:14 has its relevance: "I am who I am." The LORD simply *is* the bearer of this name. "I am the LORD; that is my name! I will not yield my glory to another" (Isa 42:8).

In the Old Testament, the divine name appears some six thousand times, vastly more often than all other designations for God put together. In the New Testament, the Tetragrammaton does not appear a single time. Instead, in conformity with the custom of Second Temple Judaism, the name is evoked indirectly, by means of a variety of surrogates, circumlocutions, and silent allusions. One of these is "Lord" (κύριος), but there are many others, including "Name," "the Power," "the Blessed," "Majesty on High," "Holiness," "I am," "He who is, who was, and who is coming," "Alpha and Omega," the divine passive, and so on.[3] By one estimate, the New Testament contains some two thousand instances of such speech. Allowing for differences of length, this means the density of allusion to the Tetragrammaton is about the same in the New Testament as in the Old, if not greater still.

Even by the exacting standards of Second Temple Judaism, Jesus of Nazareth appears to have been exceptionally zealous on behalf of the divine name. He longs for the eschatological vindication of its holiness,

---

3. See *The Divine Name(s) and the Holy Trinity*, 193–212.

as indicated by the first petition of the Lord's prayer: "Hallowed be your name." Jesus' own speech is especially dense with silent allusion to the divine name, especially in the form known to biblical scholars as the divine passive. Jesus, we surmise, refrains from pronouncing the divine name, not for custom's sake alone, and still less out of fear, but as a humble but eloquent token of his reverence for the name and its bearer.

Given Jesus' reverence for the divine name and its importance to Second Temple Judaism generally, it is not surprising that the writers of the New Testament expressed their trinitarian convictions by evoking the unspoken and unwritten Tetragrammaton. One way they do this is by citing Old Testament verses that contain the name YHWH. They apply these verses to God (e.g., Matt 4:10; cf. Deut 6:13), to the Spirit (e.g., Luke 4:18; cf. Isa 61:1), and—astonishingly—to Jesus Christ himself, *as though he himself were bearer of the divine name YHWH* (e.g., Rom 10:13; cf. Joel 2:32.) The Synoptic Gospels begin with a programmatic: "Prepare the way for the Lord" (Matt 3:3 par.). Note that God sends *John* to prepare the way of the Lord, not Jesus. God sends Jesus to be, in some extraordinary sense, the saving advent of the Lord himself.

But how can this be? How can Jesus be sent by the Lord (cf. Luke 4:18), be anointed by the Spirit of the Lord, and yet himself *be* the Lord of Old Testament attestation? Some New Testament passages make little apparent effort to answer this question, but merely affirm that it is so. Prominent among these is Paul's creed-like reformulation of the Shema, that "for us there is but one God ... and ... one Lord, Jesus Christ" (1 Cor 8:6). This confession, among the oldest in the New Testament, simply places Jesus inside Israel's ancient confession of faith alongside the one God.

Other New Testament passages, however, do shed light on how both Jesus and the God to whom he prays can bear the same divine name. Key to these passages is the affirmation God has given his own personal name to Jesus, with the result that God's saving self-manifestation to creation transpires in and through the recognition that Jesus is Lord. We encounter this astonishing idea in one of the oldest writings in the New Testament: Phil 2:5–11.

> Have the same mindset as Christ Jesus:
> Who, being in very nature God,
>> did not consider equality with God something to be used to his own
>>> advantage;
> rather, he made himself nothing
>> by taking the very nature of a servant,
>> being made in human likeness.

And being found in appearance as a man,
   he humbled himself
   by becoming obedient to death—
      even death on a cross!
Therefore God exalted him to the highest place
   and gave him the name that is above every name,
that at the name of Jesus every knee should bow,
   in heaven and on earth and under the earth,
and every tongue acknowledge that Jesus Christ is Lord,
   to the glory of God the Father.

Over the centuries, Christians have interpreted Paul's reference to "the name that is above every name" in different ways. Some have held that it referred to God's namelessness; others, the word "Lord"; and still others, the name "Jesus." When one takes into account the passage's Jewish context, however, a far more likely possibility suggests itself. "The name above every name" refers to the Tetragrammaton, the name that first-century Jews—whether Christian or not—referred to *obliquely*, by means of phrases such as this one. If this interpretation is correct, then Paul in Philippians 2 uses oblique reference to the Tetragrammaton to identify all three persons of the Trinity. He identifies the first person as the one who gives the divine name, the second person as the one who receives it, and the third person as the one who awakens its acknowledgment, in the second person, to the glory of the first. True, the text does not explicitly mention the Holy Spirit, but its activity is implied by the cosmic acclamation of Jesus as "Lord" (another conventional surrogate for the divine name), a cry that Paul says elsewhere is possible only as a work of the Spirit (1 Cor 12:3).

Impressive though it is, the trinitarian "grammar" of Phil 2:5–11 exhibits a worrisome feature, at least when judged from the perspective of the church's mature doctrine of the Trinity. It seems to suggest that Jesus *became* the bearer of the divine name after his exaltation from the dead.[4] Presumably, God—the first person—always bore the divine name, but even he *became* its *giver* at a certain point in time. Taken at face value, this seems to point in the direction of adoptionism rather than Nicene Christianity. At the very least, it certainly does not invite us to conceive of the

---

4. A similar issue presents itself in other New Testament passages. Examples include Paul's use of kinship terminology in Rom 1:4 (Jesus becomes "Son of God" by resurrection), and the Pauline use of wisdom vocabulary of Col 1:15 (Jesus as "the firstborn over all creation"). In my opinion, an "adoptionist" interpretation of these passages falls short of their intention, which is to express Christ's dignity in the strongest available terms.

giving and receiving the divine name as an *eternal* relation between the first and second persons.

Not so the Gospel of John. Unlike the Christ hymn of Philippians, John knows of a giving and receiving of the divine name that is *manifested* in time, but that takes place before the foundation of the world.[5]

John 17 records Jesus' prayer in the upper room, on the eve of his crucifixion. At the beginning and end of the prayer, Jesus speaks of himself as having revealed the divine name, which he refers to as "your name" (τὸ ὄνομα σου), the name of the One to whom he prays (17:6, 26). In the middle of the prayer, however, Jesus expresses a still more intimate relationship to the divine name. Twice he calls it "your name *you gave me*" (17:11, 12, italics added). I judge this phrase to be one of the most profoundly illuminating affirmations in the entire New Testament. It depicts the mutual relation of God and Jesus in a way that coincides substantially with the kinship vocabulary of "Father" and "Son" and the wisdom vocabulary of "God" and "Word," even as it uses a distinctive vocabulary of its own, focused on the giving and receiving of the divine name.

But just what is this name? Might it not be "Father," or just a synonym for God's reputation, as has been suggested? Not likely. Jesus' name is not "Father," nor is it possible to peel away God's reputation from God's canonical name in such a casual manner. We draw closer to John's majestic vision when we understand "your name you gave me" in light of Jesus' solemn declaration, "I am" (ἐγὼ εἰμί).

Recall that over the course of the Fourth Gospel repeatedly Jesus declares the words "I am," and he does so in two different ways. Seven times Jesus says "I am" followed by some predicate of salvation, such as "the bread of life" (6:35), "the light of the world" (8:12), and so on. But seven times Jesus simply declares the words "I am" without any predicate at all. The words just hang there, as odd sounding in Greek as they are in English.

Jesus' absolute "I am" statements in the Fourth Gospel are as decisive for the New Testament as the theophany at the burning bush is to the Old. By declaring "I am," Jesus reveals his identity as the one who has been given the divine name and who makes it known (cf. John 17), even as he

---

5. My account of the Tetragrammaton in John has been especially helped by Raymond E. Brown, *The Gospel According to John* (AB; New York: Doubleday, 1970), 2:754–56; Charles A. Gieschen, "The Divine Name in Ante-Nicene Christology," *VC* 57 (2003): 115–58; and Richard Bauckham, "Monotheism and Christology in the Gospel of John," in *Contours of Christology in the New Testament* (ed. Richard N. Longenecker; Grand Rapids: Eerdmans, 2005), 148–66.

does so in a way that continues to honor the custom of avoiding the direct use of the Tetragrammaton itself.[6]

It would be fun to dwell on the "I am" statements in greater detail, but time requires that we limit ourselves to two passages. The first is this:

> "Very truly I tell you ... before Abraham was born, I am!" (John 8:58)

What can this mean except that he who speaks these words receives the divine name before the world began? Like the Father's begetting of the Son, or God's speaking of the Word, the giving of the divine name is eternal. Indeed, these are really just different ways of saying the same thing. To say the Father begets the Son is to say God speaks the Word is to say the LORD gives his name to another.

At the same time, each way of speaking has a special charism of its own. In my judgment, the special charism of the vocabulary of the unspoken divine name is to emphasize the uniqueness of the divine life. This uniqueness encompasses mystery and identifiability in equal measure and is ultimately rooted in the first person, the primordial bearer of the divine name that Jesus receives and reveals but neither writes nor speaks. What makes the persons of the Trinity one and equally worthy of worship is the one name they share. What distinguishes them is the different ways they share it, one as its giver, one as its receiver, one as the Spirit of its glorification.

The other passage I want to examine briefly is this.

> Jesus, knowing all that was going to happen to him, went out and asked them, "Who is it you want?"
>
> "Jesus of Nazareth," they replied.
>
> "I am he," Jesus said. (And Judas the traitor was standing there with them.) When Jesus said, "I am he," they drew back and fell to the ground.

---

6. The Old Testament provides abundant grounds for drawing a connection between "I am" and the Tetragrammaton. There is Exod 3:14–15, of course, but there is also God's ubiquitous declaration "I am the LORD!" which the LXX typically renders *ego eimi kyrios*, and which is especially characteristic of Ezekiel and Isaiah 40–55. Significantly, Isaiah several times reports God's self-declaration "I am the LORD" in the abbreviated form "I am!" (41:4; 46:4; etc.). In such cases, the short form is materially identical with the longer one, i.e., "I am" = "I am the LORD." On three occasions, the LXX renders God's self-declaration with the extraordinary phrase, "I am I am"! (LXX: *egō eimi egō eimi*; Hebrew MT *'ānōkî ānoki hû'*). So, for example, Isaiah 43:25 (LXX) reads: "I am I am (Gk: *egō eimi egō eimi*, lit: "I am I am") who blots out your transgressions for my own sake, and I will not remember your sins." In this and similar passages the author of Second Isaiah creates a virtual synonymy between the phrase "I am" and God's personal proper name, which is implied rather than explicitly stated. While Second Isaiah wrote before the practice of avoiding God's name became customary, the synonymy he created has obvious relevance for understanding the Gospel of John, written during the Second Temple period when the custom was universally normative among Jews. Distinct from God's personal name yet closely linked to it, the words "I am" permit one to evoke God's name while leaving the name itself unspoken. For further discussion, consult the literature cited in the previous footnote.

> Again he asked them, "Who is it you want?"
>
> "Jesus of Nazareth," they said.
>
> Jesus answered, "I told you that I am he. If you are looking for me, then let these men go." (John 18:4–8)

What I find extraordinarily fascinating here is the interplay between "I am" and the name "Jesus" itself, which of course means "YHWH is Salvation." The soldiers know perfectly well whom they are looking for, this man who has been stirring up trouble, this Jesus of Nazareth. But the soldiers do not really know who Jesus is until he reveals himself by declaring "I am," a revelation that forces them to the ground. "Jesus" and "I am" refer to the same person, but they are not exactly synonymous, any more than are "Son of God" and "son of Mary." Jesus of Nazareth, I propose, is "I am," the receiver of the divine name YHWH, in every possible world. He is Yeshua, "YHWH is Salvation," in every world into which he is sent to save.

# 3. Relevance to Trinity and Election

Back to the contemporary debate concerning Trinity and election. Many talented theologians have spilled a lot of ink on the topic, and to suggest at this late date that biblical exegesis might help nudge things forward is to risk being lambasted by all sides. Still, that is basically what I want to do. First the debate itself.

Theologians today are discussing Trinity and election because of Karl Barth. Specifically, they are doing so because of Barth's decision to subject the inherited doctrine of double predestination to a massive reworking in *Church Dogmatics* II/2. Karl Barth was motivated to undertake this revision because of a single overriding concern: the inherited doctrine left the identity of the eternal triune God, who was the subject of election, shrouded in obscurity and ambiguity. The doctrine of election could not be good news because the God at its foundation was not manifestly the God of the gospel, the God of Jesus Christ. Of course, this is not to charge the tradition with having a completely naked and *un*determined concept of the electing God. It certainly did not. The tradition affirmed with all clarity that the Holy Trinity is the eternal subject of election, and it filled out its concept of the Trinity with a host of biblically attested names, such as Father, Son, Spirit, God, Word, Image, not to mention a bristling army of elucidating concepts such as *logos asarkos, ensarkos, incarnandus,* and so on. Still, in Barth's view, the resulting portrait of the Trinity as the subject of election remained dangerously ambiguous and *under*determined.

Dangerously underdetermined from what point of view? On this point Barth is crystal clear: underdetermined from the point of view of the name of Jesus Christ. This point is worth emphasizing. To a truly remarkable degree, Barth conceives and executes his doctrine of election as a sustained reflection on a single biblically attested name. Barth had done this once before in the *Church Dogmatics*, in his doctrine of the Trinity. In that case, the name around which everything turned was *Yahweh-kyrios*. This is interesting in itself, of course, and I will have more to say about this curious and fateful quasi-name later. In the doctrine of election, however, Barth makes no mention of *Yahweh-kyrios*. Instead, he insists, as emphatically as possible, that the doctrine of election is to be unfolded as meditation on the name Jesus Christ. The light of this name, Barth trusts, will banish the obscurity that has clouded the identity of the electing God and will disclose the God of love and freedom revealed in Jesus Christ himself.

Seen against this backdrop, there is a certain inevitability to Barth's thesis that Jesus Christ is the electing God and the elected man. The thesis is stunning in its simplicity and power. Certainly it accomplishes what Barth wanted to accomplish. It makes the name of Jesus Christ decisive for our reflections on the doctrine of election, and it banishes all obscurity from the eternal identity of the electing God.

And yet, for all that, there is something troubling—almost eerie and disconcerting—about the claim that Jesus Christ is the electing God.[7] I at any rate remember feeling that way when I first encountered the thesis as a graduate student. A friend and I chewed over it one sunny afternoon for what seemed like hours. I do not recall that we ended our conversation any more enlightened then when we began.

One of the merits of the vigorous debate conducted by Bruce McCormack, George Hunsinger, Paul Molnar, and others is to have clarified our understanding of the basic issues at stake. Here we can take our starting point from Bruce McCormack's formulation of Barth's insight: "The second person of the Trinity has a name, and his name is Jesus Christ."[8] But the thorny question is this: How does the second person of the Trinity become the bearer of this name? Does it belong to him by virtue of the same divine act by which the second person simply is the second person? Or does it belong to him by virtue of a logically and ontologically

---

7. According to Bruce McCormack, Barth himself did not settle on the thesis until after 1936. Bruce McCormack, "Seek God Where He May Be Found: A Response to Edwin Chr. Van Driel," in *Orthodox and Modern: Studies in the Theology of Karl Barth* (Grand Rapids: Baker Academic, 2008), 262.
8. Ibid., 266.

subsequent divine act, by virtue of which the second person chooses to be the second person for us and for our salvation? Or, to put the matter as simply as possible, might the second person of the Trinity have been the second person without being Jesus Christ? And if so, who would he then have been?

Now here is my contention. Our efforts to give a satisfying answer to these important questions are in some substantial measure hobbled—not crippled, but hobbled—precisely insofar as we have become color-blind to the scriptural pattern of naming the Trinity that orbits the unspoken Tetragrammaton.

Suppose we say, with Paul Molnar and George Hunsinger, that the second person of the Trinity could have been the second person without bearing the name Jesus Christ. This contention has the important and, to my mind, decisive advantage that it preserves the freedom and gratuity of the covenant of grace. Nevertheless, the position has an Achilles' heel. The difficulty appears when we try to speak in a biblically convincing manner about who the second person is prior to and apart from the name Jesus. It is not that we lack a biblical vocabulary to answer this question. The problem rather is with limitations inherent in the vocabulary itself. We may say that the second person is the eternal Son, Word, Image, and so on, and we may buttress this by speaking of the other persons of the Trinity as Father, Spirit, Love, Gift, and the like. But the difficulty is that kinship terms and common nouns are applicable by nature to endlessly many subjects in heaven and on earth. History teems with fathers, sons, and spirits who have been worshiped and adored. So long, then, as we are content to specify the Trinity's eternal identity by means of such generic terms *alone,* we are left with a version of the problem that troubled Karl Barth in the first place. We are left with a picture of the eternal subject of election that is—I will not say false—but rather *ambiguous and underdetermined.*

But suppose we say, with Bruce McCormack, that it is essential and necessary to the second person to bear the name Jesus, that he bears this name by virtue of the same act by which he is the second person. This contention has the advantage of addressing full throttle the problem of an underdetermined picture of the eternal Trinity. But it is an overcorrection that comes at an exorbitant price. As many have pointed out, it makes the eternal Trinity wholly contingent on the decision to be for us and for our salvation, and so impoverishes our ability to express the freedom and gratuity with which the biblical God creates, redeems, and consummates. This is a remedy that is worse than the disease it is meant to cure.

In passing, I would like to register a further concern I have about McCormack's position. He supposes, and invites us to suppose, that it offends the nature of the biblical God to try to speak meaningfully about who God is apart from his decision to be the God of Israel. I believe this is exactly wrong. The glory of the God of Israel is that he makes abundantly clear who he is prior to and apart from his gracious decision to be the God of Israel. He is the LORD, *yod heh vav heh*. He is this already in himself, prior to and independent of his gracious decision to become "the God of Abraham, Isaac, and Jacob" and "the Father of our Lord Jesus Christ." Affirming this has nothing to do with buying into metaphysics ancient or modern, essentialist or historicist. It has to do with harkening to the voice of the burning bush. That voice distinguishes with all clarity between who God is *in se* and who God is *pro nobis*, between "I AM WHO I AM" and "I AM has sent me to you." The staggering thing is—the voice in both cases is the same, the voice of the LORD.[9]

What then should we want to say? With Paul Molnar and George Hunsinger, we should want to say that it is possible to speak meaningfully about who the second person of the Trinity is prior to and apart from the decision to bear the name Jesus Christ. Yet with Bruce McCormack, we should want to speak about the eternal second person in a way that leans maximally on the unsubstitutable specificity of the personal proper name Jesus Christ. *We do both of these things simultaneously when we supplement our talk about the eternal Trinity by drawing more vigorously on the neglected pattern of naming the Trinity to which I previously drew attention, the pattern that orbits the unspoken Tetragrammaton.* Before he is Jesus Christ, the second person of the Trinity is the eternal Son of God, the eternal Word of God, the eternal Image of God, *and*—the eternal recipient of "the name above every

---

9. McCormack admits that Christians must be able to say "God would be God without us" in order to preserve the gratuity of God's grace, but insists that they must refrain from trying "to specify precisely what God would be without us" on pain of obscuring the identity of the biblical God with "metaphysical speculation" (cf. ibid., 274.) But the real question the Bible invites us to ask is: "Would YHWH be YHWH without us?" ("God" of course is an appellative name that stands throughout the Bible for the proper name YHWH.) And the difficulty I see with McCormack's position is that it does not allow him to answer this question acceptably, either way. If he says (as I believe he should), "Of course YHWH would be YHWH without us!" then he must abandon, or at least substantially qualify, his premise that it is impossible to speak meaningfully about the identity of the biblical God apart from his decision to be "for us and for our salvation." But if cleaves to that premise and says, "God would be God without us but he would not be YHWH," then he posits a divine agent antecedent to YHWH. This would be to engage in mythology and metaphysical speculation at once. It would reanimate a conception of God as the un- and underdetermined "x" whose banishment from Christian theology was the animating purpose of McCormack's position in the first place. (McCormack might also say, "God would be God but we cannot say whether or not he would be YHWH," but this would merely be a version of the second answer).

name," given to him by the Father of lights. Jesus of Nazareth is Ye-shua, "the Lord is Salvation" because he is first of all the Lord.

## 4. Why Did Barth Forget a Name He Had Previously Discovered?

In the final section of this essay I want to engage in a brief bit of genealogical work. Hitherto I have suggested that in his doctrine of election, Karl Barth paid insufficient attention to a pattern of naming the persons of the Trinity that orbits the unspoken Tetragrammaton, and that this in turn has had a hobbling effect on our contemporary debate about Trinity and election. But there is a puzzle here. Karl Barth was scarcely ignorant of the Tetragrammaton or its importance for Christian theology. As I mentioned earlier, in the *Church Dogmatics*, Barth goes so far as to single out the name *Yahweh-kyrios* as the key to the whole doctrine of the Trinity, declaring that it "does not seek to be anything but an explanatory confirmation of this name."[10] But then why does Barth himself neglect this name when he comes to write the doctrine of election only a few years later? Why does Barth himself not invoke it as a way of specifying the eternal identity of the electing God revealed in the name Jesus Christ?

While I think there are many correct answers to this question, I want to draw attention to one in particular: Barth was misled in his exegesis by the influence of an early modern esoteric tradition, the Christian *kabbalah*. While little noted by interpreters of Barth, the subterranean influence of the Christian *kabbalah* goes at least some way toward explaining why Barth accorded the Tetragrammaton the role he did in his doctrine of the Trinity, and the role he didn't in his doctrine of election.[11]

The *kabbalah* (Heb. "tradition") is a form of Jewish mysticism that is centrally concerned with the Divine Name, the Tetragrammaton. Christian Europe took little notice of the *kabbalah* until the late 1400s, when a circle of Renaissance humanists began to popularize it in a modified Christian form. The Christian kabbalists celebrated the *kabbalah* both for

10. Karl Barth, *Church Dogmatics* (ed. Geoffrey W. Bromiley and Thomas F. Torrance; trans. Geoffrey W. Bromiley; Edinburgh: T&T Clark, 1975), I/1, 348.

11. Barth's exposure to the ideas of the Christian kabbalists was likely mediated by figures such as Luther and the German idealists. On the Christian *kabbalah*, see Soulen, *The Divine Name(s) and the Holy Trinity*, 83–104; Joseph Dan, ed. *The Christian Kabbalah: Jewish Mystical Books and Their Christian Interpreters* (Cambridge, MA: Harvard University Press, 1998); G. Scholem, "The Beginnings of the Christian Kabbalah," in Dan, *The Christian Kabbalah*, 17–51; George F. Moore, "Notes on the Name YHWH," *American Journal of Theology* 12 (1908): 34–52.

what they supposed were its ancient roots, and because they believed it gave external evidence for Christianity's superiority to Judaism.

According to the Christian kabbalists, the Tetragrammaton is indeed a name of surpassing significance. But to understand it rightly, one must interpret it, as Christians do, in light of the distinction between the Old Testament and the New. To wit (and this is their problematic thesis) the Tetragrammaton is a temporary prophetic forerunner of a greater name yet to come. Like circumcision and other ceremonies of the Old Testament, it is destined to be fulfilled according to the spirit and rendered obsolete according to the letter. The provisional nature of the Tetragrammaton is evident in the fact that Jews recoil from pronouncing it and are (by their own confession) ignorant of the name's true meaning. What is that meaning? The Christian kabbalists actually knew of two possibilities. One was the name "Jesus," and the other was the name "the Father, the Son, and the Holy Spirit." In either case, they supposed, the pronounceable names of the new covenant *take the place* of the unpronounced name of the old covenant and consign it reverently but firmly to the past.

Turning to Karl Barth, one detects little evidence of the influence of the Christian kabbalists in his earliest runs at the doctrine of the Trinity, for the simple reason that the early Barth does not yet assign much weight of any kind to the Tetragrammaton. He is instead much preoccupied with one of its common surrogates: "Lord." In *The Christian Dogmatics* (Barth's abortive first-run at a multivolume dogmatics), Barth unveiled his famous thesis that the root of the doctrine of the Trinity is the affirmation, "God reveals himself as Lord." But what exactly does "Lord" mean? In an important discussion, Barth explains that biblical scholars of the day were divided on the point. Some maintained that *kyrios* was "a translation [*sic*] of the Old Testament name of God *Jahweh*," while others that it was "the fervent trumping of everything which the world of Hellenistic religion worshiped in the way of gods, half gods … lords, and lordships." Barth concludes that either way "Lord" really means the same thing. He explains:

> In either case, it [i.e., Lord] means a reality that one conceives personalistically, before which one bows in awe, thanksgiving, love, trust, petition, obedience.… One bows before the Lord, because the quintessence of superiority, power, and dignity is present in Him. (233)

For the Barth of *The Christian Dogmatics,* then, "Lord" gets its meaning from the existential encounter between God and humanity. So long as this is clear, it is a matter of indifference whether one traces it back "the Old Testament name of God."

When *Christian Dogmatics in Outline* appeared in print, it met a barrage of withering criticism. A particularly juicy target was Barth's doctrine of the Trinity. Barth had castigated others for deriving their concept of the Trinity from common experience (the notorious *vestigia trinitatis*). But what was Barth's thesis "God reveals himself as Lord" other than his own *vestigium trinitatis,* drawn from idealism and foisted on the Bible? Barth evidently felt the justice of the criticisms, and he abandoned the *Christian Dogmatics* as a false start.

Several years later, Barth published a revised version of his doctrine of the Trinity in the first volume of *The Church Dogmatics*. He sticks to the thesis that "God reveals himself as Lord" is the root of the doctrine of the Trinity. But now Barth declares that this "root" actually rests on something even more basic: "the revealed name *Yahweh-Kyrios*." In fact, Barth claims, the whole doctrine of the Trinity is nothing but an "explanatory confirmation" of this name.[12]

The point of Barth's revision is clear and utterly laudable. Barth means to anchor the affirmation "God reveals himself as Lord" in the uniqueness of the biblical God, not in human religious experience generally. Barth appreciates now (as he previously did not) the singular role played by the Tetragrammaton in demarcating the uniqueness of the biblical God. This is exactly the insight that I have urged throughout this essay.

Yet a funny thing happens to Barth's insight that sadly prevents it from having a lasting role in *The Church Dogmatics*. In the course of Barth's exposition, the name "*Yahweh-Kyrios*" changes into something else, like a potion in an alchemist's bottle. Specifically, the first half of the name, "*Yahweh*," dissolves away. What takes its place seems to shimmer a bit in Barth's mind. At times it seems to change into the name "Jesus." More often, it dissolves into the master concept "Lordship." Of course, both of these do play outsized roles in the *Church Dogmatics*. But in either case the Tetragrammaton itself is left behind. A particularly important passage is this.

> Into the place ... of the name of Yahweh that in the end really dwells in Jerusalem in a house of stone—there now comes the existence of the man Jesus of Nazareth, "My Lord and my God."[13]

---

12. Barth, *CD* I/1, 348.
13. Ibid., 318.

Stripped to its basics, the sentence exactly echoes the favorite motif of the Christian kabbalists, with a slight "existentialist" twist. According to Barth, the Tetragrammaton is replaced by Jesus' "existence," not by his name. But having said that, Barth then embraces the latter view, too, because of course Jesus' existence is denoted by his name. As Barth writes a few sentences later, the name Yahweh is replaced by "the historical figure of this Man on his way from Bethlehem to Golgotha, the 'name' of *Jesus*."[14]

We now have our answer to why Barth's "discovery" of the Tetragrammaton in his doctrine of the Trinity bears no fruit in his doctrine of election. He has been led astray by the Christian kabbalists. Like them, Barth confines the divine name to the Old Testament and imagines that it has been superseded by a different name in the New Testament. He fails to see that the divine name is the preeminent sign of God's uniqueness throughout the Christian canon, Old Testament and New. Barth fails to see this because, like the Christian kabbalists, he is predisposed to think of the Tetragrammaton as a Jewish symbol inherently foreign to the New Testament, and because he is largely color-blind to the very Jewish way Jesus and the apostles signal their reverence for the divine name, by avoiding its pronunciation.

Can we rescue what Barth says about Jesus and the divine name in the brief quotation I cite above? Yes, easily. We need only make one change. The Old Testament reality superseded by the name "Jesus" is the stone temple in Jerusalem, not the divine name that dwelt therein. The divine name itself is never superseded, though now it dwells in a temple of flesh, the man Jesus, who freely reveals the secret of his identity to all: "I am."

# CONCLUSION

I would like to return in closing to a claim I made at the beginning of this essay: there are three equally basic ways of naming the persons of the Trinity. I have emphasized one in this essay, not because I regard it as more important than the others, but because I believe its retrieval will ultimately redound to the health and vitality of all three.

---

14. Ibid. (italics original).

# CHAPTER 7

# OBEDIENCE AND SUBORDINATION IN KARL BARTH'S TRINITARIAN THEOLOGY

DARREN O. SUMNER

THE YEAR 1953 SAW THE PUBLICATION of the first part-volume in Karl Barth's Doctrine of Reconciliation (Volume IV of *Die kirchliche Dogmatik*).[1] By this point in his career Barth was an internationally renowned figure, secure in his position in Basel for more than twenty years. His sharp criticisms of the liberal Protestant theology of the previous century, his aggressively theological approach to biblical exegesis, and his provocative revision of the doctrine of election had helped to inaugurate a widespread theological renaissance. It is Barth, along with his Catholic contemporary Karl Rahner, that we have most to thank for the contemporary revival of the doctrine of the Trinity, a project carried on in various forms by Jürgen Moltmann, Wolfhart Pannenberg, John Zizioulas, and others.

As significant a piece of sustained theological reflection as it is, Volume IV of the *Church Dogmatics* is not without its controversies. Barth at

---

1. In English, *Church Dogmatics* (4 vols. in 13 parts; ed. G. W. Bromiley and T. F. Torrance; Edinburgh: T&T Clark, 1956–75). This volume would appear in English three years later.

times arrives at theological judgments that strike the average reader as odd, and perhaps not in keeping with what he has said elsewhere. As one who believes that Barth still has a great deal to offer, my worry is that our misunderstanding of Barth stands in the way of receiving his theology in any full sense—including its sharp edges. My agenda here is to examine one of these controverted passages critically in the light of Barth's broader trinitarian theology, in order to cast some light on why Barth makes the claim that he does.

The particular passage in question concerns Barth's description of the Son's relationship to the Father as one of willing subordination: the way of the Son into the far country is the way of obedience, in which God takes up the cause of sinners as his common cause when he takes on human flesh. For Barth God is "both One who is obeyed and Another who obeys."[2] Within the Trinity itself, it is in this relation—a relation of superiority and subordination—that the unity of the Father and Son consists.

> We have not only not to deny but actually to affirm and understand as essential to the being of God the offensive fact that there is in God himself an above and a below, a *prius* and a *posterius*, a superiority and a subordination. And our present concern is with what is apparently the most offensive fact of all, that there is a below, a *posterius*, a subordination, that belongs to the inner life of God that there should take place within it obedience.[3]

It is by no means unusual, of course, for Christian theologians to make the claim that God the Son is obedient to the Father—an obedience that extends from his eternal sending even to death on a cross. Philippians 2:8 speaks of Christ humbling himself "by becoming obedient to death." In John's gospel Jesus says to the crowd, "I have come down from heaven not to do my [own] will but to do the will of him who sent me" (John 6:38; cf. 4:34, 5:30), and that it is the Father who has granted the Son "to have life in himself" as well as the authority to execute judgment (John 5:26–27). Thus, theologians have long been content to speak of the Son's obedience and submission to his Father—but strictly *kata sarka*, in the context of the incarnation. This submission and subordination would seem to be a consequence of the Son's assumption of the *forma servi*.

What is therefore remarkable and "offensive" about Barth's words is that he does not restrict this relation to the economy, but suggests that

---

2. *CD* IV/1, 201
3. *CD* IV/1, 200–201

the superiority and subordination (*Vor- und Nachordnung*) "belongs to the inner life of God." Furthermore, Barth has made this claim in the context of an explicit disavowal of the ancient heresy of Subordinationism (*Subordinationismus*), which taught that the Son is ontologically inferior to the Father. This view was offered by pro-Arian theologians because it allowed them more easily to resolve a certain set of difficulties—namely, the strict singularity and immutability of God in light of the human life and death of one who is confessed to be God's Son. It was rightly rejected by the church. The language of subordination, then, bears a great deal of unfortunate baggage in Christian theology. Can theologians have it both ways—some sort of subordination in the Trinity without heretical Subordinationism?[4]

This passage continues to vex Barth's interpreters. G. C. Berkouwer suggests that Barth's is "an unacceptable conclusion" and "can only be characterized as speculation."[5] Rowan Williams calls the passage "a very long and tortuous treatment.... What, if anything, this can possibly mean, neither Barth nor his interpreters have succeeded in telling us."[6] Kevin Giles concludes that Barth's rhetoric here finally reaches a "breaking point" and collapses into "convoluted, poetic language."[7] Paul Molnar believes that Barth is guilty of illegitimately reading elements of the economy back into the immanent Trinity. Barth has made "a subtle mistake which places his thinking in conflict with itself."[8] Among other problems, Molnar concludes, this inadvertently introduces hierarchy into the immanent Trinity, blurs the distinction between processions and missions, and "could open the door both to subordinationism and to modalism in some form or another; it might even open the door to monism, dualism or tritheism."[9]

---

4. As the differences in Barth's choice of vocabulary show above, Bromiley may bear some responsibility for this linguistic confusion in his English translation. "Vor- und Nachordnung" suggest that there is a proper *ordering* of the three divine persons, not a hierarchy or inferiority among them—"before and after," rather than "superiority and subordination."

5. G. C. Berkouwer, *The Triumph of Grace in the Theology of Karl Barth* (London: Paternoster, 1956), 304

6. Rowan Williams, "Barth on the Triune God," in *Wrestling with Angels: Conversations in Modern Theology* (ed. Mike Higton; Grand Rapids: Eerdmans, 2007), 129. Originally published in *Karl Barth: Studies of His Theological Method* (ed. Stephen Sykes; Oxford: Clarendon, 1979), 147–93. Williams can only conclude that in *CD* IV Barth has moved "towards a very much more 'pluralist' conception of the Trinity than is allowed for in I/1."

7. Kevin Giles, "Barth and Subordinationism," *SJT* 64 (2011): 346. An account of the debate over subordination in Barth that has taken place in Australia is given in Giles, *Jesus and the Father: Modern Evangelicals Reinvent the Doctrine of the Trinity* (Grand Rapids: Zondervan, 2006), 275–305.

8. Paul D. Molnar, "The Obedience of the Son in the Theology of Karl Barth and of Thomas F. Torrance," *SJT* 67 (2014): 50–69 (quotation on p. 59). I am grateful to Professor Molnar for providing me with a prepublication copy of this essay.

9. Ibid., 65–66; cf. 63–64.

The question of whether Christian theology rightly may speak of a strictly *functional* subordination in the Trinity certainly extends beyond Barth studies. This qualifier has recently generated a great deal of controversy in evangelical quarters. That debate concerns whether "eternal, functional subordination" in the Trinity ought to inform our understanding of human gender relations, and is only tangentially related to my task here.[10] What I wish to do is to identify the place that Barth's account of divine obedience has in his trinitarian theology, and whether it is fitting to describe it using the language of "functional" and "ontological" subordination—terms that belong to the contemporary conversation and which, to my knowledge, were never employed by Barth. To do this I will subject Barth's position to three lines of criticism: (1) Can Barth affirm that this subordination is *eternal*, yet still restrict it to function and so avoid the trap of heretical Subordinationism? (2) If Barth's theological ontology bears an actualist character,[11] can he affirm that the subordination of the Son to the Father is strictly functional and not also ontological—since God's being and God's activity are always mutually implicated? (3) Does Barth's location of obedience within the inner life of God not imply two divine wills, and therefore necessarily a social model of the Trinity?

These are questions that Barth himself did not ask—at least not in the ways in which I will press them. The method of this study is to attempt to describe Barth's position by bringing his theological commitments to bear on these three challenges. I will begin with a summary of his case for the obedience of the Son of God in §59.1. The critiques will then occupy the bulk of what follows. I will conclude with some brief thoughts on the implications of Barth's position for the current debate over subordination.

## THE OBEDIENCE OF THE SON OF GOD: *CHURCH DOGMATICS* IV/1

Barth's intention in the final pages of §59.1 is to understand the way in which Christ's deity is *mystery*—since here true deity is affirmed of a

---

10. A collection of essays on the topic may be found in Dennis W. Jowers and H. Wayne House, eds., *The New Evangelical Subordinationism? Perspectives on the Equality of God the Father and God the Son* (Eugene, OR: Pickwick, 2012).

11. This interpretation is not without its critics. Paul Molnar has argued at length that Barth's actualistic impulse ought not be pressed into the sphere of divine ontology. See, for example, "Can Jesus' Divinity be Recognized as 'Definitive, Authentic and Essential' if it is Grounded in Election? Just How Far Did the Later Barth Historicize Christology?" *Neue Zeitschrift für Systematische Theologie und Religionsphilosophie* 52 (2010): 40–81. For a collection of essays related to this debate see Michael T. Dempsey, ed., *Trinity and Election in Contemporary Theology* (Grand Rapids: Eerdmans, 2011).

human person.[12] He sharply critiques Modalism and Subordinationism for failing precisely at this point: both of these ancient heresies resolve the christological mystery "by juggling it away," by circumventing the difficulty of predicating full divinity to the human Jesus rather than engaging this difficulty "in frontal assault."[13] Subordinationism takes the mystery of Christ's deity only in an improper sense, "trying to understand it as the designation of a second divine being or less divinity."[14] The humanity of the suffering Christ may then be affirmed without risk of implicating the being of the true and highest God. Modalism, by contrast, makes the opposite mistake: it attempts to maintain the full deity of Christ but regards him as a mere mode of appearance or activity of the one true God, which deprives him of "any true and proper being."[15] The Son's divinity is affirmed, but his lowliness and obedience are restricted to a "forecourt of the divine being,"[16] which is not identical with God himself. Both the Modalist and the Subordinationist solution refuse to predicate the Son's humility properly to God himself, and so evade the cross of Christ.

Barth's approach must therefore follow a different form. What he calls the first and inner moment of the mystery of the deity of Christ is that "the way of the Son of God into the far country is the way of obedience."[17] This is the mystery of Jesus' life as it is evident from the gospel narrative: God has sent his Son into the world to walk the road to Golgotha, to die for sin, and in so doing to reconcile wayward creatures to their Creator. Now Barth turns to the second and outer moment of the mystery: that walking this path, in all of the humility and the humiliation that it entails, can belong to the inner life of God—and, indeed, it does belong to the inner life of God. If we will set aside our preconceptions about what the divine being is and what God can and cannot do or be, the event of Jesus Christ will teach us that "for God it is just as natural to be lowly as it is to be high, to be near as it is to be far, to be little as it is to be great, to be abroad as to be at home."[18]

The humanity of the Son is therefore not alien to God—not a form that is donned only to be set aside at the ascension or the eschaton—but indeed is proper to God. If this were not the case, Barth concludes, our

---

12. My focus here is particularly on *CD* IV/1, 192–210 (approximately the final third of §59.1).
13. *CD* IV/1, 200, 197.
14. *CD* IV/1, 196.
15. *CD* IV/1, 197.
16. *CD* IV/1, 196.
17. *CD* IV/1, 192.
18. Ibid.

atonement would not be accomplished and the world would not be reconciled to God.[19] Indeed, God is high and majestic, exalted and praiseworthy, *precisely in that God does this*—precisely in that God is low and humble, that in the Son he enters into the condition of men and women and dies their death. This humiliation and obedience are the very expression of his deity.

Next Barth turns to three presuppositions that, at all costs, we must accept and affirm.[20] The first is that the acting subject of the reconciliation of the world with God is Jesus Christ. It is he alone who bears the judgment that is on the world, in order to bear it away. If we follow the New Testament, we see further that "when we have to do with Jesus Christ we have to do with God. What He does is a work which can only be God's own work, and not the work of another."[21] Second, the act of atonement is an event that takes place not only for the world but in the world, not only touching creation from without but affecting it from within in converting it to God. The economy with which we have to do in the existence of Jesus Christ, then, is not "the kind of economy in which His true and proper being remains behind an improper being, a being 'as if.'"[22]

Connecting these two—the acting subject who is the true God, and the world as the sphere in which God himself is truly acting—is the New Testament's affirmation that God's "presence and action as the Reconciler of the world coincide and are indeed identical with the existence of the humiliated and lowly and obedient man Jesus of Nazareth."[23] This is the vital step: the locus of the divine activity in the world is the obedient teacher who was arrested, put on trial by men who had no right to judge him, humiliated, and tortured until he was dead. This, and nowhere else, is where God's authentic presence and God's act of reconciliation take place. Everything depends on our accepting this proposition—that "the proper being of the one true God [is] in Jesus Christ the Crucified."[24] God does not dwell in an infinite, neutral repose but has a history.[25] Where we exclude the activity of humility and obedience from God's proper being,

---

19. *CD* IV/1, 193.
20. For what follows see *CD* IV/1, 197–99.
21. *CD* IV/1, 198.
22. Ibid.
23. *CD* IV/1, 199.
24. *CD* IV/1, 199. This is in contradiction not with his divine nature, but with "all human ideas about the divine nature."
25. "He is God in their concrete relationships [Father, Son, Holy Spirit] the one to the other, in the history which takes place between them. He is God only in these relationships and therefore not in a Godhead which does not take part in this history" (*CD* IV/1, 203).

we have not the God of the New Testament but only a false God, a "pure and empty Godhead."[26]

It is from these three presuppositions that Barth concludes that we can, and indeed we must, affirm and understand "the offensive fact that there is in God Himself an above and a below, a *prius* and a *posterius*, a superiority and a subordination"[27] — and that this is essential to the being of God. Two qualifications are immediately called for: this ordering in the Trinity does not equate to quantities of "more" and "less" in God's being as God, nor does it signal inequality or division.[28] In the one equal and united Godhead, "God is both One and also Another, His own counterpart, co-existent with Himself."[29]

To be able to affirm this differentiation in God, Barth argues, we must free ourselves from two arbitrary ways of thinking. The first is "the idea that unity is necessarily equivalent with being in and for oneself, with being enclosed and imprisoned in one's own being, with singleness and solitariness."[30] The unity of God is not like this, Barth says: it is a unity that is "open and free," that is outwardly moving, existing not in solitude but in solidarity with the objects of God's love.

If we correct this misconception, we are still blocked by a second arbitrary way of thinking. This is the idea that "there is necessarily something unworthy of God and incompatible with His being as God" in supposing that there is an "above" and a "below" in God. It is the idea that such an ordering entails "a gradation, a degradation and an inferiority in God" — which would certainly preclude the Nicene *homoousia*.[31] But this is an all-too-human way of thinking, which stands in need of correction according to the ontological equality of the divine persons. For God, subordination entails no inferiority, no deprivation or lack, but is a way of being that possesses its own dignity. This is why the way of humility, the way of the Son of God into the far country, is at the same time his glory.

With these two misconceptions removed, we are able to see that obedience and humility are not only possible for a God who exists in outward movement but are entirely fitting for a God who is glorified in his gracious condescension. The history of Jesus Christ — his kenosis, his humiliation, his unity with creaturely existence, and the way to his death — is from

---

26. Ibid.
27. *CD* IV/1, 200–201.
28. *CD* I/1, 381; *CD* IV/1, 201.
29. *CD* IV/1, 201.
30. *CD* IV/1, 202; cf. *CD* III/2, 323–4, *CD* I/1, 354.
31. *CD* IV/1, 202.

first to last a divine activity. More than this, though, God does all this in supreme continuity and correspondence with who he already is as God.[32] This, finally, is the real mystery of the deity of Christ—not that there is in him a suspension of deity, but that it is as Jesus of Nazareth that God is what he is as God.

What Barth has offered is an understanding of subordination that still affirms the full equality of the Father and the Son, against ancient Subordinationism and Modalism. In this sense we might tentatively label his view "functional." With Barth's larger argument now in view, we can move on to consider three avenues of potential critique.

# CRITIQUE 1: ETERNITY AND THE TRIUNE BEING

The first critique attends to the fact that Barth describes the obedience of the Son of God as eternal. But if his view of subordination is strictly *functional*, it would seem that in fact it cannot be eternal. After all, Barth agrees with the classical tradition that to speak of eternity is to speak of God himself: eternity is neither a thing nor a condition that exists apart from God, but is uncreated. And so eternity simply *is* the divine essence: as Thomas Aquinas puts it, "[God] is His own eternity."[33] Therefore an *eternal* subordination would speak directly to God's essential nature apart from creation.

The distinction between ontological and functional subordination finally rests upon a metaphysical division between God's being and act. As Scott Swain and Michael Allen put it in a recent essay on this topic: "mode of acting follows mode of being (*modus agenda sequitur modus essendi*)."[34] Therefore the divine being has (by definition) ontological priority over the divine works. God's triune life *ad intra* and in eternity precedes and grounds God's activity *ad extra* of command and obedience; there is no

---

32. *CD* IV/1, 203–4. And so "He does not change in giving Himself. He simply activates and reveals Himself *ad extra*, in the world. He is in and for the world what He is in and for Himself"— One who commands, and Another who obeys (*CD* IV/1, 204).

33. Thomas Aquinas, *Summa Theologica* (trans. Fathers of the English Dominican Province; London: Burns, Oates, and Washbourne) I, q.10, a.2; cf. *CD* II/1, 638–39.

34. Scott Swain and Michael Allen, "The Obedience of the Eternal Son," *IJST* 15 (2013): 117. Swain and Allen are committed to this ordering as a "guide for dogmatic reasoning" (121), and this forces them to restrict the Son's obedience to the economy—though it is grounded in his eternal procession: "the obedience of the Son is the economic extension of his eternal generation to a Spirit-enabled, creaturely life of obedience unto death" (117). What is thus offered as a constructive defense of Barth (on Thomist soil) unfortunately ends up having little to do with Barth's material argument.

basis for speaking of "function" or "activity" in the eternal repose of the divine Trinity. In this context, subordination therefore cannot be eternal without also being ontological.

That Barth's theological ontology shares this point in common with the classical tradition should not mislead us. Barth rejected the division between God's being and act. His ontology is actualistic, suggesting that God's being is in his eternal decision, actualized in the history that God has elected for himself. Being does not precede act, but the two are mutually grounding: "The whole being and life of God is an activity, both in eternity and in worldly time, both in Himself as Father, Son and Holy Spirit, and in His relation to man and all creation."[35] God is free to specify God's own being, and he does so according to the event of Jesus Christ—an event in which God the Son is obedient to the Father. Thus, "eternity" does not describe God's being *apart from* the history that God is, since there is no moment at which God is not the Son who obeys and the Father who is obeyed.

Here the Thomist account of the Son as a "subsisting relation" has been received but also actualized: the nature of the relation of the Son to the Father results from God's self-committing orientation toward creation. This is the covenant. This eternal act of gracious relating, in turn, is not to be restricted to a so-called "economic Trinity."[36] No, if God is his own executed decision, then what Barth calls his self-determination (*Bestimmtheit*) also determines the subsisting relations of Father, Son, and Holy Spirit. It is clear, therefore, why Barth locates his doctrine of election within the doctrine of God and grounds it in Christology: outside of the relationship of covenant, which the Son mediates in his obedience, "God no longer wills to be and no longer is God."[37]

Thus, it is *only* because Barth has an actualist ontology that he can extend the Son's subordination into eternity without compromising the Trinity's equality and unity of essence. God is his own eternity, yet he does not will to be this without the covenant to which God has committed his very life as Father, Son, and Spirit.

---

35. *CD* IV/1, 7. For an early appreciation of Barth's actualistic impulse in the English language, see Robert W. Jenson, *Alpha and Omega: A Study in the Theology of Karl Barth* (New York: Nelson, 1963).

36. In this same passage, to be clear, Barth does acknowledge that God has a "being in and for Himself," which stands distinct from God's being in this relationship. But, vitally, he qualifies this distinction by insisting that "we cannot speak correctly of God in His being in and for Himself without considering Him always in this attitude," that is, in the work of God which "belongs to God Himself, and cannot in any way be isolated from Him." See *CD* II/2, 6–7.

37. *CD* II/2, 7.

# CRITIQUE 2: ACTUALISM AND SUBORDINATION

A second line of critique suggests itself as an immediate consequence of Barth's revised ontology. By mutually implicating God's being and act, Barth would seem to frustrate any attempt to distinguish between the ontological and the merely functional. Would not God have his being in this activity of subordination, too? Certainly so, according to Barth: God's being is not grounded in "activity" or "history" generally speaking (as in Hegel's World-Spirit) but in a particular history, the history in which God has freely chosen to make himself known—the event of Jesus Christ.[38] If this event includes the Son's humility, his way into the far country, then it includes his obedience to God the Father. It would seem that Barth cannot avoid a subordinationism that is characteristically ontological.

This critique makes it clear that we must differentiate two uses of the term "ontological" with respect to subordination. In one sense, ontological subordinationism is the sort suggested by the ancient heresy: the deity of the Son is lesser than the deity of the Father. Barth clearly wishes to avoid this. In a second sense, the term "ontological" may simply refer to the fact that the obedience of the Son *pertains to* God's being. For Barth, obedience indicates not a subordination *of* being, but a subordination *within* the one, undivided, and undiminished being of the triune God. It is vital to Barth's presentation that the Son's submission is not the necessary and therefore passive consequence of his being (e.g., by virtue of his eternal procession), but the active consequence of his willing. The Son *chooses* the way of obedience (cf. Heb 5:8); he does not have it thrust upon him.

Subordination is therefore "ontological" in the sense that it pertains to the actual existence of the Trinity. What we have in Barth is a so-called "functional" subordination that is ontologically grounded. The real distinction between "functional" and "ontological" has been relativized—though it is clear that Barth's version of subordination is wholly unlike that which the church rejected in the fourth century.

# CRITIQUE 3: DIVINE WILLING AND GOD'S SINGLE SUBJECTIVITY

The third critique to bring against Barth's understanding of divine obedience is perhaps the most serious. Barth's location of obedience within the inner life of God would seem to imply two divine wills, and therefore

---

38. *CD* II/1, 264.

necessarily a social model of the Trinity—regardless of his underlying ontology. This is because obedience itself, by virtue of the sort of act that it is, involves two discrete agents who stand over against one another—one who commands and another who obeys (though he might will otherwise). The real merit of obedience, we might say further, is predicated on the possibility of disobedience. Thomas Joseph White states this challenge most incisively: there is but one divine will, and though the Son obeys the Father *secundum quod homo* ("by virtue of his humanity"), "the Son cannot obey the Father *as God* because his will is the same as the Father's will. But divine obedience in the Son would entail this kind of qualitative differentiation of persons, and therefore would endanger the very unity of God."[39] In order to obey the Father *secundum quod Dei* the Son must be *other than* the Father even in his deity.

For many who advocate eternal, functional subordination today, the way out of this dilemma is indeed to embrace a social model of the Trinity—three persons in the Godhead each with his own will and distinct center of consciousness, perichoretically indwelling one another in a model of fellowship. But Barth rejects social trinitarianism.[40] Without appeal to multiple wills in the Trinity, then, how can Barth answer this challenge? He must find another way to locate otherness in God's willing and acting. We may respond with three observations.[41]

First, Barth's account of the Son's obedience in *CD* IV/1 continues to operate under his critique of the term "person" in *CD* I/1.[42] God self-differentiates as Father, Son, and Holy Spirit by positing within himself a fellowship of I and Thou, "confronting Himself and yet always one and the same."[43] God is one and also another—not God over against God

---

39. Thomas Joseph White, "On Christian Philosophy and Divine Obedience: A Response to Keith L. Johnson," *ProEccl* 20 (2011): 288.

40. While he does not give it the full nuances of contemporary social trinitarianism, Barth dismissed the notion of "three different personalities" in God, each with its own will and self-consciousness, as "obviously ... three gods." See *CD* IV/1, 204–5; cf. "tritheism," *CD* I/1, 351. It is the multiplication of "self-consciousness" in God that he found particularly disquieting (see n. 42, below). J. Scott Horrell is mistaken when he suggests to the contrary that "Barth in various ways pointed the way toward social trinitarianism." See Horrell, "The Eternal Son of God in the Social Trinity," in *Jesus in Trinitarian Perspective* (ed. Fred Sanders and Klaus Issler; Nashville: B & H Publishing, 2007), 54.

41. It should be noted that here I am attempting to tease out the implications of Barth's Christology for the question of the possibility of God obeying Godself. This is not a question that Barth himself engaged directly.

42. *CD* I/1, 351–63; cf. *CD* IV/1, 204–5. Barth's primary reason for avoiding the language of "person" in favor of *Seinsweise* ("way of being") is that from the nineteenth century "person" has received the added sense of personality, i.e., a discrete center of self-consciousness. Thus the linguistic presuppositions on which the term was accepted by the ancient church no longer obtain today.

43. *CD* III/2, 324.

but the one God in threefold repetition, the "repetition of eternity in eternity."[44] God is one who wills and acts three times, in three ways, and therefore in potentially diverse ways: "This one God is God three times in different ways, so different that it is only in this threefold difference that He is God, so different that this difference, this being in these three modes of being, is absolutely essential to Him, so different, then, that this difference is irremovable."[45] Though distinct, these activities always remain unified by virtue of the one divine essence and God's single subjectivity. (There is little appreciable difference here between the distinct activities of Barth's *Seinsweisen* and the classical doctrine of appropriations.)

And yet, in this personal self-differentiation, God remains indissolubly one knowing, willing, and acting Subject—a Subject behind which one cannot get.[46] The persons of the Trinity thus *act* in diversity—including command and obedience, sending and being sent—despite the fact that their subjectivity, and therefore their will, is one. The Father and Son act differently; but their activities are always in harmony with one another. If these external works of the Trinity are undivided, then, what the Son does ought to look very much like obedience.

Second, Barth, I think, would not be quick to grant the presumption that the act of obedience necessarily entails two willing agents. If God can differentiate an I and a Thou within the one divine life, God has it within himself to "command" and to "obey" within the structure of that relation. (This is particularly evident when we recognize that the relation is not abstract, but concretized in God's history.) Such is the tenor of CD IV/1, in particular: God is free to be this sort of God. God is able to be the same one who speaks and who hears, who sends and is sent, and who commands and obeys, despite the fact that this runs counter to human intuition. The creature's theological language must be accommodated to the reality of God's activity, rather than *vice versa*.[47]

Third, while there are two natures and two wills in Jesus Christ, Barth insists that each of these is determined (or "commonly actualized") according to their personal union.[48] The human essence is drawn into obedient conformity to the divine, while the divine essence is given a

---

44. *CD* I/1, 350.
45. *CD* I/1, 360.
46. *CD* I/1, 381.
47. *CD* IV/1, 186; cf. 202.
48. See Darren O. Sumner, "Common Actualization: Karl Barth's Recovery and Reappropriation of the Communication of Natures," *Neue Zeitschrift für Systematische Theologie und Religionsphilosophie* 53 (2011): 465–79.

new determination that, without the incarnation and the *unio hypostatica*, it would not otherwise have.[49] What Jesus does in his divine essence he does not only in conjunction with his humanity but in the "strictest relationship" with it.[50] If the divine essence is determined by its union with humanity, then Barth is able to say further that God's willing in his second way of being is not *necessarily* identical with God's willing in his first way of being. While there is one divine will, in God's second way of being that will is in relation to a particular human will as well—a relation of openness and receptivity to the humanity of Christ. In its common actualization the will of the Son may thus be differentiated from the will of the Father—who does not possess a human will.

Barth's doctrine of the communication of operations as "common actualization" might be described as a sort of *radical theandricism*. What is materially decisive here is not the distinction of the operations of the two natures but rather their concurrence. Barth's concern, after all, is not with the metaphysics of natures and energies but with the common activity of the God-human seen in the New Testament.

To that end, it is worth stepping back a bit to find our footing in the way in which Barth actually talks about Jesus Christ. According to Barth, Christ's work of redemption ought to be regarded in two important ways. From the divine side, what takes place in the atonement is the accomplishment of "the original and basic will of God."[51] When the Son obeys the Father, he is executing the one divine will. And yet Barth insists that this obedience is a genuinely human decision, rendered by one who in humility does what Adam did not. In his exegesis of the story of Gethsemane Barth is in fact utterly disinterested in the competitive influence of a divine will in Jesus' prayer ("not my will, but yours be done," Luke 22:42). Instead, he is concerned to show how this prayer shows that Jesus' obedience is "a genuinely human decision" and "a decision of obedience. He chooses, but He chooses that apart from which, being who He is, He could not choose anything else."[52] The obedience of the divine Son is therefore *also* a human obedience; his activity is commonly actualized.

A second facet of our third critique is implicit here. White also suggests that Barth's doctrine of obedience renders problematic the attribution of *any*

---

49. *CD* IV/2, 113–14.
50. *CD* IV/2, 115.
51. "The will of God is done in Jesus Christ, in God's own being and acting and speaking as man" (*CD* IV/1, 36).
52. *CD* IV/1, 166. See further Paul D. Jones, *The Humanity of Christ* (Edinburgh: T&T Clark, 2008), 229–42.

divine agency at all to the Son, since the Son is constituted by his consent of will to another.[53] If there is but one divine agency, in other words, does obedience indicate that the Son does not actually possess it? Either the Son *shares* the will of the Father, or the Son *consents* to the will of the Father—the two appear to be incompatible. Since command and obedience require some basis of duality, White suggests that the better solution is to locate the Son's obedience where the tradition already finds duality—in the economy of the incarnation and not in the divine willing. It is *only* by virtue of the Son's human agency that theologians have any place to speak of God obeying God.[54]

This is not all that far from where I want to suggest Barth ends up. He criticized Thomas Aquinas for having overlooked a vital aspect of the doctrine of election—namely, that Jesus Christ in his humanity is not merely the passive recipient of an oath sworn by God, but is himself "in the beginning with God." Jesus, the God-human, is the electing God. And by virtue of his unity with the Father, "the Son, too, is an active Subject of the *aeterna Dei praedestinatio*"—and he is this *as the Son of Man*.[55] God the Son can obey the Father because he is eternally the God-human, with two natures and two wills. "He shows Himself the One He is by the obedience which He renders as man."[56] White is thus correct to suggest that the differentiation of "One who is obeyed" and "Another who obeys" is located in the two natures of the incarnation. What he has not accounted for is the fact that, for Barth, this diversity of natures in Jesus Christ is true of the eternal Son.

Barth is therefore able to make three moves that the Thomist tradition cannot. First, he can extend the relation of obedience from the Son's temporal mission into eternity—since (proleptically speaking) the Son has never been without his humanity. Second, Barth suggests that this eternally anticipated relation of divinity and humanity in God's second way of being is a mutually conditioning relation: just as the human essence of the Son receives its determination from the divine, so also the divine essence of the Son receives a special determination in and for his humanity.[57] Here in

---

53. Thomas Joseph White, "Intra-Trinitarian Obedience and Nicene-Chalcedonian Christology," *NV* 6 (2008, English edition): 391. White's goal seems to be less one of deconstruction and more one of constructive rehabilitation. He concludes that Barth's theory "contains a multitude of rich intuitions," despite being "latent with difficulties" (401).

54. Ibid., 400.

55. *CD* II/2, 108. Barth's charge is that Thomas makes the decision of God a "hidden decree" that has as its ground and basis something quite different from Jesus Christ, thus reducing Jesus to a mere mechanism for the outworking of God's decision (109) and failing to see him as the very content of God's Word that is given to creatures in their predestination.

56. *CD* IV/1, 208.

57. *CD* IV/2, 113–16. In this relation the divine essence remains superordinate; Christ's divinity is not conditioned *by* humanity, strictly speaking, but by its divinely appointed relation with humanity—by God's openness to the humanity of Christ.

§59, however, Barth is clear that he is speaking of obedience according to Christ's *divinity*, not merely an anticipation of his humanity—obedience is the "inner moment" of the mystery of Christ's deity. Third, then, comes a welcome insight also from Thomas Joseph White: that, for Barth, the mode in which God exists in God's second way of being is a mode of *receptivity* to his humanity.[58] The Son receives from his humanity a humble submission to the divine will. Contra White, however, an actualist ontology means that Barth need not predicate obedience to the pre-incarnate Son in a strictly figurative sense—for here it has become proper to God the Son.

## CONCLUSIONS: THE GOD WHO COMMANDS AND OBEYS

Barth's doctrine of the obedience of the Son of God calls into question the terms of the debate over eternal, functional subordination. He undermines the judgment that God's self-distinction cannot accommodate command and obedience, "an above and a below," without a multiplication of divine wills and centers of consciousness. He rejects such multiplication in favor of the unity of God's subjectivity and action. On the other hand, he also opposes the position that the Son's obedience is a strictly economic phenomenon. In understanding God as being-in-act Barth has relativized the very distinction being made today between "functional" and "ontological" subordination. He categorically rejects the latter insofar as it is taken to mean the Son's having a lesser deity, a being unequal to God the Father. But he does ground subordination in theological ontology: the Son's obedience to the Father is proper to God, and not sealed off in the foreignness of the assumed flesh. In his being as God, the Son obeys the Father *humanly*.[59]

To identify Barth's version of divine subordination as "functional" and not "ontological" is a concession to the contemporary conversation, and it is worth reminding ourselves that Barth does not use these categories.

---

58. See White, "Intra-Trinitarian Obedience," 378–79, 397–401. The widespread embrace of the notion of the Son's "receptivity"—applied variously to the Father's communication of divine essence, to the will and command of the Father, or to the humility of his assumed humanity, etc.—suggests that this concept may provide fruitful common ground in the debate over the Son's obedience. Bruce McCormack, for example, has characterized the receptivity of the Son to his humanity in terms of the Protestant scholastic idea of the "genus of humility"—a communication of the attributes of humanity directly to the divine nature of Christ. See McCormack, "Karl Barth's Christology as a Resource for a Reformed Version of Kenoticism," *IJST* 8 (2006): 243–51. Swain and Allen follow White in making use of the principle of the Son's "receptive filiation" in a Thomist sense. See Swain and Allen, "The Obedience of the Eternal Son," 123 n.34, 129 n.56 and *passim*.

59. This point is emphasized by Bruce L. McCormack, "The Doctrine of the Trinity after Barth: An Attempt to Reconstruct Barth's Doctrine in the Light of His Later Christology," in *Trinitarian Theology after Barth* (ed. Myk Habets and Phillip Tolliday; Eugene, OR: Pickwick, 2011), 107–8.

Whatever term we use to describe Barth's view, it is clear that he does not fall neatly under either one. Therefore, with respect to the debate currently taking place in evangelical circles, he cannot readily be appropriated by either side.

One question remains for us, and that regards the usefulness of Barth's views on eternal subordination for this debate. I conclude with three observations.

First, Barth's trinitarian theology challenges the way in which central concepts are used in the debate—including *essence* and *equality*, *appropriation* and *distinction*, and especially the notion of *necessity* (including conflations of *eternity* with necessity). Barth's contribution suggests that the strongest affirmation of the Son's exaltation and authority is precisely in his self-humiliation and servitude; and, in turn, that his submission to God the Father is precisely that which demonstrates his coequality. It also prompts theologians to rethink whether Christ's kenotic submission may properly be limited to the sphere of creation.

Second, were the evangelical theologian to appeal to Karl Barth as a potential ally in arguing for eternal, functional subordination,[60] she must be willing to bring on board the whole of Barth's actualist commitments—including an ontology that challenges the conviction that God's being precedes God's act, a material identification of the immanent and economic Trinity, and a rejection of the notion that the Son's assumed humanity is an instrument isolated from the divine life. Without these commitments Barth's theology is not comprehensible. The obedience of the Son to the Father relies on God's self-determination in election.

Now, I believe there is much in this to commend for evangelical theology. But I suspect that, at present, taking on Barth's broader theological commitments is not something many conservative, North American evangelicals are willing to do. If I am right about that, then Barth can be no happy ally; his account of the obedience of the Son, of God's submission to God, is simply not compatible with the evangelical case for trinitarian subordination.

Finally, Karl Barth was not known as a great champion of gender equality.[61] But I believe he would be mystified by the transplantation

---

60. Such appeals to Barth's advocacy of divine subordination are not common, but have been made. See, for example: Bruce A. Ware, "Equal in Essence, Distinct in Roles: Eternal Functional Authority and Submission among the Essentially Equal Divine Persons of the Godhead," in *The New Evangelical Subordinationism?* 35; Giles, *Jesus and the Father*, 275–305.

61. For an introduction to Barth's complicated views on gender see Katherine Sonderegger, "Barth and Feminism," in *The Cambridge Companion to Karl Barth* (ed. John Webster; Cambridge: Cambridge University Press, 2000), 258–73.

of this debate from the sphere of trinitarian doctrine into that of gender roles in marriage and in the churches. Why is that? Why not pattern human relationships on the relations of the divine persons? For at least two reasons. First, without a social model of the Trinity there is insufficient correspondence for such an analogy. God the Father and the Son do not exist as two subjects, and trinitarian distinctions are utterly unlike human gender distinctions. If the one God exists in subordination to the one God, no space remains for insisting on a corresponding subordination of wives to husbands.

There is an analogy of *relation* here (and not of being), Barth says, in that God created men and women for fellowship just as God himself exists in fellowship. The likeness of creatures to God is not in their ordering of super- and subordination but in their fellowship, their being in relation.[62]

This more basic analogy notwithstanding, we should understand further that the patterning of human relationships on the relations of divine persons is dogmatically disordered: the proper model for human existence and human relationships is not to be found in the doctrine of the Trinity but in Christology. Jesus Christ reveals true humanity to us, Jesus Christ is the bridegroom of the church, and Jesus Christ is given to all human creatures as an example of their own obedience and submission to God. Men and women participate in the triune life of God as they are united with Christ in the power of the Holy Spirit, as together they are the "body of Christ"—a body that is in need of him as its head. They are not "heads" and "bodies" of one another. Dogmatically speaking, then, anthropology properly follows Christology and not the doctrine of God. There is no creaturely access to the triune life that does not pass through the person of the Mediator, the one who "did not regard equality with God as something to be used to be exploited" (Phil 2:7 NRSV), and who demonstrates true humanity in his humility and servitude.

---

62. See *CD* III/2, 324. Ware's use of analogy, in contrast to this, is self-referential: he takes a human phenomenon (the ordinary submission of sons to their fathers) and reads it into the divine economy in order to then read it back out again and apply it to human gender relations. In other words, Ware attempts to overcome the lack of sufficient correspondence through the artificial imposition of an *analogia entis*. See Ware, *Father, Son, and Holy Spirit: Relationships, Roles, and Relevance* (Wheaton, IL: Crossway, 2005), 71–87.

# CHAPTER 8

# THEOLOGY IN THE GAZE OF THE FATHER

## Retrieving Jonathan Edwards's Trinitarian Aesthetics

KYLE C. STROBEL

THIS CHAPTER OUTLINES Jonathan Edwards's understanding of beauty for contemporary dogmatics.[1] It falls into two parts. First, Edwards's doctrine of God is outlined and developed, focusing on the inner relations of the triune God. Second, building on this initial discussion, a retrieval of Edwards's doctrine is considered. I suggest that Edwards's conception of beauty is fruitful to ground the task of trinitarian theology as a distinctively affective discipline. Knowledge of the God who is beautiful requires a relational movement of the heart to know and love within the movement of God's self-revelation. In short, Edwards's trinitarian aesthetics grounds theology as a contemplative discipline, ordered by the God of beauty, for the purpose of beauty. True theology is, as it were, sapiential theology; the task of "faith seeking beautification" as it is faith captivated by beauty.

## DOCTRINE OF GOD

For Edwards, God is the fountain of all things, and therefore all flows from him and ultimately back to him (emanation and remanation respectively).

1. Several people gave me helpful feedback on this article. Special thanks to Oliver Crisp, James Merrick, Jamin Goggin, Kent Eilers, and Ty Kieser.

In Edwards's conception, God is not so loquacious as he is luminescent. Creation certainly pours forth speech, as the Psalmist declares (Ps 19), but it is written by the effusive overflow of God's beauty. This speech is seen and not heard (or only heard as it is seen). The visual takes precedence in Edwards's theology because of his doctrine of God, his understanding of the beatific vision, and its orientation for faith. One day believers will see "face to face" (1 Cor 13:12), so the spiritual sight of faith is the anticipation—through a glass darkly—of God's beatific glory.

Edwards's doctrine of God has three interrelated emphases: personhood, employing a psychological analogy;[2] perception, as the Father gazes upon his perfect image and understanding; and affection, the flowing forth of the Holy Spirit as the will and love of God. By making personhood central, Edwards can emphasize the God of eternal beatific glory, the real focus of his account. In language I believe Edwards would have approved, his doctrine of God can adequately be called religious affection in pure act.[3] This description assumes personhood, but the focus is elsewhere. Note how Edwards begins his work on the Trinity:

> When we speak of God's happiness, the account that we are wont to give of it is that God is infinitely happy in the enjoyment of himself, in perfectly beholding and infinitely loving, and rejoicing in, his own essence and perfections. And accordingly it must be supposed that God perpetually and eternally has a most perfect idea of himself, as it were an exact image and representation of himself ever before him and in actual view. And from hence arises a most pure and perfect energy in the Godhead, which is the divine love, complacence and joy.[4]

---

2. Whereas this view assumes something like a psychological analogy in his development of the Trinity, it would be a mistake to categorize it as such. One of the reasons for this is that it is unclear, to me at least, that Edwards is employing an analogy at all. Edwards utilizes the category of personhood to delineate the threefold reality of the divine essence (something like mind, understanding, and will). But Edwards is clear that this is not an analogy. This is just what it means to be personal: God or human. Edwards claims, "Though the divine nature be vastly different from that of created spirits, yet our souls are made in the image of God: we have understanding and will, idea and love, as God hath, and the difference is only in the perfection of degree and manner." Jonathan Edwards, "Discourse on the Trinity," in *Writings on the Trinity, Grace, and Faith* (ed. Sang Hyun Lee, *The Works of Jonathan Edwards*, vol. 21; New Haven, CT: Yale University Press, 2003), 113. (Hereafter, volumes from the Yale edition will be listed "Y" with volume number [e.g., Y21], the name of the work, and then the page number.) While Edwards collapses God and humanity within the broad category of "personal creatures," he reinforces his Creator/creature distinction through his use of infinity.

3. Oliver Crisp has argued, persuasively in my mind, that Edwards's doctrine of God should be understood in light of the *actus purus* tradition. See Oliver Crisp, *Jonathan Edwards on God and Creation* (Oxford: Oxford University Press, 2012); idem, "Jonathan Edwards and the Divine Nature," *JRT* 3 (2009): 175–201.

4. Y21, "Discourse on the Trinity," 113.

Edwards's God is the God of happiness whose inner life is effusive love and perfection. This God has his own image ever before him, and a "pure and perfect energy" of love, complacence, and joy pours forth in an infinite fountain of delight. The architecture of this view is the beatific vision, functioning to exposit the God of religious affection. By invoking personhood in the manner he does, God the Father becomes pure mind, but only partakes in personhood perichoretically through the generation of the divine understanding and will—both necessary features of personhood.[5]

## A BEAUTIFUL MIND

In Edwards's musings on the mind, he develops a notion of excellency as an aesthetic category and reveals his notion of beauty with its specifically pneumatological focus:

> As to God's excellence, it is evident it consists in the love of himself . . . he exerts himself towards himself no other way than in infinitely loving and delighting in himself, in the mutual love of the Father and the Son. This makes the third, the personal Holy Spirit or the holiness of God, which is his infinite beauty, and this is God's infinite consent to being in general. And his love to the creature is his excellence, or the communication of himself, his complacency in them, according as they partake of more or less of excellence and beauty; that is, of holiness, which consists in love; that is, according as he communicates more or less of his Holy Spirit.[6]

Here, void of the technical discussion of the processions, Edwards invokes psychological imagery, expositing the Spirit as the holiness, love, and beauty of God. As Edwards notes in the "Discourse on the Trinity" itself, "A mind is said to be holy from the holiness of its temper and disposition. . . . As all creature[ly] holiness is to be resolved into love, as the Scripture teaches us, so doth the holiness of God himself consist in infinite love to himself. God's holiness is the infinite beauty and excellency of his nature. And God's excellency consists in his love to himself."[7] Likewise, when arguing that the Father, Son, and Holy Spirit all share the same honor, Edwards writes, "The honor of the Father and the Son is that they are infinitely excellent, or that from them infinite excellency proceeds.

---

5. I have dealt with this aspect of Edwards's thought at length in my book, *Jonathan Edwards's Theology: A Reinterpretation* (T&T Clark Studies in Systematic Theology; London: T&T Clark, 2013), esp. 23–71.

6. Y6, "The Mind," 364.

7. Y21, "Discourse on the Trinity," 123.

But the honor of the Holy Ghost is equal, for he is that divine excellency and beauty itself."[8]

In mooring his account to the happiness and delight of God, Edwards develops the procession of the divine idea, first offering the qualification, "Though the divine nature be vastly different from that of created spirits, yet our souls are made in the image of God: we have understanding and will, idea and love, as God hath, and the difference is only in the perfection of degree and manner."[9] God is infinite, and therefore he exists in simplicity and pure act. Nonetheless, this does not mean that it is somehow meaningless to talk about God understanding and willing. God is love, a notion that grounds plurality within God as an essential feature of his life. If God is love, then God must have an object of his loving. This object is the divine idea or understanding. Because God is a simple being in pure act, his self-knowledge is a procession of the divine essence, leading Edwards to claim, "I do suppose the Deity to be truly and properly repeated by God's thus having an idea of himself; and that this idea of God is a substantial idea and has the very essence of God, is truly God, to all intents and purposes, and that by this means the Godhead is really generated and repeated."[10] As a spiritual, infinite, and eternal being, this idea creates a duplication of the divine essence.[11]

Up to this point Edwards has described the Father, or the divine mind, and the proceeding forth of the divine understanding. Now, he states, "there proceeds a most pure act, and an infinitely holy and sweet energy arises between the Father and Son: for their love and joy is mutual, in mutually loving and delighting in each other."[12] Edwards continues, "This is the eternal and most perfect and essential act of the divine nature, wherein the Godhead acts to an infinite degree and in the most perfect

---

8. Ibid., 135.

9. Ibid., 113. Edwards makes this claim right after admitting that the divine understanding is well beyond our own reason, leading one to expect that what follows will be tentative. Edwards's following claim, quoted above, is decisively less tentative than one might think. Elsewhere, Edwards does claim, "Thus we have briefly insisted upon the glorious—infinitely glorious—perfections of that God which we profess. All that we can say is but clouds and darkness to the reality: the attributes of God, these infinite perfections, cannot be set forth by the eloquence of an angel, much less by mortal tongue" (Y10, "God's Excellencies," 424). Likewise, Edwards utilizes the hidden and infinite nature of God's life to argue that God is all the more beautiful because of these things, claiming that the more hidden the beauty, the more satisfying, and the more complex the beauty, the more hidden (Y6, "Beauty of the World," 306).

10. Y21, "Discourse on the Trinity," 114.

11. Notice Edwards's turn to our own experience with spiritual ideas to buttress his point: "If a man had a perfect reflex or contemplative idea of every thought at the same moment or moments that that thought was, and of every exercise at and during the same time that that exercise was ... and so through a whole hour: a man would really be two" (ibid., 116).

12. Ibid., 121.

manner possible. The Deity becomes all act; the divine essence itself flows out and is as it were breathed forth in love and joy."[13] The pure actuality of God's life is the procession of the Spirit as the divine will, love, holiness, and beauty. Edwards explains how these processions end up grounding the relations within the Godhead:

> though the Holy Ghost proceeds both from the Father and the Son, yet he proceeds from the Father mediately by the Son, viz. by the Father's beholding himself in the Son. But he proceeds from the Son immediately by himself by beholding the Father in himself. The beauty and excellency and loveliness of the divine nature, though from the Father first and originally, yet is by the Son and nextly from him. The joy and delight of the divine nature is in the Father by the Son, but nextly and immediately in the Son.[14]

Troubled by anti-trinitarian subordination, Edwards wants to protect the Son's dignity and equality. Whereas the Spirit flows forth from the Father originally, it does so by the mediation of the Son. The Son's act in the procession of the Spirit is secondary, but immediate. "For though it be from the Son by his beholding the Father," Edwards explains, "yet he beholds himself in himself." The Son's gazing upon the Father "is nothing else but his existing: for 'tis nothing else for an idea of a thing to behold that thing that it beholds, but only for an idea to exist. The idea's beholding is the idea's existing."[15] The Son's very existence is his beholding of the Father, and embracing that the Father is in him, and he is of the Father.

Edwards's account struggles (and he recognized this) to turn the corner from one divine mind with understanding and will, to three divine persons partaking of one singular divine essence. It is here that Edwards turns to perichoresis, asserting, "the whole divine essence is supposed truly and properly to subsist in each of these three—viz. God, and his understanding and love—and that there is such a wonderful union between them that they are after an ineffable and inconceivable manner one in another; so that one hath another, and they have communion in one another, and are as it were predicable of one another."[16] He continues, "the Father understands because the Son, who is the divine understanding, is in him. The Father loves because the Holy Ghost is in him. So the Son loves because the Holy Spirit is in him and proceeds from him. So the Holy

---

13. Ibid.
14. Ibid., 143.
15. Ibid.
16. Ibid., 133.

Ghost, or the divine essence subsisting in divine love, understands because the Son, the divine idea, is in him."[17]

Furthermore, in God's self-revelation in Jesus, his image, he is doing more than simply passing along information about himself. God is beautiful, and in the Son and Spirit beautifies his people by harmonizing them with his own life of beauty. This entails communion with the Father, in the Son, by the Spirit, and as such is a partaking of God's love, holiness, and beauty.[18] The Father and Son exist within the Spirit as the bond of love—a bond that exists as the affection and pure action of the divine mind. In the economy this love overflows to the elect, and by receiving the Spirit believers receive God's own holiness, love, and beauty—an infusion, Edwards tells us, that reorients the human person by pulling them up within the divine life.[19]

In this account, Edwards ends right where he begins—with a God who is infinite happiness, delight, and joy. God's life is, as it were, the truly religious life; God's life is one of affection, delight, and the vision that "happifies." God is the great contemplative, we can say, captivated with truth divine by consenting in union with Truth itself—the Logos. As Edwards claims, God's excellency "is the highest theme that ever man, that ever archangels, yes, that ever the man Christ Jesus, entered upon yet; yea, it is that theme which is, to speak after the manner of men, the highest contemplation, and the infinite happiness, of Jehovah himself."[20] God's life serves as the archetype for perfect knowledge and therefore casts knowledge in a specifically affectionate and contemplative mold. This is why religious affection is a central issue for Edwards's understanding of Christian life, knowledge, and conversion. To know God, one must know him as God knows himself—by gazing upon his perfect image in the affection and beauty of the Spirit.

---

17. Ibid. Edwards admits that there is room to push back on his account, but he is able to simply ask, How does your account of God fare against mine? The orthodox, he notes, have always asserted one divine essence, along with one understanding and one will (see ibid., 134–135). If God has an understanding and a will, and if Edwards's biblical material is convincing, this understanding was made incarnate in Jesus Christ, and this will is given over for believers to commune with God.

18. "This is the divine partaking or nature that we are made partakers of (II Pet. 1:4)," Edwards claims, "for our partaking or communion with God consists in the communion or partaking of the Holy Ghost" (ibid., 122).

19. "When men are regenerated and sanctified, God pours forth of his Spirit upon them, and they have fellowship or, which is the same thing, are made partakers with the Father and Son of their good, i.e. of their love, joy and beauty" (ibid., 124). The claim that God "pulls creatures up" into the divine life is my own language to describe this reality. This does not undermine the creature/Creator distinction, but should be read in terms of communion or fellowship.

20. Y10, "God's Excellencies," 417.

## BEING'S CONSENT TO BEING

While the preceding emphasis on perception and affection assumes beauty, we still have not defined it. Here, briefly, it is necessary to hone in on Edwards's definition of beauty and excellency. In his work on religious affection, Edwards claims that "God is God, and distinguished from all other beings, and exalted above 'em, chiefly by his divine beauty, which is infinitely diverse from all other beauty."[21] Edwards's conception of beauty entails a description of God's own life, a life that is, in some sense, sui generis. This is why divine beauty is "infinitely diverse" from other notions of beauty. Yet beauty is the very category Edwards utilizes to link humanity to the life of God.[22] Beauty is, in some sense, the common ground between God and his creatures; the difference is the degree of virtue and greatness of being—concepts linked in Edwards's thought.[23]

God is beautiful, therefore, as he is personal and as he partakes in the "consent, agreement and union of being to being" within his own life.[24] Primary beauty, what Edwards will also call spiritual beauty, is persons uniting in love.[25] Spiritual beings are the primary instance of beauty, whereas physical beauty points beyond itself to the primary.[26] Edwards takes it for granted that "this is an universal definition of excellency: The consent of being to being, or being's consent to entity. The more the consent is, and the more extensive, the greater is the excellency."[27] Consent, as will become clear, is a work of the will within persons to unite personally to another. In nature, by contrast, the phenomenon of union or agreement

---

21. Y2, "Religious Affections," 298 (my emphasis).

22. See Y10, "God's Excellencies," 415–435.

23. Roland A. Delattre, *Beauty and Sensibility in the Thought of Jonathan Edwards: An Essay in Aesthetics and Theological Ethics* (The Jonathan Edwards Classic Studies Series; Eugene, OR: Wiph & Stock, 1968), 30–35. For a critique of Delattre's model, see Kin Yip Louie, *The Beauty of the Triune God: The Theological Aesthetics of Jonathan Edwards* (Princeton Theological Monograph Series; Eugene, OR: Wipf & Stock, 2013), 82–83. Edwards notes that "God's beauty is infinitely more valuable than that of all other beings ... viz. the degree of his virtue and the greatness of the being possessed of this virtue" (Y8, "True Virtue," 551).

24. Y8, "True Virtue," 561.

25. This is why the word "consent" is used, which is used in a way that directly relates to the will. In his notes on excellency, Edwards states, "When we spake of excellence in bodies, we were obliged to borrow the word 'consent' from spiritual things. But excellence in and among spirits is, in its prime and proper sense, being's consent to being. There is no proper consent but that of minds, even of their will; which, when it is of minds toward minds, it is love, and when of mind towards other things it is choice. Wherefore all the primary and original beauty or excellence that is among minds is love, and into this may all be resolved that is found among them" (Y6, "The Mind," 362).

26. Y8, "True Virtue," 561–63.

27. Y6, "The Mind," 336. Paul Ramsey notes, "God's peculiar excellency is his 'beauty within himself, consisting in being's consent with his own being, or love of himself in his own Holy Spirit; whereas the excellence of others is in loving others, in loving God, and in the communications of his Spirit'"( Y8, "Edwards on Moral Sense," 701).

happens among objects, shapes, and so on.[28] Recall the threefold focus of Edwards's doctrine of God: personhood, perception, and affection; these are all key attributes of beauty. Edwards's God is the God of beauty, within his own life, because he is the pure actuality of persons perceiving in the consent of love. On this understanding, for God to be beautiful, God has to be triune. As Edwards states explicitly:

> One alone, without any reference to any more, cannot be excellent; for in such case there can be no manner of relation no way, and therefore, no such thing as consent. Indeed, what we call "one" may be excellent, because of a consent of parts, or some consent of those in that being that are distinguished into a plurality some way or other. But in a being that is absolutely without any plurality there cannot be excellency, for there can be no such thing as consent or agreement.[29]

This is why the Spirit is the beauty of God. Beauty, properly perceived, is consent, proportion, and affection, and the type and degree of beauty is determined by the nature of the being's consenting. The Spirit is the consent of the divine life and the infinite proportion of love between Father and Son. This is divine beauty, the infinite consent of love as the pure actuality of God's life. Edwards outlines this life of love accordingly:

> There must have been an object from all eternity which God infinitely loves. But we have showed that all love arises from the perception, either of consent to being in general, or consent to that being that perceives. Infinite loveliness, to God, therefore, must consist either in infinite consent to entity in general, or infinite consent to God. But we have shown that consent to entity and consent to God are the same, because God is the general and only proper entity of all things. So that 'tis necessary that that object which God infinitely loves must be infinitely and perfectly consenting and agreeable to him; but that which infinitely and perfectly agrees is the very same essence, for if it be different it don't infinitely consent. Again, we have shown that one alone cannot be excellent, inasmuch as, in such case, there can be no consent. Therefore, if God is excellent, there must be a plurality in God; otherwise, there can be no consent in him.[30]

God's pure actuality is the Spirit's consenting spiration, serving as the union between Father and Son. As an infinite being of virtue existing as the pure actuality of the Spirit's consent between Father and Son, God is

---

28. Y8, "True Virtue," 565.
29. Y6, "The Mind," 337.
30. Y13, "Miscellanies 117: Trinity," 283–84.

infinite beauty. The infinite greatness of the divine being, the pure actuality of God's goodness and love, and his infinite consent as the procession of the Spirit establishes God's life of beauty. By locating beauty in the procession of the Spirit, Edwards binds beauty together with goodness, holiness, love, and consent. As the foundation and fountain of these realities, the Spirit's work in the economy carries these over to creatures. By having *this* Spirit one is now in a relation of beauty with God that requires affection and contemplation to be true knowledge of God. As holiness itself, infused into the nature of a person, the Spirit creates freedom to consent in affection, in ever greater and greater ways, to the life of God.

## SPIRITUAL KNOWLEDGE AND THE WAY OF BEAUTY

By embracing a notion of beauty as being's consent to being, the archetype of which is God's own life, Edwards casts spiritual knowledge into the mold of this trinitarian beauty. To know God is to be caught up in a vision of the Son in the union of the Spirit, just as in the archetype. The Reformed of this period employed the archetypal/ectypal distinction to uphold the Creator/creature distinction, but also to delineate the task of theology as a distinctively relational enterprise.[31] All knowledge of God sifted into the two broad categories of archetypal (God's self-knowledge) and ectypal (any creaturely knowledge of God). For the Reformed High Orthodox, ectypal knowledge was often broken down into three categories, knowledge by union, pilgrim knowledge, and beatific knowledge.[32] Jesus has knowledge of God by union, believers have pilgrim knowledge of God, and the glorified saints will have a beatific knowledge of God in glory.[33]

Even though knowledge by faith (pilgrim) and knowledge by vision (beatific) were separate categories, that did not stop Reformed thinkers from orienting the knowledge by faith to the knowledge by vision. The visual is emphasized by many Reformed thinkers for this very reason: pilgrim knowledge was heading somewhere, and the destination formed the

---

31. See Michael Scott Horton, *Lord and Servant: A Covenant Christology* (Louisville: Westminster John Knox, 2005), 17; and Willem J. van Asselt, "The Fundamental Meaning of Theology: Archetypal and Ectypal Theology in Seventeenth-Century Reformed Thought," *WTJ* 64 (2002): 325.

32. I explore a Reformed notion of the beatific vision in the chapter "Jonathan Edwards's Reformed Doctrine of the Beatific Vision," in *Jonathan Edwards and Scotland* (ed. Ken Minkema, Adriaan Neale, and Kelly van Andel; Edinburgh: Dunedin Academic, 2011), 171–88.

33. Francis Turretin uses the ectypal distinction to develop a threefold division in theology: natural, supernatural, and beatific. In his words, "the first is from the light of reason, the second from the light of faith, and third from the light of glory." Francs Turretin, *Institutes of Elenctic Theology* (ed. James T. Dennison; trans. George Musgrave Gige; Phillipsburg, NJ: Presbyterian & Reformed, 1992), 1:5.

mode of the journey. John Owen claims that "no man shall ever behold the glory of Christ by sight hereafter, who doth not in some measure behold it by faith here in this world."[34] Faith is a kind of beholding for Owen, and he is clear that the spiritual sight believers have in this world is exactly that, a kind of sight. Edwards, perhaps more than his fellow Reformed theologians, merged the pilgrim with the beatific, so that regeneration places a person on a beatific journey that never ceases. In Edwards's case, the barrier between pilgrim and beatific collapses, and each category merges with the other. In Edwards's thought, all spiritual knowledge is a form of vision, and all vision entails a pilgrimage into the never-ceasing fountain of God's beauty.

By employing the archetypal/ectypal distinction, the later Reformed were able to affirm that only God has perfect knowledge of himself. But this does not somehow make knowledge of God impossible. Archetypal knowledge gives the form and orientation for all ectypal knowledge—a form that becomes decisively Christocentric. In the condescension of the Logos, the image of the invisible God, human persons can truly know God. For Edwards, archetypal knowledge is necessarily affectionate, as the Father gazes upon the Son and the Spirit billows forth between them as love. Therefore, there is no true knowledge of God that is not affectionate, because ectypal knowledge takes on the contours of the archetypal. Heaven is a world of love, as Edwards never tired of saying, because God is the fountain of love at its center. The vision of God's beauty fuels this world of love and captivates the hearts of all who have eyes to see. This is the darkened vision of faith that drives religious affection in sanctification, and, necessarily, will be the form of all theological work.[35]

Ectypal knowledge, formed according to the pattern of the archetype, is knowledge in love, and knowledge that beautifies. According to this pattern, something is known as it is perceived, and right perception necessitates a movement of the heart to embrace in beauty. Truth, then, is the foundation for goodness and beauty, both of which flow forth from the perception of the "true" (understanding that the "true" here is being itself, i.e., God). This is the baseline for Edwards's doctrine of illumina-

---

34. John Owen, *The Glory of Christ* (The Works of John Owen, vol. 1; ed. William H. Goold; London: Banner of Truth Trust, 1965), 288.

35. Note how Edwards orients knowledge by faith: "The knowledge which the saints have of God's beauty and glory in this world, and those holy affections that arise from it, are of the same nature and kind with what the saints are the subjects of in heaven, differing only in degree and circumstances: what God gives them here, is a foretaste of heavenly happiness, and an earnest of their future inheritance" (Y2, "Religious Affections," 133).

tion, religious affection, virtue, and the beatific vision. Just as the Father's self-knowledge is the procession of the Son, known affectively within the Holy Spirit, so also is all ectypal knowledge known in the Son by the Holy Spirit. Edwards claims, "Jesus Christ, who alone sees immediately, [is] the grand medium of the knowledge of all others; they know no otherwise than by the exhibitions held forth in and by him."[36] In Christ, believers gaze on the finite, created image of the infinite, uncreated Logos that the Father gazes upon eternally. Both Father and believers gaze upon the Son within the Spirit; both, within that same Spirit, experience the emanating forth of the divine idea in the clear perception of truth, which the Father knows immediately and infinitely, and believers know mediately and finitely in the Son.

## GAZING UPON THE SON

Ectypal theology establishes a specifically christological mediation of all knowledge of God. By casting knowledge of God into this ectypal mold, knowledge of God takes on the contours established by God's interpersonal knowing as pure, infinite mind. God is known relationally, and therefore God is only known in the loving union of the Spirit. In this specifically relational register, Edwards unveils that "being's consent to being" is synonymous with "mind's love to mind."[37] Just as the future vision of God entails knowing as you are known (cf. 1 Cor 13:12), so does all knowledge of God entail a reciprocal self-knowledge. The way of wisdom necessitates knowledge of God and knowledge of self in relation to God. True wisdom is to know oneself in a certain kind of relation to the Father in the Son, knowing the Father in the Son by the Spirit with a new identity, and being wrapped up in the beauty of God that beautifies.

God's infinite beauty is his infinite love to himself, and this beauty is the pattern of all, such that the perfection of creatures is perfection in the beauty and love of God.[38] As noted above, beauty is cast in a trinitarian mode because it is the procession of the Spirit to bind the Father and Son

---

36. Y18, "Miscellanies 777, The Happiness of Heaven Is Progressive," 428.

37. Y6, "The Mind," 362. These are, of course, identical, but are made more personal with an explicit focus on "mind" and "love" rather than "being" and "consent."

38. Ibid., 363. Perceiving being, Edwards continues to clarify, is the only proper being. Being, of course, is a term Edwards utilizes to describe God. God is persons, and therefore being itself is personal. Personal being, what Edwards sometimes calls simply "spirit" or "spiritual being," is perceiving being—mind loving mind. The divine essence—true being—is the Father perceiving the Son and the Son perceiving the Father, and the infinite pure actuality of love and delight pouring forth between them.

together in love.[39] As archetypal knowledge, God's own self-knowledge is knowledge within beauty and love: "As to God's excellence, it is evident it consists in the love of himself.... But he exerts himself towards himself no other way than in infinitely loving and delighting in himself, in the mutual love of Father and the Son. This makes the third, the personal Holy Spirit or the holiness of God, which is his infinite beauty, and this is God's infinite consent to being in general."[40] This reality of God's inner life establishes the pattern of the economy. Jesus is the one beheld as "Son" by the Father in the Spirit of love, and Jesus is the Son deemed beautiful as he is caught up in the beautifying knowledge of God, a knowledge of who the Father is and who he is in relation to the Father.

Just as the Father gazes upon the Son in the Spirit in the inner life of God, so too in the economy; but now this gaze provides the context for our theologizing. In Matthew's account of Jesus' baptism we are told that "as soon as Jesus was baptized, he went up out of the water. At that moment heaven was opened, and he saw the Spirit of God descending like a dove and alighting on him. And a voice from heaven said, "This is my Son, whom I love; with him I am well pleased" (Matt 3:16–17). The heavens were open to Jesus, a comment claiming more, no doubt, than the parting of clouds. The Father calls from heaven that this is his Son whom he loves, in whom he has pleasure, while the Spirit descends like a dove to rest on Jesus.[41]

According to Edwards's understanding, the dove is the Holy Spirit as the pleasure and belovedness of the Father's gaze upon his Son. In this scene, sonship and beauty are wrapped together in one. This picture in

---

39. "When the true beauty and amiableness of the holiness or true moral good that is in divine things, is discovered to the soul, it as it were opens a new world to its view. This shows the glory of all the perfections of God, and of everything appertaining to the divine being: for, as was observed before, the beauty of all arises from God's moral perfection.... He that sees the beauty of holiness, or true moral good, sees the greatest and most important thing in the world, which is the fullness of all things, without which all the world is empty, no better than nothing, yea, worse than nothing. Unless this is seen, nothing is seen, that is worth the seeing: for there is no other true excellency or beauty. Unless this be understood, nothing is understood, that is worthy of the exercise of the noble faculty of understanding. This is the beauty of the Godhead, and the divinity of Divinity (if I may so speak), the good of the infinite Fountain of Good; without which God himself (if that were possible to be) would be an infinite evil: without which, we ourselves had better never have been; and without which there had better have been no being. He therefore in effect knows nothing, that knows not this: his knowledge is but the shadow of knowledge, or the form of knowledge, as the Apostle calls it" (Y2, "Religious Affections," 273–74).

40. Y6, "The Mind," 364.

41. David Bentley Hart insightfully notes, "a distinctively Christian understanding of beauty is contained in trinitarian theology, whose nature is intimated with exquisite brevity in the words of the Father at Christ's baptism. The most elementary statement of theological aesthetics is that God is beautiful: not only that God is beauty or the essence and archetype of beauty, nor even only that God is the highest beauty, but that, as Gregory the Theologian says, God is beauty and also beautiful, whose radiance shines upon and is reflected in his creatures (*Oration* 28.30–31)." David Bentley Hart, *The Beauty of the Infinite: The Aesthetics of Christian Truth* (Grand Rapids: Eerdmans, 2003), 177.

the economy images the processions, such that the Father gazes upon the Son with the Spirit of love binding them together. We, however, stand on the other side of Jesus. We look upon the one who has the heavens open to him, and if we have seen him we have seen the Father.[42] This sight is only possible within the Spirit, because true sight of Jesus is not passive gazing, but necessitates a movement of the whole person.[43] The Spirit both illumines Christ and reveals him as beautiful. To see Jesus truly, therefore, is to see Jesus for me. This entails the recognition that Jesus is the one sent from God, he is the true Son, as well as the recognition that he is beautiful. In the self-revelation of God in his Word, we can proclaim, with Psalm 27: "One thing I ask from the LORD, this only do I seek: that I may dwell in the house of the LORD all the days of my life, to gaze on the beauty of the LORD and to seek him in his temple" (Ps 27:4). In Christ we are caught up in the temple of the Lord, dwelling with him all the days of our lives, to gaze upon his beauty. In him we are partakers of the beauty that binds him with the Father, as Jesus prayed, "that all of them may be one, Father, just as you are in me and I am in you. May they also be in us" (John 17:21).

As the Father beholds his Son in the pleasure of his Spirit, so too do

---

42. The Christ whom Edwards presents to his audience is the "excellent" Christ, recalling that excellence is an important aesthetic term. It is a position taken from a close meditation on Heb 1:3, which claims that Christ is the radiance of the Father's glory and the exact representation of his nature. Christ himself, of course, affirmed that no one has ever seen the Father, but then qualifies this statement to claim that no one, except the one who is from God, referencing himself (John 6:46). Likewise, Jesus claims that anyone who has seen him, has seen the Father (14:9), and that eternal life is knowing both the Father and Jesus Christ whom he has sent (17:3). Christ is the revelation of God to his people, people with eyes but cannot see and ears but cannot hear. Just as Jesus healed the blind and the deaf, so too does the Spirit open ears and illuminate eyes to the spiritual depths of God's revelation of himself in the Son. Believers truly see God the Father in the Son as they are caught up in the movement of the Spirit to bind them to the life of God. The pattern of God's life is eternal and infinite happiness that is known and experienced within the pure actuality of love. God's economy is an emanation of this life; that he might allow the beauty of his life to overflow to creation. In Edwards's words, "How good is God, that he has created man for this very end, to make him happy in the enjoyment of himself, the Almighty, who was happy from the days of eternity in himself, in the beholding of his own infinite beauty: the Father in the beholding and love of his Son, his perfect and most excellent image, the brightness of his own glory; and the Son in the love and enjoyment of the Father.... 'Twas not that he might be made more happy himself, but that [he] might make something else happy; that he might make them blessed in the beholding of his excellency, and might this way glorify himself" (Y14, "Nothing upon Earth Can Represent the Glories of Heaven," 153).

43. What I am thinking of here will follow along the trajectory of Matthew Levering's exposition of Augustine: "In seeking to speak about the Trinity, who is the one God, Augustine at the same time seeks to remember and understand and love rightly, and in so doing to become what the trinitarian missions aim to make him, namely a participant in the trinitarian acts. The work of theological understanding, proceeding as it does from faith and love, cannot be separated from the movement of restoring and perfecting the imago dei. Put another way, theological understanding belongs within the context of supernatural friendship—and the restoration and perfection of the imago dei, which includes the intellectual acts of the soul, has to do with establishing and enhancing this spiritual friendship" (Matthew Levering, "Friendship and Trinitarian Theology: Response to Karen Kilby," *IJST* 10 [2007]: 50).

we gaze on the Son in the Spirit. There is a symmetry made apparent in the sending of his image that the Father beholds from all eternity. In this Spirit "we all, who with unveiled faces contemplate the Lord's glory, are being transformed into his image with ever-increasing glory, which comes from the Lord, who is the Spirit" (2 Cor 3:18). But we are not only external to the Son, captivated by a vision of his life and beauty, but we are bound up in his life by the Spirit. We do not remain external to the beauty that captivates us, but we are made beautiful as we partake in his beauty.

Along these lines, Edwards notes that in the economy there is a new image of the Trinity that emerges: the Son takes the place of the Father, and the church takes the place of the Son.[44] The Spirit is the same Spirit of beauty and holiness that binds them together in love. As in the immanent Trinity, so in the economy; the Son as Father pours forth love to the church, in whom he sees himself. The church, in the place of the Son, pours forth the consenting love of the Spirit as she sees herself caught up in the life of God. But this image only goes so far. In being united to the Son, the church is ushered before the Father in Christ's priestly office, so she knows that, in Jesus' words, "the Father himself loves you because you have loved me and have believed that I came ... from the Father and entered the world" (John 16:27–28) and that "I am in My Father, and you are in me, and I am in you" (John 14:20). In his ascension, "Christ did not enter a sanctuary made with human hands that was only a copy of the true one; he entered heaven itself, now to appear for us in God's presence" (Heb 9:24).

Christ is the one to whom we consent in the beauty and love of the Spirit, a beauty and love that first embraces us: "We love because he first loved us" (1 John 4:19).[45] In being embraced by Christ, we are united with the Father in a filial union of love within the Son and by his Spirit. We are children wrapped up in the life of the Son as we have the Spirit, such that we spiritually appraise all things and have the very mind of Christ (1 Cor 2:14–16). Our call is not simply to gaze on the beauty of Christ, to see

---

44. "In this also there is a trinity, an image of the eternal Trinity; wherein Christ is the everlasting father, and believers are his seed, and the Holy Spirit, or Comforter, is the third person in Christ, being his delight and love flowing out towards the church" (Y13, "Miscellanies 104, End of the Creation," 273).

45. Edwards notes that there is an ordering to seeing the loveliness of Christ and the love he has for them: "They don't first see that God loves them, and then see that he is lovely; but they first see that God is lovely, and that Christ is excellent and glorious, and their hearts are first captivated with this view ... and then, consequentially, they see God's love; and great favor to them" (Y2, "Religious Affections," 246).

Christ as beautiful, but to be caught up into this beauty itself—that our whole being would consent to his, and that we would partake in his filial relationship with the Father. A believer's identity as "child" and the beauty she partakes in are bound together in the life of the Son, and therefore must be bound together in the work of Christian rationality. What unfolds from this is an understanding of Christian rationality caught up in the grace of God. Theology, in this mode, is sapiential theology—theology done within and by the gaze of the Father on his people within his Son; it is here that we say, "in the sight of God we speak in Christ" (2 Cor 2:17). In the Son, the church hears that this is my beloved child in whom I am well pleased, and therefore theological proclamation reverberates in response to this Word.[46]

## BECOMING BEAUTIFUL: THE CALL OF THE THEOLOGIAN

With this as our backdrop, it is now possible to focus on retrieving something of Edwards's doctrine. It is not imperative that we employ every aspect of what Edwards was trying to do. Retrieving doctrine, as I am suggesting here, is not to recreate a mosaic piece by piece, but rather to take the large image and abstract it away from its individual tiles. This should be done, I believe, in a way that is not foreign to Edwards's account, but we should not hesitate to leave aside some of the idiosyncratic notions that are gratuitous for our purpose. Rather than retrieving Edwards's aesthetics for its own sake, therefore, I assess his trinitarian aesthetics to help outline the task of the theologian. Depicting beauty as he does requires a specific kind of relation between the knower and the known, and it is this relation I am looking to retrieve.

So what is the overarching image of this mosaic? *It is a vision of the beautiful known through spiritual sight in the Son by the uniting love and holiness of the Spirit.* This pushes the theological task into a distinctively affective and contemplative mode, as it is moored in the affection and contemplation of the Son. Therefore, more narrowly, theology is understood as the task of the human person *coram deo*; recognizing that theologizing in the

---

46. With Barth, "Theology itself is a word, a human response; yet what makes it theology is not its own word or response but the Word which it hears and to which it *responds....* In short, theology is not a creative act but only a praise of the Creator and of his act of creation—praise that to the greatest possible extent truly responds to the creative act of God." Karl Barth, *Evangelical Theology: An Introduction* (Grand Rapids: Eerdmans, 1963), 16–17.

presence of God is always also within the gaze of God.[47] Faith seeking beautification is faith working within the love of God as you are caught up within God's own beauty. It is not an extrinsic gazing on a God beautiful but distant, but the recognition that God's beautifying gaze is the foundation of your identity and being. Within the beautifying gaze of God we find the call for sapiential theology, locating the task of the theologian within the harmony of God's life, for the harmony of God's church in the world. By focusing on beauty, the emphasis rests on the movement of the *whole* person to God (rather than the intellect or will alone); by focusing on beautifying, the emphasis is on theological knowledge as spiritual knowledge (knowledge in the Spirit), and entails a new identity as one who now knows God as he knows himself (but through the limitations of our creatureliness).

For the remainder of this paper, therefore, let me use three biblical terms to describe the gaze in which we work. God beholds his people as *children*, as *bride*, and as *saints*. "Sapiential theology," as noted above, requires that this is not simply true of God's perception, but that the theologian is the one coming to know herself within the truth of these identifiers as well; faith seeking beautification requires this. To receive the truth of this gaze, we could say, means that we must receive it along the same contours as Christ—knowing ourselves as those known by the Father. This is more than imitation, but is knowing the Father in the Son, and knowing oneself in the Son as well. This kind of knowledge is upheld in the love of the Spirit, just as one's threefold identity as child, bride, and saint is upheld in the union of love with the Son.

We could contrast this with what we might call "disciple theology," which is the rationalism of fundamentalism.[48] This is pre-ascension theology—

---

47. This is to reject the notion that we can break up the disciplines of theology in various academic programs, sifting systematic, practical, moral, and spiritual theology in different directions. Rather, these are bound together in beauty, as they are caught up in God's life. These aspects of theology are called to witness—to harmonize—with this beauty of God, a beauty that refuses to let the spiritual, practical, moral, and systematic part ways.

48. Ellen Charry argues, "Sapiential truth is unintelligible to the modern secularized construal of truth. Modern epistemology not only fragmented truth itself, privileging correct information over beauty and goodness, it relocated truth in facts and ideas. The search for truth in the modern scientific sense is a cognitive enterprise that seeks correct information useful to the improvement of human comfort and efficacy rather than intellectual activity employed for spiritual growth. Knowing the truth no longer implied loving it, wanting it, and being transformed by it, because the truth no longer brings the knower to God but to use information to subdue nature. Knowing became limited to being informed about things, not as these are things of God but as they stand (or totter) on their own feet. The classical notion that truth leads us to God simply ceased to be intelligible and came to be viewed with suspicion." Ellen Charry, *By the Renewing of Your Minds: The Pastoral Function of Christian Doctrine* (Oxford: Oxford University Press, 1997), 236.

theology done without the high priestly work of Christ.[49] I call it disciple theology because it depends on extrinsic or what Edwards would call "natural" rationality, and it is pre-ascension theology because it fails to recognize the shift in identity that takes place in the ascension. In the ascension, believers radically shift from disciples to adopted children, bride, and saints.[50] In other words, this kind of theology is purely rationalistic without an overarching call of contemplation; it is not caught up in the life of God but remains external to his grace. What follows, by contrast, is a brief explication of this threefold form of sapiential theology: theology as children who proclaim "*Abba*, Father"; theology as the bride affectionately beholding her lover; and theology as saints that inseparably binds theology and spirituality together.[51] These are not three separate forms of theology or somehow distinct in their own right, but are three angles of one ultimate reality. In other words, doing theology in the gaze of the Father requires that one is knowing and being known, both by God and oneself, as child, bride, and saint.[52]

## CHILDREN

Sapiential theology cannot be done on different grounds than God's self-presentation in Christ, as if we are ushered before the cross for salvation and are sat down at a desk for theology. In salvation, the sonship of the Son is broken open to believers to partake in the life of the Son before the Father. This is why God sends the Son; he was on a "sonly" mission. Furthermore, the procession of the Logos is the Image of God in the incarnation who can claim that "anyone who has seen me has seen the Father" (John 14:9). The Word sent forth in the economy reveals the Father, as the

---

49. Bernard claims that "the Son makes us disciples. The Paraclete comforts us as friends. The Father raises us up as sons.... The first teaches us like a master. The second comforts like a friend or brother. The third embraces us as a father does his sons." Bernard of Clairvaux, *Bernard of Clairvaux: Selected Works* (New York: Paulist, 1987), 117. In this sense, because fundamentalist theology is pre-ascension, it is theology without the Spirit (hence its extrinsic rationalizing and biblicism).

50. This explains why Paul rejects, entirely, the word *disciple*. This does not mean that we rid ourselves of the term entirely, but only that we move it into the realm of ecclesiology. Discipleship, following Jesus' command to make disciples of all nations, is a call to be the church and to call people into the church.

51. One might argue that this loosely follows Bernard's division: "The first food, then, is humility. It purges by its bitterness. The second is the food of love, which consoles by its sweetness. The third is the food of contemplation, solid and strengthening" (ibid., 105). While humility, love, and contemplation serve as helpful glosses on child, bride, and saint respectively, I am not using them as a progression but as three angles of one united reality.

52. One of the advantages of the child and bride images is that they quickly reveal themselves to be communal rather than individual. By the time Paul starts writing, for instance, "brother" and "sister" were now the primary terms by which Christians recognized each other. In a similar sense, "bride" is a term referring to the church as a whole, thereby making it difficult to understand in an overly individualistic manner.

image of the invisible God, and true sight in faith is a real partaking of the Son's own knowledge of God. Like the archetype, the ectype always ties together sonship with love and beauty. The Son stands in a filial relation to the Father that defines him. In the economy, it is Jesus' identity as Son that is primary. He is the antitype of Israel, who was originally deemed God's son called out of Egypt (Matt 2:15). He is the Son declared beloved at his baptism (Matt 3:16–17). He is the Son of man who has existed from eternity past at the right hand of God (Dan 7:13–14). His sonship in the economy is an extension of his filial identity in the immanent Trinity. Likewise, it is Jesus' sonship that is broken open in adoption for believers to partake in his nature (2 Pet 1:4).

To embrace the call of the theologian is to grasp one's identity as a child of the Father within Jesus' sonship: knowing oneself as raised and ascended with the one who is at the right hand of God. After the resurrection, when believer's lives are understood to be "hidden with Christ in God" (Col 3:3), they are no longer referred to as disciples, but as children and saints. Jesus' immediate divine knowledge did not translate over into a rabbi with an incredible CV and reference (i.e., the Father);[53] rather, the divine knowledge is revealed in the Son as the Son. This is not a contingent form of the economy, but a necessary feature of God's immanent life. To know this God, one must share the filial relation of the Son to the Father—explicated in Scripture with the related images of adoption and marriage. The theologian, in this sense, is one who knows themselves within the filial gaze of God; she is the one who hears this is my beloved child in whom I am well pleased, and in response proclaims "*Abba*, Father." To know God as my God, one must know God as Father and themselves as child. This is the proper ground for theological reflection, because it is here that one is caught up within the beauty of God to proclaim the truth of this beauty from within.

## BRIDE

The second delineation overlaps significantly with the first. The soteriological frameworks of adoption and marriage share the same family emphasis, but marriage shifts the metaphor to a more erotic register. For

---

53. The language of CV is not arbitrary. Here, I am thinking of Philippians 2 and the descent of Christ. This is an important image against the backdrop of the Roman understanding of honor and status. The notion of CV might be the closest to depicting what Paul is representing here, as well as in the next chapter when he presents his own CV. The notions of *cursus honorum* vs. *cursus pudorum* come into play here. See Joseph Hellerman, *Reconstructing Honor in Roman Philippi: Carmen Christi as Cursus Pudorum* (Cambridge: Cambridge University Press, 2008).

our purpose, this is a helpful place to ground the distinctively affective nature of the theological task. For Edwards, knowledge is bound together in love, but what this binding reveals is that God is beautiful and beautifying.[54] This means that the theologian's primary task is a spiritual task; it is, as Paul says, a task of spiritual appraisal—as those who have "the mind of Christ" (1 Cor 2:10–16). Ectypal theology is spiritual theology, and as such, it is theology in the relation of beauty—of mind consenting to mind in love—and is distinctively affective.[55]

Affective knowledge is a way to speak meaningfully about the holistic nature of the theological task.[56] The ascent of knowledge is, necessarily, an ascent into love, and any ascent into love is equally an ascent into beauty. To know beauty one must be caught up in it, consenting to it internally. As von Balthasar states so well, "Before the beautiful—no, not really before but within the beautiful—the whole person quivers. He not only 'finds' the beautiful moving; rather, he experiences himself as being moved and possessed by it."[57] Affectionate knowledge, in this sense, is captivated knowledge, but also, continuing in the sphere of beauty, it is deeply personal. As Calvin notes, "it is certain that man never achieves a clear knowledge of himself unless he has first looked upon God's face, and then descends from contemplating him to scrutinizing himself."[58] This is more than an assent to truth, but the captivation of a lover, and entails the peace of one known as beloved.

---

54. Since primary beauty is only available in the Spirit, the notion of beauty is inseparable with union, love, and holiness. Human persons are so constituted as to receive and be embraced by this reality of God's life, and theology must mirror this. One of the problems with fundamentalist notions of theology is that they fail not only on the side of revelation (employing an overly reduced account of God's self-giving) but also on the side of anthropology (assuming that humans are only rational agents).

55. "According to this model, the relation of trinitarian persons to one another, and the relation of God and humanity, are relations constituted by knowledge and love. Knowledge, like love, is a unitive force ... thus knower is bound to known, love to the beloved, and knowledge and love are united to one another." A. N. Williams, "'Contemplation' in Knowing the Triune God," in *Knowing the Triune God: The Work of the Spirit in the Practices of the Church* (ed. James J. Buckley and David S. Yeago; Grand Rapids, Eerdmans, 2001), 123.

56. What I am thinking about here is well articulated by von Balthasar: "Augustine and Bernard usually describe this dimension with the categories of the voluntative and the affective, as opposed to the purely intellectual and the theoretical, but this is only partly accurate. What an older theology so designated, for want of other categories, may be more correctly understood using the more central categories of the existential and the personal, which allow one to see the act of faith at its roots as the attitude and behaviour of the total person as determined by God and his revelation of grace.... Only when by 'will' and 'affect' we understand the engagement of the person in all his depth—only then does intellectual faith become a genuine answer to God's disclosure of his depth as person; for God too does not primarily communicate 'truths' about himself, but rather bestows himself as absolute truth and love." Hans Urs von Balthasar, *The Glory of the Lord: A Theological Aesthetics*; I. *Seeing the Form* (San Francisco: Ignatius, 2003), 165–66.

57. Ibid., 247. The notion of *experiencing* oneself within the beautiful is a particularly important notion here that will tie together the task of theology and spirituality.

58. John Calvin, *The Institutes of the Christian Religion*, 1.1.2.

In the sphere of beauty, and this is seen in the theologians who emphasize beauty, the adoption image tends to be superseded by the marital one. When the Son sends the Spirit, he is sending his love. The gaze of the Son upon his bride is not a passive gaze, but a generative one; the groom so loves the church that his love binds her to himself in a substantial union.[59] Christian theology is done within this gaze, the gaze, Edwards notes, that leads one to conclude "that he, though Lord of the universe, is captivated with love to them, and has his heart swallowed up in them, and prizes 'em."[60] The work of the theologian, therefore, while still laborious, should be the labor of a poet, overcome *with* and *by* love, and therefore unable to keep silent.

The gaze of Christ upon his church creates the space to do theology in a sapiential mode—a mode that follows the contours of sonship and bride, and as we will see, saint.[61] It is theology done while being captivated by the God without, and the realization that this God is within. The theologian's foundation for herself is outside of herself, but includes the awareness that this God has descended to her depths. To be captivated by this God is to know the unity of beauty and love with knowledge, to proclaim with the Psalmist that "deep calls to deep in the roar of your waterfalls; all your waves and breakers have swept over me" (Ps 42:7). It is within this interiority that one comes to grasp that God gives himself in his revelation, and to know God in this self-revelation is to be known in him (1 Cor 13:12).[62]

---

59. As Balthasar notes, "God's gaze is not passive (otherwise it would not be a divine gaze); he does not merely 'read off' or ascertain: his gaze is creative, generative, originative, by his utterly free decree." Hans Urs von Balthasar, *Prayer* (San Francisco: Ignatius, 1955), 40.

60. Y2, "Religious Affections," 245.

61. It is here where we might heed Luther's warning against theologies of glory, by recalling that Christ's life revealed both God and the harmonization of creaturely existence within the life of God. The disfigurement of the cross must serve as the gestalt-shift that reorients beauty, or, to continue to harmony metaphor, the cross must serve as the note discordant to the world but the very note that the human heart must harmonize with to embrace the depths of reality. The theological contemplation this leads to is not ecstasy, but to society. A vision of God's presence and life does not take one's eyes off of others and the world, but creates the space within which to love God and love neighbor. This kingdom always remains somewhat foreign, however harmonized to it we become, it still runs contrary to our orientation. To forget this is to open oneself up to the temptation to reject foolishness and embrace a wisdom without foundation in reality. As put by Mark McIntosh concerning theologians and academic culture, "The danger is that we will attempt to blend in all too well; we will master the academic and ecclesiastical arts so proficiently that people will not notice how outrageous is the subject of our work. We may even manage, perhaps without realizing it, to substitute for the outlandishness of the Christian faith, a gray orderliness in which nothing unexpected ever happens or ever could. Mark A. McIntosh, *Divine Teaching: An Introduction to Christian Theology* (Oxford: Blackwell Publishing, 2008), 3–4.

62. For Edwards, this entails a knowledge of God *pro nobis*: "He is graciously present with them, and when they see him they see him and know him to be so. They have an understanding of his love to them; they see him from love manifesting himself to them" (Y17, "The Pure in Heart Blessed," 64). The focus of Edwards's thought here is that believers not only see and know God, but know him as love to them and for them.

Theology done as bride is churchly theology that embraces Christ as the true lover of the Song of Songs, calling to the depths of the human person to be known, cherished, and captivated by God.[63] This does not sanctify specific emotions—as if affection detailed the texture of specific existential responses to God, but is the calling forth of the whole person that can be only understood utilizing relational and erotic terminology.[64] This focus orients theology to the call and formation of God through union to the Son in love.

## SAINTS

The final aspect of the theologian's identity within the gaze of God is saint. As Paul wrote to the delinquent church of Corinth, "To the church of God which is at Corinth, to those who have been sanctified in Christ Jesus, saints by calling" (1 Cor 1:2, pers. trans.). The theological task is only fully achieved as one is caught up in the harmony of God's life, a harmony only possible by a deeply relational captivation of one's heart. This is to be sanctified in Christ, the sanctified One. "Both the one who makes people holy [namely, Christ] and those who are made holy are of the same family" (Heb 2:11).[65] Saintly theology, if I can put it that way, must not simply describe this reality from without, but from within. Edwards notes that "a true saint" is one who has his mind "captivated and engaged by what he views without himself," in such a way that that reorients his identity around Christ. In his words, "to stand at that time to view himself, and his own attainments: it would be a diversion and loss which he could not bear, to take his eye off from the ravishing object of his contemplation."[66] Sapiential theology, therefore, is saintly theology; it is Christian rationality from within the holiness of the Spirit and the

---

63. "Theology, therefore, participates in a special manner in the bridal holiness of the Church." This theology, according to von Balthasar, is a "dialogue between bride and bridegroom in the unity and communication of the Spirit." Therefore, "the purpose of contemplation is to cause the life of the bride to be transformed: glory is the splendor of holiness, which is not only mirrored in the bride, but takes her up into the 'metamorphoris.'" Hans Urs von Balthasar, *Word and Redemption* (New York: Herder and Herder, 1965), 78–79.

64. It is interesting that this kind of terminology, used so readily in the tradition, has fallen out of favor. It could be that theology needs an erotic corrective in order to break it out of its comfortable academic slumber. For an interesting counter to this trend, see Belden C. Lane, *Ravished by Beauty: The Surprising Legacy of Reformed Spirituality* (Oxford: Oxford University Press, 2011).

65. Edwards argues that "Christ's beauty, for which his person is delighted in and chosen, is especially his holiness" (Y21, "Notebook on Faith, 121," 458). Similarly, then, the saintly nature of the theological task is directly related to the beauty of believers who are caught up within Christ's beauty in his Spirit.

66. Y2, "Religious Affections," 252–53. Edwards's specific point here concerns discerning the nature of true affection, but the point is relatable here.

righteousness of Christ. This is theology that serves the spiritual integrity of life in God, all the while embracing its task as *pilgrim*-theology.[67]

Sapiential theology is a distinctively spiritual task that is caught up in the "beauty of holiness." This means that Christian spirituality and theology are bound together, and to attempt one without the other is to destroy them both. In terms of theology, and this is evident everywhere in the academy, theology without spirituality becomes mapping exercises and a discussion of how theology should be done without actually getting around to doing it.[68] The texture of this theology is from the outside looking in rather than from within for the sake of worship. For spirituality, again, the results are all too obvious. We are confronted with a spiritual impulse that is doctrinally ignorant and a practice that is random at best and sub-Christian at worst. Overall, as von Balthasar was so quick to note, "The impoverishment brought about by the divorce between the two spheres is all too plain; it has sapped the vital force of the Church of today and the credibility of her preaching of eternal truth."[69]

Sapiential theology founded upon the trinitarian gaze of beauty and glory, two themes often found hand in hand, is a theology of contemplation.[70] As such, sapiential theology, theology of the saints, is theology at prayer.[71] It is contemplative because it seeks to set one's "mind on things above" (Col 3:23), and it is prayerful because the "things above" are the Father, Son, and Holy Spirit, who have revealed themselves in the economy and called us into this life of love. Talking about classic works of ancient theology, von Balthasar notes, "Theology was, when pursued

---

67. Pilgrim theology is not something to supersede, but to receive as grace. A theology of glory, in a negative sense, is a rejection of the *pilgrim* nature of theology. Barth helpfully reminds us of this when he states, "It should be remembered that our knowledge is achieved as a pilgrim theology in the light of grace and not of glory, in the light of the *parousia* of Jesus Christ." Karl Barth, *The Christian Life: Church Dogmatics*, vol. 4, part 4: *Lecture Fragments* (trans. Geoffrey W. Bromiley; London: T&T Clark, 1981), 8.

68. Admittedly, something that could be said about aspects of this chapter.

69. Von Balthasar, *Word and Redemption*, 65.

70. A. N. Williams argues, "Augustine's conception of the knowledge of God ... encompasses both theology and spirituality, because he portrays it as the fruit of contemplation. A contemplative knowledge does not seek to establish truth by hard-won deduction, but rather to nourish understanding and 'enable it to rise up to the sublimities of divine things.'" A. N. Williams, "'Contemplation' in Knowing the Triune God," 125.

71. Barth, one of the great prayerful theologians, writes, "Dogmatics is possible only as an act of faith, when we point to prayer as the attitude without which there can be no dogmatic work." Karl Barth, *CD* I/1, 23. Likewise, "The old saying, *Lex orandi lex credendi*, far from being a pious statement, is one of the most profound descriptions of the theological method.... The free and true theologian lives from it. In the invocation, in the giving of thanks, and in the petition, this turnabout is realized and the theologian is allowed to live out the freedom of thought which he enjoys as a child of God." Karl Barth, *The Humanity of God* (Richmond, VA: John Knox, 1963), 90. Barth's beautiful chapter "Prayer" in his *Evangelical Theology*, 159–70, should also not be ignored.

by men of sanctity, a theology at prayer; which is why its fruitfulness for prayer, its power to foster prayer, is so undeniable."[72] Theology in this register is known by its love and its ability to direct the church in love; it is not known by its credentials (although it may, in fact, have them). Like Paul, these theologians look at their own CVs and declare, "I consider everything a loss because of the surpassing worth of knowing Christ Jesus my Lord.... I consider them garbage, that I may gain Christ" (Phil 3:8–9).[73] In this way, saintly theology focuses on the truth that our status as saints is outside of ourselves, even though it is given over to us in the Spirit.[74] As von Balthasar goes on to note:

> True theology, the theology of the saints, with the central doctrines of revelation always in view, inquires, in a spirit of obedience and reverence, what process of human thought, what modes of approach are best fitted to bring out the meaning of what has been revealed.... Any intellectual procedure that does not serve this purpose is assuredly not an interpretation of revelation, but one that bypasses its true meaning and, therefore, an act of disobedience.[75]

# CONCLUSION

In conclusion, sapiential theology can be described as being caught up in the grace of God such that one knows himself within the Lord.[76] This movement into love is an embrace of the truth of God's gaze—that we are seen and known as children, bride, and saints—and are therefore beautiful

---

72. Von Balthasar, *Word and Redemption*, 84. "As time went on, theology at prayer was superseded by theology at the desk, and this brought about the cleavage now under discussion. 'Scientific' theology became more and more divorced from prayer, and so lost the accent and tone with which one should speak of what is holy, while 'affective' theology, as it became increasingly empty, often degenerated into unctuous, platitudinous piety" (ibid., 85).

73. An important connection with Philippians 2, as noted above.

74. The saints, declares Balthasar, "never at any moment leave their center in Christ. They give themselves to their work in the world, while 'praying at all times' and 'doing all to the glory of God' (1 Thess 5:17; 1 Cor 10:31).... Their thinking is an act that is ultimately performed in the service of their faith, of Christ's revelation, which is its norm and guiding principle" (von Balthasar, *Word and Redemption*, 68–69).

75. Ibid., 69–70. The saints "wish to contemplate nature with no other eyes than those of Christ. They have no desire to know God as simply *ens a se*, but solely as the Father of Christ; the Spirit, too, not as an abstract world of universal laws and prescriptions, but as the Spirit of the tongues of fire, the Spirit who breathes where he wills" (ibid., 81). "Their one desire is to be receptive, men of prayer in other words. Their theology is essentially an act of adoration and prayer.... Christian dogmatics must express the fact that one whose thinking is dictated by faith is in a constant relationship of prayer with its object" (ibid., 82).

76. This self-knowledge is imperfect, as Bernard will remind us, placing the fourth level of love as loving oneself for the sake of God. "Happy is he who has been found worthy to attain to the fourth degree, where man loves himself only for God's sake." Bernard of Clairvaux, *Bernard of Clairvaux: Selected Works*, 195.

as we partake in his beautifying life. This puts contemplation at the heart of theology, so that the theological task is not simply faith seeking understanding, but faith seeking beautification. This is not a separate category of knowledge outside of our rationality, but is our rationality caught up in grace. This rationality entails a knowing and being known that is revealed in the life of the Son. The act of faith is an embrace of the Father in the Son by the Spirit so that faith seeks beautification, and beautification proclaims the goodness of the beloved.[77] Theology before this God, therefore, must take on the posture it will take in eternity. To close, then, let me narrate this posture from Edwards's own words:

> All shall stand about the God of glory, the fountain of love, as it were opening their bosoms to be filled with those effusions of love which are poured forth from thence, as the flowers on the earth in a pleasant spring day open their bosoms to the sun to be filled with his warmth and light, and to flourish in beauty and fragrancy by his rays. Every saint is as a flower in the garden of God, and holy love is the fragrancy and sweet odor which they all send forth, and with which they fill that paradise. Every saint there is as a note in a concert of music which sweetly harmonizes with every other note, and all together employed wholly in praising God and the Lamb; and so all helping one another to their utmost to express their love of the whole society to the glorious Father and Head of it, and [to pour back] love into the fountain of love, whence they are supplied and filled with love and with glory. And thus they will live and thus they will reign in love, and in that godlike joy which is the blessed fruit of it, such as eye hath not seen, nor ear heard, nor hath ever entered into the heart of any in this world to conceive [cf. 1 Corinthians 2:9]. And thus they will live and reign forever and ever.[78]

---

77. It does not take much imagination to see how Edwards's conception of the Trinity, beauty, and knowledge serve as the foundation for his great work on the religious affections. It should also be clear why, in that work and elsewhere, Edwards posits a "sense of the heart" that is necessary to have true spiritual knowledge. This sense is not based on new information the person did not have before, nor is it based on new physical sight. Rather, the sense of the heart calls out the texture of real personal knowledge of God. It is knowledge only known in love, because God's archetypal knowledge is always knowledge known in love. Edwards claims, "From what has been said, therefore, we come necessarily to this conclusion, concerning that wherein spiritual understanding consists; viz. that it consists in a sense of the heart, of the supreme beauty and sweetness of the holiness or moral perfection of divine things, together with all that discerning and knowledge of things of religion, that depends upon, and flows from such a sense" (Y2, "Religious Affections," 272). Religious affection, for Edwards, locates anthropology within the revelation of God's triune life, by orienting the human person to knowledge of God qua beauty. In the processions God has perfect and immediate self-knowledge, but that self-knowledge is always known in love, beauty, and delight. This is the form of all true knowledge of God.

78. Y8, "Charity and Its Fruits," 386.

# CHAPTER 9

# A CONFESSING TRINITARIAN THEOLOGY FOR TODAY'S MISSION

JASON S. SEXTON[1]

OVER THE PAST SEVERAL DECADES a steady effort has sought to expound what it might mean to be trinitarian to the point where just about everything conceivable might somehow fit the category for some theologians.[2] With much to celebrate about this renewed interest in the deepest ocean of Christian theology, the question often remains, especially for practitioners and ministers: To what end is this trinitarian reflection? How might it serve to bless our world?

The trinitarian emphasis has been complemented by a flurry of interest in what it might mean for today's church to be "missional" and to carry on the task of genuine Christian mission. In part, this has flowed from the wider world of global ecumenical missionary activity over the past century,[3] and especially from work over the past two decades,[4] lagging somewhat behind the trinitarian resurgence, but not by much.

---

1. I am grateful to Rev. Dr. Paul Weston for reading and commenting on an earlier draft of this chapter.
2. For an account of this among evangelicals, see Jason S. Sexton, *Evangelicals and the Trinity: Tracing the Return to the Center of Christian Theology* (Downers Grove, IL: InterVarsity Press, 2015).
3. See *Edinburgh 2010: Mission Then and Now* (ed. David A. Kerr and Kenneth R. Ross; Pasadena: William Carey International University Press, 2009).
4. See Craig Van Gelder and Dwight J. Zscheile, *The Missional Church in Perspective* (Grand Rapids: Baker, 2011).

Also apparent is that these efforts have not produced much consensus about either what is "trinitarian"[5] or what is "missional" in the best possible forms. This is not necessarily a bad thing; however, we must hold forth yet better ways of expounding the trinitarian gospel in its well-developed contours and still better ways of understanding the role that the church is to play in fulfilling the mission to which God has called it in our ever-changing world. But the lack of consensus has also paved the way for the enthusiastic celebrators to carry on with exuberant proposals following fashionable trends,[6] or else, with wide popularizing effects to enable other disciplines to co-opt theology as a handmaiden while a little leaven does its work.

Of course, if everything can be understood as trinitarian or missional, then it's likely that neither mean anything, and theologians may remain free to construct their own hyperrealities similar to Lewis Carroll's Alice, who surmised,

> If I had a world of my own, everything would be nonsense. Nothing would be what it is, because everything would be what it isn't. And contrariwise, what is, it wouldn't be. And what it wouldn't be, it would. You see?[7]

Instead of attempting to bend whatever may or may not be real in these worlds or what may pass for "trinitarian" or "missional" theology through the selective editing processes for which theologians are notorious, it seems best rather to create space for addressing trinitarian theology plainly as it has developed, especially in organic ways and in indigenous settings.[8] In so doing, we may learn again to be "trinitarian without pretending to know more than in fact we do."[9] And we may even learn how to be better missionaries in the process.

At the risk, then, of adding to the lack of consensus and contributing further confusion, with the explorative nature of trinitarian theology in

---

5. See the essays and responses from leading classical trinitarians (Stephen R. Holmes and Paul D. Molnar) and relational trinitarians (Thomas H. McCall and Paul S. Fiddes) in *Two Views on the Doctrine of the Trinity* (ed. Jason S. Sexton; Grand Rapids: Zondervan, 2014).

6. The most forceful argument against the trend is Stephen R. Holmes, *The Quest for the Trinity: The Doctrine of God in Scripture, History and Modernity* (Downers Grove, IL: InterVarsity Press, 2012); see also Thomas A. Noble and Jason S. Sexton, eds., *The Doctrine of the Holy Trinity Revisited: Responses to Stephen R. Holmes* (Milton Keynes, UK: Paternoster, 2015).

7. This quote is from the Walt Disney adaptation, *Alice in Wonderland* (1951), www.imdb.com/title/tt0043274/ (accessed 22 Jan 2014).

8. Such a full-orbed task would seem to require at least sustained effort from both systematic theologians versed in the interpretation of Scripture and the history of Christian doctrine as well as either missiologists or other social-scientists capable of tracing belief-systems in various cultures.

9. This phrase has been borrowed from Professor Karen Kilby.

view, this essay attempts to attend to concerns from the disciplines of systematic theology and missiology in hopes of suggesting better ways of confessing our developing trinitarian theology for the sake of the church's mission today.

# FORMULATING TRINITARIAN DOCTRINE

## FROM INCHOATE AND TACIT TRINITARIANISM ...

Lesslie Newbigin sought something more than what he found with the inchoate trinitarian missiology implied in the International Missionary Council's (IMC) 1952 Willingen conference on "The Missionary Obligation of the Church," which identified "the Church's mission as participation in God's mission to the world through the Son and the Spirit."[10] With the church's missionary effort facing serious challenges from Communism, secularism, and religious pluralism, by the 1960s Newbigin began arguing that the church had resources within the Christian understanding of God as Father, Son, and Holy Spirit to address the perplexing moment. As a result he invited the missions movement "to bind itself to the strong name of the Trinity."[11]

Newbigin's call to develop "a fully and explicitly trinitarian doctrine of God" for a theology of missions was his response to what he considered a more "church-centric view of missions" that had been vogue since the IMC conference at Tambaram in 1938. He thought that this was perhaps "too exclusively founded upon the person and work of Christ and [having] perhaps done less than justice to the whole trinitarian doctrine of God."[12] This "fully trinitarian doctrine of God" he proposed would be aimed at "setting the work of Christ in the Church in the context of the over-ruling providence of the Father in all the life of the world and the sovereign freedom of the Spirit who is the Lord and not the auxiliary of the Church."[13]

Newbigin's concerns were not unlike those of Colin Gunton decades later, who warned of treating the presence of the Spirit in the church as

---

10. Geoffrey Wainwright, *Lesslie Newbigin: A Theological Life* (New York: Oxford University Press, 2000), 177–78. For an excellent discussion on the tributaries to the IMC Willingen conference and the origin of the *missio Dei* theology, see John G. Flett, *The Witness of God: The Trinity, Missio Dei, Karl Barth, and the Nature of Christian Community* (Grand Rapids: Eerdmans, 2010), 123–62.

11. Lesslie Newbigin, *Trinitarian Doctrine for Today's Mission* (Eugene, OR: Wipf & Stock, 2006), 33; first published as a pamphlet titled *The Relevance of Trinitarian Doctrine for Today's Mission* (London: Edinburgh House, 1963).

12. Ibid. See also Newbigin's explanation of his earlier work as "too exclusively church-centered" in Lesslie Newbigin, *Unfinished Agenda* (London: SPCK, 1985), 198–99.

13. Newbigin, *Unfinished Agenda*, 198–99.

something of a "claimed possession" to the point where the actions of the church and the actions of the Spirit become convoluted. "It is not," Gunton asserted, "as has often been suggested, if not actually taught, that the Spirit is in some way at the disposal of the church, so that what the church does the Spirit is doing. It is rather that the Spirit's first function is to realize in the life of particular human beings and groups of human beings the reality of what God in Christ achieved on the cross."[14] Shirking a similarly unformed christological emphasis, and for similar reasons, Gunton was also uncomfortable regarding the phrase "the body of Christ" as a metaphor designating the church.

Such cautions are worth emulating, especially in light of the postcolonial situation.[15] They emphasize the theological priority of *God's mission*, and that our mission both "flows from and participates in" his mission.[16] Arguments of retrieval have recently been made on behalf of different ecclesiologies, highlighting how the emphases on Father, Son, or Spirit designate a tacit trinitarianism.[17] Yet such optimistic and even revisionist readings of the history have been interpreted as justifying a confessional reductionism. While acknowledging that few Latin American Protestants would actually deny the Trinity, late in the last century Argentinian theologian José Míguez Bonino noted that in the Latin American Protestant traditions it remained largely "a generic doctrine which does not profoundly inform the theology, and what is worse, the piety and life of our churches."[18] But what does this trinitarian feature look like in some recent indigenous, localized theologies?

## ... TO INDIGENOUS TRINITARIAN EMPHASES

There are many examples that can be selected to highlight the recent localized developmental nature of trinitarian theology that show organic developmental doctrines of the Trinity at work. While these examples

14. Colin E. Gunton, *The Christian Faith: An Introduction to Christian Doctrine* (Oxford, UK: Blackwell, 2002), 121.

15. It is said the ecumenical movement contributed to the demise of the earlier and highly unfortunate colonial model of missions; this was part of the argument of Lesslie Newbigin, "Mission to Six Continents," in *The Ecumenical Advance: A History of the Ecumenical Movement*, Vol. 2, *1948-1968* (2nd ed.; ed. Harold E. Fey; Philadelphia: Westminster, 1986), 173–97.

16. Christopher J. H. Wright, *The Mission of God: Unlocking the Bible's Grand Narrative* (Downers Grove, IL: InterVarsity Press, 2006), 22–23.

17. Chief among these retrieving resources from a largely underexplored evangelical tradition is Fred Sanders, *The Deep Things of God: How the Trinity Changes Everything* (Wheaton, IL: Crossway, 2010).

18. José Míguez Bonino, *Faces of Latin American Protestantism: 1993 Carnaham Lectures* (trans. Eugene L. Stockwell; Grand Rapids: Eerdmans, 1997), 113.

could be mounted in near endless expressions—from nonliterate cultures (e.g., those where African Independent Churches exist) to the mentally ill or severely disabled peoples, and everything in between—this section aims to provide a brief sketch of select emphases from different indigenous groups working through how to better understand and relate the doctrine of the Trinity in their theologies.

Míguez Bonino sought to develop an understanding of the doctrine of the Trinity as a hermeneutical criterion informing the rest of theology. It would reference the range of the *loci theologici*, with particular significance for ecclesiology, sanctification, and eschatology, but then consider all doctrinal subjects as related to life and mission.[19] Kept in mind would be that the doctrine of the Trinity is nothing more or less than an attempt of the church to formulate and speak of "that inscrutable and inexhaustible wealth that we call Father, Son, and Holy Spirit."[20] Thus Míguez Bonino pled for a move that placed various theological emphases within the total framework of revelation, yielding "a trinitarian perspective that will broaden, enrich, and deepen the Christological, soteriological, and pneumatological understanding which is at the very root of our Latin American Protestant tradition."[21]

Peruvian theologian Samuel Escobar recently confirmed Míguez Bonino's diagnosis from his own personal history and that of his generation within the *Fraternidad Teológica Latinoamericana*. He noted that the "Cochabamba Declaration," with which the FTL was born in Bolivia (1970), included no reference to the Trinity, although there are brief references to the work of God, of Christ, and of the Holy Spirit. Here Escobar reiterates the need for Míguez Bonino's emphasis and has found Latin American theology largely moving in this direction, connecting Christology and the other doctrines more closely with the broader biblical revelation. The five Latin American Congress on Evangelization (CLADE) meetings have also confirmed this.[22]

Escobar sees the work of Justo L. González also moving in a similar direction. As part of a Hispanic minority in the US, González has developed an economic doctrine of the Trinity concerned with socioeconomic consequences, something he also sees in the great theologians of the fourth

---

19. Ibid., 117–27.
20. Ibid., 112.
21. Ibid.
22. Samuel Escobar, "New Directions for Evangelical Theology in Latin America: A Literature Review," *JLAT* 8 (2013): 82–84.

century. Rather than reflecting on the Trinity in purely speculative or metaphysical terms, he affirms belief in "a God whose essence is sharing," and thus the doctrine of the Trinity says, "God is love." González then calls Hispanics "to discover, to imitate, and to apply to our societal and ecclesial life the love of the Triune God," helping the wider church to see what this might look like for their brothers and sisters in the North Atlantic communities.[23] Ghanaian theologian Kwame Bediako finds that second-century orthodox Greek theologians wrestled through the same concerns as mid-twentieth-century African theologians,[24] struggling with issues of identity and philosophical integration in order to understand the divine-creature relationship amidst the development of a trinitarian doctrine of the divine life and love, and divine intimacy with the created order.[25]

Korean theologian Paul Chung calls his proposal a "reconstruction of an irregular theology of the Trinity," drawing from different epistemologies, including the Jewish wisdom of Kabbalah and the philosophical Daoism rendered through *Daodejing*. He begins with the Christian self-understanding of God revealed through Israel's history and in Jesus Christ through the Spirit, but then uses these incipient epistemologies to develop a notion of divine economic speech bearing witness to God's trinitarian life "as an eschatologically open movement of divine action and becoming in light of God's coming." This "provocative irregularity" maintains an eschatological reserve that understands God as "free to speak in a completely different and unexpected manner than that which is limited to the Church."[26] Yet, in light of this, "human language and words may be a genuine witness and attestation when viewed as an analogical medium of God's grace of speech."[27]

Catholic theologian Peter Phan attempts to develop a Vietnamese American theology employing *tam tai* philosophy for a construction of a doctrine of the Trinity. Here the Father is correlate to "heaven," the Son

---

23. Justo L. González, *Mañana: Christian Theology from a Hispanic Perspective* (Nashville: Abingdon, 1990), 111–15.

24. Andrew Walls, "The Rise of Global Theologies," in *Global Theology in Evangelical Perspective: Exploring the Contextual Nature of Theology and Mission* (ed. Jeffrey P. Greenman and Gene L. Green; Downers Grove, IL: InterVarsity Press, 2010), 25.

25. Kwame Bediako, *Theology and Identity: The Impact of Culture upon Christian Thought in the Second Century and in Modern Africa* (Oxford, UK: Regnum, 1992).

26. Paul S. Chung, *Constructing Irregular Theology: Bamboo and Mingjung in East Asian Perspective* (Boston, MA: Brill, 2009), 81–101. Note the discussion of how this orients the church in mission and genuine openness toward religious pluralism and ethical responsibility in the face of the Other in light of trinitarian openness, peace, and reconciliation in the world.

27. Ibid., 100.

to "humanity," and God the Spirit "to earth and to elaborate [trinitarian] roles in the history of salvation in the light of those of heaven, earth, and humanity."[28] These roles are truly distinct, yet intimately linked together in a *perichoresis* or *koinonia* of life and activity, where divine transcendence and immanence are intrinsically related, conceived as internally connected with and even *dependent on* humanity and earth to fulfill divine action in the economy. Accordingly, "the Trinity is conceived as inscribed in the structure of reality itself."[29]

While some of the above reflections may push the limits of what might denote genuine trinitarian doctrine, say, with the notion of divine eschatological reserve or with various panentheistic renderings,[30] Kärkkäinen still wants these and other localized forms of naming to complement the traditional ways of naming the Trinity.[31]

What Amos Yong means by "fully trinitarian" is a Christ-centered and Spirit-oriented theology, normed by Scripture and deeply embedded in the great theological tradition.[32] But of course, if this is Christ-centered and Spirit-oriented, it must include ecclesiology, at least if the church has any sense of self-consciousness in the salvation economy. This is not church as an institution, but as the called, gathered, and simultaneously sent community—both brought into and sent out by the divine life and being. Yong's view and some of the others would benefit from a proposal like R. Kendall Soulen's, which suggests that there is a threefold pattern yielding three different appropriate ways of naming the persons of the Trinity: the theological, the christological, and the pneumatological. The latter pattern is most significant here, looking to the life of the churches for how this pattern most fully unfolds the name of the Trinity with extraordinary breadth, intersecting with the range of human language and experience.[33] This pattern adapts itself to time and place, making use

---

28. Peter C. Phan, *Christianity with an Asian Face: Asian American Theology in the Making* (Maryknoll, NY: Orbis, 2003), 244.

29. Ibid.

30. See also the earlier treatment of Stephen R. Holmes, "Trinitarian Missiology: Towards a Theology of God as Missionary," *IJST* 8 (2006): 71–90, which risks having the economy or "missionary" constitute the divine being in ways that risk introducing *necessity* into the divine life (I am grateful to Keith E. Johnson of Florida for this point). Liberation theologies and other social models easily fall into this; yet the matter is avoided when Holmes notes, "it is a necessary perfection of God's being that he is not sent" (ibid., 77).

31. Veli-Matti Kärkkäinen, *The Trinity: Global Perspectives* (Louisville: Westminster John Knox, 2007), 398–99. See also the selective survey in this vol. of various "global" trinitarian theologies.

32. Amos Yong, "Asian American Evangelical Theology," in *Global Theology in Evangelical Perspective*, 207–8.

33. R. Kendall Soulen, *The Divine Name(s) and the Holy Trinity, vol. 1: Distinguishing the Voices* (Louisville: Westminster John Knox, 2012), 247–51. See also ch. 6 of the present volume.

of what is readily available, insisting on "no single fixed vocabulary of its own, but unfolds the inexhaustible glory of the triune Name through the general forms of speech and possibilities of speech present in the discourse of all peoples, tribes, and nations."[34]

Here Jonathan Wilson's attempted "apocalyptic" corrective is set against these, suggesting that the already-not yet scheme draws us "back into the kind of historical captivity that opens the door to 'theology-with-reserve,'" and thus places Christian mission in "a space where authorities and powers other than the Messiah circumscribe the sphere, range, and possibilities for Christian mission."[35] Apocalyptic theology shows its weakness here, however, by not having a real "place" in the already-not yet situation, where amidst our fallenness we truly participate in being Christ's body in the world. In so doing, the church becomes the place of "his righteousness, the extension of his presence, the very inbreaking of his reign in the world," which does not separate Christians from the world. Yet the church has a major role in history, preceding the world epistemologically on this account with God's reign being "manifest in the midst of the church as a foretaste of what is to come in the world."[36] In this way, the eschatological nature of the gospel finds history as the medium of truthful witness.[37] And if indeed it is a real place where witness occurs, it seems it is also the place where witness—indeed, witness to the triune action in salvation history—is enacted, formulated and developed.

While the above emphases resemble various attempts to reconcile theologies with Scripture and the church's doctrinal heritage with a goal of being self-consciously "trinitarian," often tending toward social models of the Trinity,[38] what they do not do is provide a sound means for precisely how the doctrine of the Trinity is both formulatedly and irreducibly mis-

34. Ibid., 252.

35. Jonathan R. Wilson, "Aesthetics of the Kingdom: Apocalypsis, Eschatos, and Vision for Christian Mission," in *Revisioning, Renewing, and Rediscovering the Triune Center: Essays in Honor of Stanley J. Grenz* (ed. Derek J. Tidball, Brian S. Harris, and Jason S. Sexton; Eugene, OR: Cascade, 2014), ch. 8.

36. David E. Fitch and Geoffrey Holsclaw, "Mission amid Empire: Relating Trinity, Mission, and Political Formation," *Missiology* 41/4 (2013): 398–99.

37. Stanley Hauerwas, "Beyond the Boundaries: The Church Is Mission," in *Walk Humbly with the Lord: Church and Mission Engaging Plurality* (ed. Viggo Mortensen and Andreas Østerlund Nielsen; Grand Rapids: Eerdmans, 2010), 61.

38. About which, see the critical comments by Stephen R. Holmes, Karen Kilby, and Lewis Ayres in this volume (chs. 3, 4, and 5). See also the recent attempts by Robert K. Lang'at, "Trinity and Missions: Theological Priority in Missionary Nomenclature," in *Trinitarian Theology for the Church: Scripture, Community, Worship* (ed. Daniel J. Treier and David Lauber; Downers Grove, IL: InterVarsity Press, 2009), 161–81; and in the same vol., Leanne Van Dyk, "The Church's Proclamation as a Participation in God's Mission," 225–36.

sional. For this matter, we return to Lesslie Newbigin's insights to seed the argument of this essay.[39]

## NEWBIGIN AND EARLY TRINITARIAN FORMULATION

Newbigin argued that the significance of trinitarian doctrine is seen in the church's earliest struggles to articulate it in the pagan world. The vehemence of this struggle highlighted how central the process of formulating the doctrine was to Christian witness, and it showed how early trinitarian theology was grounded in missionary activity. Despite the fact that there is no formally developed doctrine of the Trinity in the New Testament, any attentive reader finds a trinitarian pattern therein, with prominence given to the Spirit active in the life of the church. As the church took the gospel to the world, as the argument runs, "it very soon found itself compelled to articulate a fully trinitarian doctrine of the God whom it proclaimed."[40] The most significant early doctrinal dispute about the nature of the Trinity (the mutual relations of the Son and Father) developed *right in the midst of the struggle* between the church and the pagan world. Thus as the church invested intellectually in the task of stating the gospel in the Greco-Roman culture's terms without compromising the gospel message, "it was the doctrine of the Trinity which was the key" to this, which allowed Christians to state both "the unity and distinctiveness of God's work in the forces of man's environment and God's work of regeneration within the soul of man."[41]

Just so, outside of the Christianized Western world that Newbigin called "Christendom," one learns that "the doctrine of the Trinity is not something that can be kept out of sight; on the contrary, it is the necessary starting point of preaching. Even in the simplest form of missionary preaching, one finds that one cannot escape dealing with this doctrine."[42] Thus while an understanding of the triune nature of God was the presupposition (*arche*) without which no gospel preaching can be done, it was also the struggle to communicate this gospel that *was* the trinitarian confession! It gave way to the content that was proclaimed. Nothing about this

---

39. Along with C. S. Lewis, Lesslie Newbigin is said to have given evangelicals in the age of late modernity "an intellectual armoury of a very different kind from that offered by the sterling efforts of conservative theologians" (Brian Stanley, *The Global Diffusion of Evangelicalism: The Age of Billy Graham and John Stott* [Nottingham, UK: Inter-Varsity Press, 2013], 149). For an excellent introduction to Newbigin's life and writings, see Paul Weston, *Lesslie Newbigin, Missionary Theologian: A Reader* (Grand Rapids: Eerdmans, 2006).

40. Newbigin, *Trinitarian Doctrine for Today's Mission*, 34.

41. Ibid., 34–35.

42. Ibid., 35.

confession was tacit, but was dynamically and explicitly trinitarian since Trinity just *is* the confessional explanation of the nature and identity of this God in Christ reconciling the world.

## CONFESSING TRINITARIAN DOCTRINE TODAY

Trinitarian theology properly becomes such while confessing faith in the God of the gospel through the medium of missionary engagement. This manner of confessional theology locates historic creeds and ecclesial confessions as forms of contextualized gospel renderings insofar as they work centrifugally from the scriptural witness and Spirit-born confession, "Jesus is Lord" (1 Cor 12:3a), which then takes expansive trinitarian shape in dynamic relation to all things the triune God stands in reference to. The meaning of this as faithful confession lies in its being shaped by Scripture and is thus consistently evangelical as well as inexhaustibly expansive in particular contexts. Accordingly, "trinitarian" theology covers the traditional loci and everything the triune reality touches, yet has a confessional home chiefly in *prayer* and *evangelism*, while reflecting the reality of eschatological hope and re-creation of all things (Rev 21:5). Therefore trinitarian confession—confessing this triune God—is the shape of mission today. Sent to proclaim salvation in Jesus' name (Acts 4:12), when asked, "Who is this Jesus?" the question can only be answered in terms of trinitarian faith.[43]

While making this point Newbigin drew from his own evangelistic experience in Indian villages, noting that the evangelist and converts (in retrospect), upon believing the message of Jesus (essentially a message about the Father and Son), discover ways that the hearers have been prepared by the Spirit's prevenient work to receive the gospel. It is this same Spirit who "made preaching his instrument and continues to work in those he has enabled to believe." Such a trinitarian starting point provides grounds for fresh articulation of the missionary message amidst "the pluralistic, polytheistic, pagan society of our time."[44]

Accordingly, if wise the missionary must take ample time to listen before talking. But when asked for the identity of the church in and bear-

---

43. Lesslie Newbigin, *The Open Secret: An Introduction to the Theology of Mission* (rev. ed.; Grand Rapids: Eerdmans, 1995), 28. See also discussions from the 2013 Los Angeles Theology Conference, "Christology, Ancient and Modern," which continually moved to discussions about the Trinity, especially in the final panel (http://latheology.com/past-years).

44. Newbigin, *Trinitarian Doctrine for Today's Mission*, 36–37; see also Wainwright, *Lesslie Newbigin*, 179.

ing witness to Christ, there is a pneumatological answer to be given, as with all providentially-governed affairs of the triune God's work, and especially with the community of faith. When asked of the kind of union with God our faith indicates (and *which* God), it is that with the God of Israel, maker of heaven and earth, all things seen and unseen, whom believers confess as "*Abba*, Father" (Rom 8:15; Gal 4:6).[45]

## TRINITARIAN MISSIONARY TEXT

Newbigin was emphatic that true missionary work should start not by attending to aspirations of people in a particular culture, nor by answering questions on their terms, nor by offering solutions to problems as the world sees them. Rather, it begins and continues "by attending to what God has done in the story of Israel and supremely in the story of Jesus Christ. It must continue by indwelling that story so that it is our story, the way we understand the real story. And then, and this is the vital point, to attend with open hearts and minds to the real needs of people."[46] Newbigin's commitment to Scripture's supreme authority is complemented by his commitment to understanding it within the context of the church congregation. He noted the creeds as constituting a point of reference for all engagement with Scripture, paying special attention to the *homoousios* concept, a word expressing in contemporary philosophy the truth on which everything depended. Thus there is a sense in which, as Newbigin found when crucial biblical teaching is explicitly formulated, like the trinitarian formulations, the church "can never go back on what it has decided."[47]

Trinitarian doctrine therefore has taken no better shape than in what is worked out in the church's exposition of its own faith, set forth in its creeds, and manifestly located in various ways. Confession of the Trinity is the shape of trinitarian mission in the world, but in this way, trinitarian theology is normed by Scripture,[48] worship, prayer, and the translational practice of trinitarian evangelism (Rom 15:16).

There is therefore an archetypal trinitarian confession inherent to the life of God that works out centrifugally by means of mission in creation, the primary features of which find the redeemed community correspondingly

---

45. This matter emphasizing the pneumatological and the union with the God of Israel aims to move beyond Newbigin's answer to the question of the missionary's authority (*The Open Secret*, 16–18).

46. Lesslie Newbigin, *The Gospel in a Pluralist Society* (Grand Rapids: Eerdmans, 1989), 151.

47. Newbigin, *The Open Secret*, 27; Wainwright, *Lesslie Newbigin*, 319.

48. Not the fully developed doctrine of the Trinity, but the trinitarian pattern, for example as developed in Soulen, *The Divine Name(s) and the Holy Trinity*; and Newbigin, *Trinitarian Doctrine for Today's Mission*, 34.

confessing after the character of this triune God, in Holy Scripture,[49] creeds, councils, doctrinal statements, and all statements of gospel that, and insofar as they, testify mimetically to the reality of God's life.

## MISSIONARY TRINITY

The seeds of the nature of the confession give way to an apologetic and missional elasticity that appears in fresh ways wherever the Spirit blows (John 3:8). This message, of course, is about a Son (a true one going after wayward ones) and a Father. This cannot be preached without speaking of the Father and the Son[50] and carries proclamational power by virtue of the Spirit who creates life where there is none. This primary designation of God as "Father" denotes not only the trinitarian nature of God but also the sending nature of God,[51] whereby mission becomes constitutive of the triune God.[52] As David Bosch says, "Mission has its origin in the heart of God. God is a fountain of sending love. This is the deepest source of mission. It is impossible to penetrate deeper still; there is a mission because God loves people."[53]

While the above statement delineates an epistemological and indeed missiological framework, grounding mission in the triune life also resists the polarizing of evangelism over social justice since mission involves God putting the whole of himself, channeling his "creative, redemptive, eschatological energy ... into a mission whose ultimate goal is the total transformation of the whole of reality."[54] This whole movement of sending and bringing others within the sphere of his communion is beyond one-directional.[55] Indeed, it is the promise of the triune God to be involved in every missionary endeavor, circumventing human failure, redeeming flawed attempts, and through creation extending his prior claim on all peoples, tongues, tribes, and nations (Ps 96:10). It is the triune God "who by His Son has provided a way back for His alienated, rebellious creatures (John 14:6) ... [and] who by His Holy Spirit selects, equips, and sends His

---

49. Note the argument from the theological priority of God's mission that the Bible itself is grounded in a missional basis (Wright, *The Mission of God*, 22–23).

50. Newbigin, *Trinitarian Doctrine for Today's Mission*, 36.

51. Scott W. Sundquist, *Understanding Christian Mission: Participation in Suffering and Glory* (Grand Rapids: Baker, 2013), 190.

52. David Fergusson, "Ecumenism and the Doctrine of the Trinity Today," in *The Oxford Handbook of the Trinity* (ed. Giles Emery and Matthew Levering; Oxford: Oxford University Press, 2011), 552. See also Holmes, "Trinitarian Missiology," 72–90.

53. David J. Bosch, *Transforming Mission: Paradigm Shifts in Theology of Mission* (20th anniv. ed., Maryknoll, NY: Orbis, 2011), 402.

54. Martin N. Accad and John Corrie, "Trinity," in *Dictionary of Mission Theology: Evangelical Foundations* (ed. John Corrie; Downers Grove, IL: InterVarsity Press), 398.

55. Ross Hastings, *Missional God, Missional Church: Hope for Re-Evangelizing the West* (Downers Grove, IL: InterVarsity Press, 2012), 261.

servants to all nations (Acts 1:8)."[56] Not only is God a missionary in the above senses, but the church also witnesses to the triune missionary activity.

## MISSIONARY WITNESS TO THE TRINITY

Witness is not primarily an act of the church, of course, but of the Spirit, who indelibly marks the church and sets God's people apart as witnesses (Matt 10:16–20; John 15:26–27; Acts 1:8; 1 Cor 6:11). This is no contrived witness but a martyrological act made possible by the Spirit, who unites and indwells the church. It may be in "a quite unexpected way and from a quite unexpected quarter that the Spirit will bear witness, using perhaps some small piece of simple fidelity, or some unstudied word, to illuminate with the authority of light itself what the Church has been trying to say about the purpose [and, indeed, nature] of God."[57] Here a recovery of the centrality of the Holy Spirit for the missionary task should be plain: "The Spirit is the Spirit of the Father and of the Son. His work is to enable us to participate in Christ's Sonship, to be one with him in his obedience to the Father. And only he can enable us to participate in, and thereby be the occasions of, his witness."[58]

The church, then, witnesses to Jesus' "supra-religious life,"[59] to his role as the subversive fulfilment of every cultural narrative. The church is not the source but rather the locus of witness, and carries the Spirit-enabled task of translation. It is the Spirit who *translates* the message from one culture to another (1 Cor 12:8–10; 14:26–28), and whose own action and translation work enable the nations to hear "the mighty acts" (*ta megaleia*) of God in their own tongues (Acts 2:4–11). The missionary activity of Bible translation functions in a similar capacity, having had the effect of recognizing and even preserving other cultures and dialects, as an action reflecting the translatability of the gospel message and its humanizing quality. As such the church is precarious, vulnerably present, open and hospitable for the work of translating and inviting all to experience this love. Lamin Sanneh notes this feature, stating that "solidarity with the poor, the weak, the disabled, and the stigmatized is the sine qua non of Christianity's credibility as a world religion."[60]

---

56. Herman Buehler, "Pietism's Most Challenging Task: A Trinitarian Renewal," in *The Good News of the Kingdom: Mission Theology for the Third Millennium* (ed. Charles Van Engen, Dean S. Gilliland, and Paul Pierson; Maryknoll, NY: Orbis, 1993), 238.

57. Newbigin, *Trinitarian Doctrine for Today's Mission*, 50.

58. Ibid., 81.

59. Accad and Corrie, "Trinity," 396–401.

60. Lamin Sanneh, *Translating the Message: The Missionary Impact on Culture* (rev. and exp.; Maryknoll, NY: Orbis: 2009), 11.

Avoiding come-and-see versus go-and-tell paradigms of missions, which quite easily perpetuate the homogeneity principle or ecclesio-centric hegemonies, Andrew Walls's "principle of translatability" provides contours that find confessional Christianity anchored in the life of the triune God, yet shows God's own translation as his mode of action for salvation. "Christian faith," Walls argues, "rests on a divine act of transla-tion: 'the Word became flesh and dwelt among us.'" God's own translation into humanity, fully being expressed in and as humanity while remaining fully grounded in divinity, is a cultural reality completely unlike ours and stands as the basis for all translation of his missionary action.[61]

This proposal avoids potential problems with so-called pneumatologi-cal naming of the Trinity[62] as it locates mission in the Spirit's work through the localized ecclesia and in the biblical text, making relevant the global as well as localized ecclesial expressions of trinitarian confessions. As such, this view possesses a unifying power for the churches, even while locat-ing the possibility of a constant dynamic and dialogue between solid and liquid churches, enabling the missionary church to articulate its confession in many ways (cf. Acts 13 and *passim*) consistent with the inexhaustible and dynamic nature of the gospel, the *dynamis* of God.[63] Here our mission-ary activity—rather than exercising a confident knowing of traditional missionary models, the implications of particular models, of other disci-plines that may shed light on contemporary models, or even of the particu-lar ways we have articulated our trinitarian confession—as a missionary movement sets out in prayer with, "Our Father," "Lord Jesus," or "Come, Holy Spirit." And it blesses: "May the grace of the Lord Jesus Christ and the love of God and the fellowship of the Holy Spirit...." It advances the trinitarian proclamation of Jesus as Lord and of the one faith, one hope, and one baptism in the name of the Father, Son, and Holy Spirit in hopes that the Lord may do again what he's promised in Scripture to do, speak-ing life and bringing healing and hope in this name among all peoples.[64]

---

61. Andrew F. Walls, "The Translation Principle in Christian History," in *Bible Translation and the Spread of the Church: The Last 200 Years* (ed. Philip C. Stine; Leiden: Brill, 1990), 25–39. Insights in this paragraph are owed to Paul Weston.

62. Soulen, *The Divine Name(s) and the Holy Trinity*, 247–52.

63. Ken Gnanakan, "To Proclaim the Good News of the Kingdom," in *Mission in the 21st Cen-tury: Exploring the Five Marks of Global Mission* (ed. Andrew Walls and Cathy Ross; Maryknoll, NY: Orbis, 2008), 10.

64. For an expansive argument grounded in the history of revelation and proper rejection of the argument that a theocentric or christocentric emphasis leads to reductionism, see John Howard Yoder, *Theology of Mission: A Believer's Church Perspective* (ed. Gayle Gerber Koontz and Andy Alexis-Baker; Downers Grove, IL: InterVarsity Press, 2014), 138–42.

## MISSIONARY TRINITARIAN THEOLOGIES

So what will witnessing to the triune action yield? Shaped and nuanced by different competing epistemologies in our ever-changing, globalized world, today's missionaries might hope for unique ways that distinct trinitarian theology/ies can be developed while on mission in particular places: Siberian trinitarian theology, Thai trinitarian theology, Iranian prison trinitarian theology, Los Angeleno suburban trinitarian theology, "Hakka" trinitarian theology, Native American "Hopi" trinitarian theology, with different languages, experiential, and conceptual terms available.

The practice of theology itself is always exercised as a way of gathering conceptual and real tools available in a particular culture to expound the wonderful truth that God was in Christ reconciling the world and all that baptism into his name entails. As God's triune life has been revealed in Christ by the Spirit, just like there remains today unfathomable mysteries of the human brain to be explored, so also the wonders of the triune reality disclosed to us in Scripture and shaping the cosmic universe that bears the imprint of the triune God may yet hold forth ways of better expressing *homoousios*, or eternal generation, or other wondrous truths of the gospel.

So my argument is largely methodological. And while various proposals have been offered for relating trinitarian theology to mission, since mission is not *out there* as much as it is *right here* wherever we find ourselves (Acts 17:26–27), there is language readily available to us for the translation of the shape of the God who is Father, Son, and Spirit. Some of the best of it, I'm arguing, will perhaps never appear in print or be the subject of a global ecumenical council. When I was in a Parisian hospital waiting to hear about the results of my youngest child's emergency brain surgery following a cavernoma vascular malformation that had hemorrhaged on her left frontal lobe, our trinitarian reflection was not in our struggle to nuance the meaning of *homoousios*, but in our reckoning of the reality of its implications for the healing of all things now broken, for my wife, myself, and our small baby girl, and for all who may find themselves resting in the strong name of the triune God of grace.

The way we enacted the confession of our hope in Jesus before a Parisian neurosurgeon and his amazing medical team, as we prayerfully reflected on the hope of the incarnation and what this means, we found ourselves engaged in this kind of trinitarian reflection through prayer, setting our hearts on God in relation to his world and on God in triune relation to Godself that we see and are brought into by virtue of the incarnation, by virtue of which we find ourselves *right there* in the very life of the triune God, in the Son by the Spirit, crying "Abba, Father." That event—that hospital, those rooms, that small bandaged body on a hospital bed, that hot July Parisian sun—shapes everything I think about the incarnation, its implications, and how I articulate these.

## TRINITARIAN CREEDAL CONFESSIONS

As this all relates to our creeds and confessions of the Trinity, it's important to note that when the church starts writing things down for codification and recognition, whether local, regional, or ecumenical, it forfeits the first-order activity that a trinitarian theology of mission may best thrive under, open to new possibilities of expressing the strong name of the Trinity in an expansive exposition. As such, we acknowledge that our creeds and confessions are *ours*, capturing moments of our confession of the triune God in a *developable* doctrine. It's not that we capture the Trinity itself in our confession, who in the Spirit's ever-opening, ever-renewing, ever imparting hope amidst the rubble and in the place of alienation brings loving reconciliation. But it moves out like a world-class doctor, scientist, or any researcher (*apostolos*) ever eager to confront unaddressed challenges and problems plaguing individuals and communities that can be aided with the healing power of just the right cure.

Various theological expositions so rendered have at times compromised other important theological loci with reductionism or misplaced emphasis, as may be seen in any context. These risk short-circuiting the coherent exposition of the gospel, especially when set forth as universal norming systems on par with Scripture, which as God's inspired Word flows from the very life of God in revealed movement that shapes the way disciples of Jesus walk together in the present world for the sake of the future one, where the triune God will be all in all.

The dynamic impulse of the creeds and confessions, then, if understood properly as formulated dogma—polemical and apologetic—ought to propel us in our missional task, free to articulate in various imaginatively resourced and resourceful ways the nature of this God revealed in Scripture. Barth also sees continuity between this missionary practice and the early church by pointing out that "the [trinitarian] analogies adduced by the fathers are in the long run only further expositions and multiplications of the biblical terms Father, Son, and Spirit, which are already analogical."[65]

---

65. Karl Barth, *CD* I/1, 340.

With further space, a rubric might be sketched for what confessional trinitarian theology on mission ought to look like through a reversed reading of the creed insofar as the realities in our present world—including cultural impulses and deeply personal longings for healing, renewal, forgiveness, community, purpose, and everlasting life (eschatology)—can be properly understood in light of the creed's third article. This missionary exposition of the third article gives way to the second and then first articles. It makes sense of our stories, bringing everything into the light of our confession of faith in the Holy Spirit, the Lord and Giver of life, and in the one Lord Jesus Christ, and in God the Father, Almighty Maker of heaven and earth.

For the missionary task Newbigin did not expect an "explicitly trinitarian theology" to be the substance of the missionary's initial talk or of the listener's initial understanding, but he did expect the message to be a trinitarian gospel nevertheless, resting in the reality of the revelation of God as Father, Son, and Spirit, fueling expansive exposition.[66] But how precisely do believers carry out their missional task of developing the explicit, fully trinitarian theology? May I suggest this is done by baptism—in the name of the Father, and of the Son, and of the Holy Spirit—and by following and by giving obedience to Jesus (Matt 28:18–20),[67] who in every way is like us (Heb 2:17; 4:15), and in the fullness of whose life we find ourselves living in dynamic, life-giving terms.

Does this dynamic mode of discipleship mean that concepts like *homoousios* are up for grabs, or that the means of this Father-Son relationship described as eternal generation (reflecting relations of origin in the divine life) is up for grabs if something else or better can be found? Newbigin himself observed:

> it is not enough for the church to go on repeating in different cultural situations the same words and phrases. New ways have to be found of stating the essential Trinitarian faith, and for this the church in each new cultural situation has to go back to the original biblical sources of this faith in order to lay hold on it afresh and to state it afresh in contemporary terms.[68]

I suppose, then, that the answer to the question of what's up for grabs, at least on Newbigin's terms, depends on the questions that the display of the healing reality of God's reconciliation of the world through Christ

---

66. Newbigin, *Trinitarian Doctrine for Today's Mission*, 36.

67. For an extended treatment of this text, see David J. Bosch, "The Structure of Mission: An Exposition of Matthew 28:16–20," in *Exploring Church Growth* (ed. Wilbert R. Shenk; Grand Rapids: Eerdmans, 1983), 218–48.

68. Newbigin, *The Open Secret*, 27.

are meant to subversively fulfill in the missionary moments of *euange-lizometha*—our evangelism. Therein, rather than being an action of our own, our missionary activity shows that it is actually "the presence of a new reality, the presence of the Spirit of God in power."[69]

The way to avoid not squelching this power or aborting the ongoing confession is to be constantly conscious of the difference between God's triune work in the world (which we celebrate in the form of baptism into the triune name) and that for which we labor through our prayer, worship, evangelism, and constant [extra]ordinary missionary work—first order theology as much as anything. When the time comes to develop these expositions further into full-orbed statements, confessions, or otherwise, we would do well to so saturate them with trinitarian, open-ended, and expansive explications, pointing to the triune God of love whom we love and who loves and cares for all that he has made.[70] Of critical importance today remains the need to keep central the core issues from the early church's debates: (1) how God's nature can still be one and not three, start-ing of course with the status of the Son; and (2) how the authoritativeness of the incarnation is to be explained as "the only valid point at which we can know who God is."[71]

# PARTICIPATING IN TRINITARIAN MISSION

In the 2003 book *Father, Son, and Holy Spirit*, Colin Gunton defined the-ology's task as "to essay a rational account of the creed of the Church whilst remaining deeply entrenched in the gospel."[72] Yet his work was also shaped by listening to culture and responding to it *with* the gospel. New-bigin also developed his early sketches from the 1963 volume, *Trinitarian Doctrine for Today's Mission*, into a more expansive trinitarian proposal with his 1978 book, *The Open Secret*,[73] adding additional features beyond his work in India, and reflecting further on the secularized post-Christian West. Simply because we have a roughly ecumenical understanding of the doctrine of the Trinity does not mean that further nuances are not pos-

---

69. Newbigin, *The Gospel in a Pluralist Society*, 119.

70. This has been capably done with the work of the Third Lausanne Congress on World Evan-gelization, which met in Cape Town, South Africa, October 16–25, 2010, and among many other things produced the document *The Cape Town Commitment: A Confession of Faith and a Call to Action* (Cornwall, UK: The Lausanne Movement, 2011).

71. Yoder, *Theology of Mission*, 136–44.

72. Colin E. Gunton, *Father, Son and Holy Spirit: Essays toward a Fully Trinitarian Theology* (New York: T&T Clark, 2003), 34.

73. Newbigin, *Unfinished Agenda*, 199.

sible if threats to a sound understanding of the nature of God are raised, or when new insights may be gathered that might illumine new problems, or grant better access or solutions to old ones. It might be suggested that the best way, however, of participating in the triune mission is by prioritizing conversation and life together with our neighbors, whoever they may turn out to be. This will enable the followers of Jesus to transcend various approaches and to co-labor genuinely and seriously with the triune God by contributing to what Hans Urs von Balthasar described strikingly as the "unfolding of this dramatic tension."[74]

---

74. Hans Urs von Balthasar, *Theo-Drama: Theological Dramatic Theory, vol. 1, Prolegomena* (trans. Graham Harrison; San Francisco: Ignatius, 1988), 645.

# SCRIPTURE INDEX

# SCRIPTURE INDEX

# SUBJECT INDEX

# AUTHOR INDEX